C000215102

Geoff Tristram has been a professic
years, working for a diverse range c
Embassy World Snooker, the BB(
Ravensburger Puzzles, Reeves, Win
to name but a few. He has created artwork featuring the likes of ~~~~~~~
Ross, Ian Botham, Jeremy Clarkson, Alan Shearer, Ayrton Senna, David
Vine, and virtually every snooker player of note. You may even have
spotted him on TV during the 2008 World Snooker Championship,
interviewing the players as he drew their caricatures!

Geoff has also designed hundreds of book covers, advertisements,
packaging items, and several record sleeves for bands such as UB40,
City Boy and The Maisonettes. In the 1980s he designed postage stamps
for Bermuda's Miss World edition, the Charles and Diana Royal
Wedding, Lake Placid's Winter Olympics, and Spain's World Cup
Football. Geoff's 'slightly rude and surreal' cartoon greetings-card
range, Norman and Brenda, can be found in all good card shops and
probably a few not-so-good ones as well. He now also writes jokes for
UK Greetings and Ling cards. His incredibly detailed Cat Conundrum,
Best of British, and What If? jigsaw designs for Ravensburger Puzzles
have thrilled and exasperated thousands of fans worldwide. As if this
was not enough, he has now written 14 books, almost entirely humorous
fiction. This one is the 15th, but this time it's humorous fact.

In 2016, Stratford-upon-Avon's Town and District councils asked
Geoff to create the town's 400th Anniversary Portrait of William
Shakespeare, which made him rightly proud.

Geoff's younger brother, David, was famous theatrical publishing
company, Samuel French's Comedy Playwright of the Year in 2015 and
he has also branched out into film-making with the hilarious Inspector
Drake comedies and more recently, 'Doreen the Movie'.

Their lovely mother, Ruby, is very proud of both of them, as was their
beloved and much-missed dad, Len.

A Lifetime Spent Watching Paint Dry
by Geoff Tristram

**DRAWING
ROOM**

First published in 2018 by The Drawing Room Press.

Printed and bound by 4edge Limited, 22 Eldon Way Industrial Estate
Hockley, Essex, SS5 4AD.

ISBN Number 978-0-9926208-7-5

Buy books online at www.geofftristram.co.uk or contact the author via
gt@geofftristram.co.uk

'I cannot choose my 100 favourite books
because I've only written 5.'
Oscar Wilde

'I was reading a book called 'The History of Glue'.
I couldn't put it down.'
Tim Vine

'Shakespeare's stuff is different from mine,
but that is not to say it's inferior.'
P.G. Wodehouse

'A novel should be 80,000 words or more,
but don't worry Geoffrey, you can use
some of them at least twice.'
David Tristram

'It's the way I tell 'em!'
Frank Carson

'If somebody could write a book
for people who never read
they would make a fortune.'
Nancy Mitford

'I would like to thank my wife for all her
encouragement. When can I have it?'
Geoffrey Tristram

Chapter 1

I was born early on the morning of April 19th, 1954, a mere nine years after World War 2 had ended, and I still can't quite get over how old that makes me sound. April has been a mixed month as far as birthdays are concerned. I was born on the same day as my future wife, Susan, and also the diminutive jazz pianist/comedian/film-star Dudley Moore. Either side of that date were Spike Milligan and well-known fascist dictator, Adolf Hitler. Four days later than me was William Shakespeare, of whom, more later. It was 60 years later, as a matter of fact, when our paths next crossed, if you exclude 'O' and 'A' level English exams.

I like to think that in terms of Arian character traits, I have a little more in common with the two comedians and the playwright than the prominent Nazi, though I did, reluctantly, sport a similar hairstyle to his at one stage.

My mother and grandmother were having one hell of a week. Talk about mixed emotions. My grandmother's father, a.k.a. my mother's grandad, died the day before I arrived. The Lord giveth, and the Lord taketh away. When I was being born, the midwife commented to those present, namely my Granny Bertha and presumably my mother, Ruby, that I had one of the hardest heads she had ever encountered. If I'm honest, I have no recollection of her saying that, and I have nothing meaningful to add to her observation, other than, how did she *know* it was hard? I hope to God she didn't set about me with a lump hammer, just to test how hard it was on the 'Mohs' scale, which, I've discovered, is how 'Hard Things' are measured (This book is nothing if not educational).

My mother gave birth to me at her parents' house, No.14, Thorn's Avenue, Quarry Bank, the very epicentre of the Black Country, because she and my dad, Len, were living there until they found a place of their own. My mom, as I prefer to call her (and can we put this to rest right from the beginning, it's Mom in the Black Country, as it is in the U.S.A., and NOT Mum), tells me that I was born exactly nine months after their wedding night. Apparently, she didn't have the faintest clue about sex and didn't even know for sure which hole the baby came out of. My dad presumably had a slightly better idea of what to do, otherwise I wouldn't have been created, and that, in my humble opinion, would have robbed the world of a major talent.

My grandparents on my mother's side were named Bertha and Reuben – very biblical - and if you add to that Ruby and Leonard, my parents, and David, my brother to be, and stir into the mixture a cluster of Franks on my dad's side, and then toss in the fact that we were circumcised, for good measure, it all pointed to us being Jewish as far as I was concerned. I spent several of my teenage years putting two and two together and making seven with regard to this potential scenario, fondly imagining that we had escaped Nazi Germany and were living a secret life in Quarry Bank - or Quarry Bonk as it's pronounced by the locals – having dropped our original surname of Blumenfeld or Aaronovich or whatever, in favour of Tristram to make us slightly less conspicuous. The only flaw in my reasoning was that if we really had wanted to be less conspicuous, why did we choose a very rare ancient Celtic surname that no one else in the Black Country seemed to have? Surely, Billingham or Foley or maybe Genner would have been better, as everyone and his dog had those surnames where I came from.

My main reason for coming up with this ridiculous Jewish theory was the circumcision. I resented it, largely thanks to the fact that it took away a sizable section of my willy, which wasn't all that big to begin with. In my opinion, doctors were a little bit scalpel-happy back in the day. You only needed to have a foreskin that was a bit on the tight side and some butcher would immediately hack away at it with a 10A

Swann-Morton blade. The same can be said for tonsils, adenoids and appendixes; one squeak and they were removed without as much as a 'by your leave'. To this day I feel violated and regard it as an illegal act, a bit like the genital mutilation that some poor young black girls suffer in the name of religion. Anyway, I'll try to move on with my story and put that to the back of my mind for the time being, though, knowing me and my obsessive tendencies, I may well return to the theme later on.

So, we were not Jewish after all, even though, to this day, I say things like 'Oy-oy-OY!' when I am dismayed, and I have also been known to mutter, 'Enough already!' now and again, when things aren't going my way. Maybe it's psychosomatic, or in this case, a better word would be psycho-Semitic. But seriously, a major reason for the big misunderstanding on my part was simply that the older Black Country folk took their names from biblical sources. They were often God-fearing, superstitious people, and the local dialect was littered with 'thees and thines' which had presumably been picked up in church of a Sunday and became part of everyday language. We all spoke with what is supposed to be the oldest, most authentic Anglo-Saxon dialect in the country, but I am once more getting ahead of myself. I will touch on our remarkable way of speaking later on.

I remember nothing whatsoever about the very early days, as you would expect, but my mother has an old leather-bound album stuffed with photographs from my toddler years, and what strikes me as interesting about them is the fact that they're not only black and white, which was to be expected, but also no larger than two inches square. Very occasionally the better shots had been blown up, hand coloured and framed. Photography was hardly in its infancy, but everyone in the Black Country seems to have skimped on the photographic paper to the extent that it is impossible to make out any detail on these microdot photos without the aid of a Sherlock Holmes-style magnifying glass. On close inspection I appear to have been a chubby blond-haired thing with a penchant for cross-dressing, and my mother seems to have chosen my attire from a 1940's Tyrolean mountain-wear catalogue. I could be seen in a variety of frilly, embroidered blouses which perfectly complimented my lederhosen and girly white socks.

The hand-coloured larger picture of me from this ghastly period shows me sat on the sideboard sporting my blond, Arian, Hitler hairdo, a couple of dubious, airbrushed red cheeks and a pair of blue peepers that Paul Newman would have been deeply envious of.

On the back of this photograph are the colourist's simple – some would say too simple – instructions. It reads: Eyes; blue, Skin; pink, Hair; blond, Blouse; white, Shorts; purple, embroidered flowers; green and pink. Kids these days don't know how lucky they are.

Chapter 2

Six months after I was born, Ruby and Len moved to a tiny place of their own in Sheffield Street, off the high street. My perfectionist dad was a highly-skilled toolmaker who worked in nearby Old Hill. My mom, thanks to Yours Truly, suddenly became a housewife and gave up her exciting and lucrative career as a painter of galvanized buckets to look after me, and I have to report that she made a first-class job of it (looking after me I mean, not painting the buckets, though she was good at that too). She quickly settled into her new role and adored her little child. Mom was a bit of a worrier though; so much so that if a doctor needed to inject me - and this seemed to happen every ten minutes if my memory serves me correctly - she would swoon and have to be revived by a passing nurse. In those days, she was notoriously squeamish and I was too.

It was around this time when the country was hit with a particularly severe Asian flu epidemic that was claiming many lives. My mom and I succumbed to the virus, and we were pretty ill, which of course upset my dad more than somewhat. Not only was he working all day, doing whatever toolmakers do, but also, he was doing his best to look after his young wife and child when he got home. One evening, exhausted, he made sure we were as well as could be expected and fast asleep upstairs, before returning downstairs to eat his cheese sandwich and drink a medicinal beer. He settled into his favourite armchair by the cosy fire, sighed a heavy sigh and poured the drink into a glass, when all of a sudden there was a loud whooshing noise. Around a ton of soot, which had previously been hiding up the chimney, now came blasting out like a dark, diabolical typhoon, covering every available surface with half an inch of the evil black powder. Dad, the

5

furniture, the wallpaper, the beer, the washing that was drying on the clothes-horse next to the fire, the cheese sandwich – everything in that small room became black. This was, sadly, the last straw as far as Len was concerned, and the previously stoic and now aptly-named Black Country man broke down and wept like a baby with colic. My mom, who was suffering with bouts of pure delirium thanks to the severity of the flu, was convinced that she had been visited in her boudoir that night by Al Jolson. Mercifully, mother and child made a full recovery, though many of our vulnerable, i.e. younger and older British people and those already in poor health, did not survive.

Three and a half years after I was born, my mom and dad announced that I was to be joined by a new child, namely my brother David, which meant that all that previously-owned Tyrolean mountain wear wasn't going to be wasted.

Soon after David arrived, we all moved to a brand-new council house just down the hill in a small cul-de-sac by the name of Anne Road. It was number 3, for the benefit of the blue-circle plaque manufacturers who may wish to get started on mine before my demise; not that I'm planning to keel over any time soon.

I have a lovely photograph of me and the baby David cuddled up on our settee. Me, aged four, resplendent in my Sunday-best shirt, tie, patterned jumper and shiny sandals combination, eyes heavy with a nasty cold, and David wearing something akin to a floral plastic shopping bag with a Sellotape belt. If ever my brother gets too cocky, or sarcastic, or more famous, or maybe just too wealthy, I will show him this photograph to bring him down a peg or two.

I have heard all sorts of stories about the first day at school, but my personal experience of it was not at all traumatic. My friend Steve Jolliffe, the graphic designer who works with me on a lot of my projects, tells me that his first day was also enjoyable, and whilst all around him were sobbing or even screaming to be allowed home to their mothers, he, like me, quietly got on with things. Unlike me, however, things went awry for him on Day Two, once he'd cottoned on that school was not a one-off experience. I don't think his parents had fully explained to him that he was expected to attend *every* day except weekends for the foreseeable future, and this resulted in him kicking off, bigtime. I wasn't there, obviously, but I have visions of tables being overturned, like a western saloon-bar brawl.

Apparently, I was showing signs of being an artistic fellow from a very early age; as young as four, I am told, though I can't remember anything meaningful until I was old enough to attend Quarry Bank Infants' School. I have a very clear memory of being asked to design the face masks for our production of Dick Whittington, and this is backed up with photographic proof. The cast are lined up for the school photographer, and a couple of the children are wearing my creations, namely two cat masks, though I seem to recall that the original tale only featured one cat. These schools are notorious for playing fast and loose with the texts to these classics, I find. I vaguely recall one Nativity play that featured around twenty wise men and at least seven kings and their two royal cats – well, it was a shame to waste the props after they'd been specially made for an earlier production. I still have the Dick Whittington   photograph, which is reproduced in this book, but I am slightly disappointed by the quality of the cat masks. In my mind, they were far better than that.

I loved school, most of the time. I was artistic, musical, good at English, but hopeless at P.E. I was in my element in class, often showing the teachers how to draw properly. I was precociously talented at drawing to the extent that, at nine years of age I was regularly being invited by certain less-fortunate teachers to come to the blackboard and draw diagrams - frogs, horses, human faces, suits of armour, coats of arms, birds, and what-have-you for them, much to my delight. I have always been a show-off and used my artistic talents for that purpose. Well, I was the son of Leonardo after all. I vividly remember Mr Weston, the Deputy Head, struggling one day to construct a frog with which to illustrate his biology lesson.

'I just can't seem to make it look like a frog!' he groaned, much to the amusement of the class, who were all sniggering at his incompetence. 'Come on, Geoffrey,' he would eventually say, 'You come up and draw us one.'

I cockily strode up the board, extracted the chalk from his talentless digits and began lecturing him on how amphibian leg joints were assembled, and what frog's mouths looked like. Saving the best till last, I then kicked the man while he was down by sarcastically adding, 'Oh yes sir, and it's very important to make sure they have four limbs too. Your frog appears to have two back legs but no arms.' Cue hysterical laughter from the rapt audience. Maybe this was my first taste of stand-up comedy, and I loved the attention. I couldn't dribble with a football and I was pathetic at cricket, but stood in front of a crowd with a stick of chalk, I was in my element. I am also certain that this show-off attitude to art shaped my future artistic style. If you were a little working-class boy from the Black Country in the 1960s, the only way to impress the neighbours was to draw realistically – the more realistic, the better. They would not have understood Abstract Expressionism or Cubism, as maybe middle- or upper-class London parents might have done, but if it looked like what it was supposed to be, it was a work of genius in their eyes. I also remember enjoying a regular lesson with the Headmaster, during which we had to copy out, in our neatest handwriting, a famous poem or piece of prose into our 'best' books on the left-hand page and then illustrate it on the facing page. We were raised on epic Empire poems such as 'Vitai Lampada' by Henry Newbolt, the wonderfully evocative 'Winter' by William Shakespeare and 'Cargoes' by John Masefield, to name but three, and I still get dewy-eyed if I hear them today.

My artistic bible was a set of four royal-blue Collins encyclopaedias which my parents bought me, and it was from these that I honed my drawing skills. I would spend hours with my pencils or my 13-colour biro, copying the illustrations in those books, and I still remember the pictures vividly. If I took one of my copies to school; say a portrait of Churchill, Wordsworth, Gandhi or Shakespeare, Mr Perry, our Headmaster, would spirit it away to a small room next to his office, and file it carefully in a portfolio ready for when eBay was invented. I often wonder what became of them all. Another memory is of being in bed with a nasty cold (I was always getting colds and flu in those days) when I heard the doorbell ring. It was the Headmaster delivering my homework project, the cover of the school play's programme, which was done in bed on a drawing board to meet the looming deadline. I doubt that any other artist in this country has had deadlines to cope with at such a young age, but it did prepare me for a lifetime of delivering artwork strictly on time, rather than when I felt like it.

On weekends, my parents would go to either Quarry Bonk's Liberal, Labour or Conservative Clubs, and David and I would be dragged along to sit in a dank children's room with loads of other screaming kids, as was the norm in those days. Occasionally dad would appear with a bottle of Vimto and a packet of plain crisps for us. There was always a dusty old blackboard and some sticks of chalk, so while the others screamed and ran amok, I drew things, and David drank pop, chewed crisps and shrewdly observed.

At the Liberal Club we sat with our parents in a horrible long smoke-filled room, and mom made sure I had my A3 plain-paper sketchpad and pencils to keep me quiet. The cockles, mussels and shrimps man would arrive halfway through the night with his wicker basket, and we would all have a little bag as a treat. There was a billiard room which we weren't allowed into, and the story goes that, during World War 2, a German bomber dropped two 500-lb bombs on our sleepy little town, for no particular reason other than spite. One landed in the local Mary Stevens' Park near the main gates and one landed on the Liberal Club billiard table, which must have been the best cure for constipation ever for the blokes playing on it at the time. Miraculously, neither bomb exploded, and thereafter Quarry Bonk was known as the Holy City.

At closing time, dad would drive back to the garage which he built himself, at the back of our council house, and park his Austin Cambridge Shooting Brake, or his Vauxhall Cresta, or whichever car he had at the time, and David and I, eyes streaming from the cigarette smoke, would be fast asleep on the back seat, in each other's arms. Mom would gently try to stir us and assure us that we'd be more comfortable in our beds, but nothing was as comfortable as the back seat of that car, at that precise time. Eventually we were coaxed out, slipped into pyjamas and tucked into bed, our poor little red eyes still watering prolifically. Then both parents would say 'God Bless!', surgically remove my drawing book, and switch off the main light. Some thirty years later, when I was a corporate events caricaturist working at an exhibition in Frankfurt, I was busy drawing an elderly English businessman, when he recalled frequenting a pub back in England, many years previously. He told me that a very well-behaved little boy would spend hours sketching, and one weekend the boy drew a picture of him, just as I was doing as we chatted, and the likeness was, he said, incredible. 'I often wonder,' added the businessman, 'what became of that child.' I then learnt that the pub in question was Quarry Bonk Liberal Club, and the boy was me.

I loved drawing, but I was also in love with playing music. I began by learning the recorder, as we all did back then, but I used mine as a musical instrument and not a form of aural torture akin to scraping my fingernails down a blackboard. Not for me the painful, atonal rendition of 'Pease Pudding Hot'. I played Bach on my recorder, I'll have you know. I also

10

perfected a party piece of playing it behind my back, courtesy of a long thin plastic tube which my dad got for me from work, that went down my blazer sleeve into my shirt, out the bottom of my grey school shorts and into the mouthpiece of the instrument. I could also play through my nose, though Mrs Hancock, our wonderful, kind, inspirational music teacher, whilst amused, asked me to do this using my own posh wooden Dolmesch model, rather than using the school's plastic instruments, as she was fearful of causing a new flu epidemic. I also, very immaturely, equated quality with speed in those days. I probably still hold the Quarry Bonk Junior School Recorder Record for the fastest rendition of 'British Grenadiers' and 'Mexican Whistler'.

All very silly I know, but a non-sporty child needs a chance to shine, as does, of course, the sporty child who's not overly academic. That's why it was an absolute disgrace, in my opinion, that some genius in government wanted to make school games non-competitive, and by doing so, rob some children of their only chance to make their mark. If we follow that half-soaked logic to its conclusion, we should have maths lessons where your sums don't have to add up and aren't marked, English essays that have all the typos, grammar and spelling uncorrected and cricket or football competitions where no one keeps the score and both teams draw at the end. It's like something that Lewis Carroll would have come up with in one of his Alice books.

I HATED the school gymnasium with a vengeance. I couldn't, and still can't, do a rollover. Whenever I ran at the vaulting horse, I'd invariably clatter my testicles on the leather top bit and then feel sick for the rest of the day. I never had the strength to climb up a bloody rope, as my arms and legs looked like pipe-cleaners and still do. Halfway up the climbing frame I'd get frightened senseless and go dizzy. When they lined you up against the wall and the two football captains chose a person each for their team, I was invariably last, or last-but-one if the chap with polio was there. Actually, even that was a lie. Gary, the chap with polio, was a fantastic goal-keeper and got chosen early on, now I come to think of it. I didn't even get chosen early if it was my ball. They'd rather just get another ball, but even then, when I was around ten years old, I didn't really mind that too much because I knew that when it was art time they were lining up to ask me how to paint a flat wash, or mix purple, or draw a footballer, a Nazi bomber or a thrush, and I already had a fantastic mental repertoire to deal with those random requests; I could draw all of them without much thought or effort. Fairness has never been about us all doing the same thing. It's about allowing Neil to shine on the pitch, Susan to excel at rounders, Kevin to know about nature, Gail to be good at stories, Simon to be a numbers wizard, Celia to play us a tune and sing to us, and Paul to make us laugh. Likewise, in The Adult World, equality doesn't mean Sandra needs to smother herself in tattoos and drink gallons of beer to be as good as Graham. Ladies and men are equal but different. If you put half a pound of soap on a weighing scale and half a pound of dirt on the other side, they balance exactly, in spite of being poles apart in physical make-up. The world would surely be a better place if a few more people understood this simple fact. Or to be totally flippant, can you imagine a planet that was home to 85 billion accountants and nothing else? *Vive le difference* I say!

Meanwhile, back in the real world, or Quarry Bonk at any rate, Mr Perry, our much-loved and respected Headmaster, was having a word with his artistic, daydreamy pupil about the Nativity play, and how he wanted to commission a plywood sheep to star in said theatrical extravaganza, on account of real sheep being not only hard to come by in Quarry Bonk, but also unreliable and prone to incontinence when shoved onto a stage in front of a capacity crowd. It was agreed that I would forfeit a few breaks and lunchtimes over the autumn to visit the woodwork room, where a large sheet of plywood would be waiting for me. I had to fretsaw this into the shape of a sheep, and when it was sheep-shape and Bristol fashion, to then paint it using my dad's Dulux gloss paints from 'down the shed', so that it would pass for a real sheep from half a mile away if one were seriously myopic. This I set out to do, after first getting in-depth fret-sawing tips from my dad over the fishfingers at teatime. In spite of his sagely advice, I must have snapped at least 346 blades in order to make that one plywood sheep, with a blade sawing, on average, through around an inch of plywood before it gave up the ghost and went 'ping'. It's a wonder I wasn't blinded. Nowadays, thanks to the Health and Safety brigade, children of that age aren't allowed anywhere near a fretsaw. Parents would start to fret if their kids were allowed to even pick one up just to look at it. My dad let me have his old air rifle when I was ten, and it never did me any harm. It probably did quite a few gardening neighbours and the odd mangey starling some harm, but not me.

On the night of the Nativity play, I was sat in the orchestra pit beneath the stage, which had the lush purple velvet curtains with their QBJS crest in bright yellow drawn across it. I use the word orchestra loosely. It was in fact fifteen or so kids clutching recorders they could hardly play (and one who could), Mrs Hancock at the battered old upright piano, and a couple of drippy females with national health pink spectacles clutching a variety of percussive items. The hall itself was heaving with proud parents and grandparents. The lights went down, signalling that something of great pith and moment was about to happen. Mrs H nodded to us, counted to four under her breath and we began the overture in an assortment of key and time signatures, while the curtain was jerkily drawn open to reveal a charming tableau. On a suspect astro-turf grassy bank, three shepherds with regulation tea-towel headgear sat around a campfire that consisted of a ring of building bricks filled with silver and gold foil. Right at the front centre section of the stage, in pole position, stood a plywood sheep on a dad-made plinth. It was immediately above my head, and looking, in my humble opinion, fairly magnificent. It even had a spotlight trained on it. There was a small gasp from the expectant crowd, and I heard, much to my embarrassment, the broad, loud, Black Country voice of my grandmother, Bertha, say, 'Look up theer, Reuben! Thass ower Geoffrey's sheep, that is!'

Then, dramatically, the Angel of the Lord came down from the sky on a sturdy rope, and suddenly began spinning around, out of control, like a helicopter with a faulty rear-rotor. The actor playing this important role was my relative, David Nixon, a rather thick-set and heavy-handed individual in those days, who then proceeded to kick the plywood sheep, causing it to topple into the orchestra pit, bounce heavily off my head and settle at my feet with a sickening clatter. The audience seemed to think this was a good thing and cheered. Meanwhile, I sat there, recorder in hand, with my lower lip quivering and tears forming in my eyes. Andy Warhol once said, and I'm paraphrasing here, we should all be famous for 15 minutes. My plywood sheep took the best part of three months to make and had been on stage for all of eight seconds before it returned to obscurity. To add injury to insult, my brow was now seeping blood. Looking back, I am rather grateful that my head was rated a 9.5 on the Mohs Scale of Hardness, otherwise I might have inherited a fractured skull. Can you imagine turning up at Russell's Hall Hospital's A&E Department and trying to explain how it happened?

'I was playing a hymn on the recorder when the Angel of the Lord came down from on high and kicked a wooden sheep onto my head'.

They'd patch me up and dispatch me to the nearest loony bin - I'd probably still be there now. Anyway, If I may be allowed to skip forward 43 years, just for one paragraph, there is a very strange ending to this tale.

I was visiting my old school one day, after an absence of many, many years – 43 to be precise, but you've probably already gleaned that from reading the previous sentence – and as I was leaving I asked the current Headmistress, a vision of loveliness named Helen, to look out for an old plywood sheep, having briefly explained to her what it was all about. She addressed me the way she presumably addresses her more dim-witted pupils, when patiently trying to explain to them why it is not a good idea to play football using the old greenhouse as the goal posts, and reminded me that, over 43 years, the school had changed a fair bit, believe it or not, and if there was indeed an old plywood sheep hanging around, odds-on they would have come across it by now. Duly chastised and humiliated, I smiled a sad smile and drove home, and when I got into my studio the answering machine light was flashing. It was Helen. I'd left something at the school and I needed to retrieve it, she explained. This was not unusual. I was always leaving portfolios, laptops and so on, at all manner of establishments, and I am so scatterbrained that I once drove home from Cheltenham without my car. I'm sorry, that was a ridiculous joke. So I jumped back in the trusty old Mercedes and drove back to the school. I was met in the vestibule by Helen, who had a plywood sheep under her arm, and I could tell right away that it was mine and not someone else's.

'How on earth did you find that?' I gasped, tears of joy already forming in my eyes, as opposed to the type that formed in my eyes when the thing bounced off my head.

'Well,' she replied, 'just as you left, Ken the caretaker walked past my office with a plywood sheep under his arm, and I called to ask what he'd got. He said he'd been clearing out the cavity under the old stage where we store tables and chairs – the same stage you'd sat beneath during the Nativity play in 1965 – and he found this here sheep right at the very back, covered in cobwebs. He reckoned it must have been

15

there since World War 2. He was about to sling it on the skip and I said please, no, Jeez! I know what that is!'

She handed me my sheep and I'm not ashamed to say that I cried enough to fill a small bucket. Suddenly, my dad, his shed, Mr Perry, the woodwork room and of course the Nativity play itself, all came rushing back to me. I was choked. And isn't it funny that one second you are in full control and the next, emotion hits you like a surprise right hook from Cassius Clay, and you're struggling to remain upright and get your words to come out. Nothing can make you weep like a long-lost plywood sheep, I always say.

Chapter 3

I loved my life, generally speaking, but there were certain aspects of it that caused me great distress – namely injections, school milk, the school dentist, accidental amputations, love letters, embarrassment, and Mrs 'W', as we will refer to her. There are probably other topics that exercised me but that will do for now.

I was every bit as squeamish as my mother when it came to injections, and as we all know, the needles were blunter and hurt more in those days. The very thought of one would turn me white, and I'd have to spend ages in the medical room with my head between my legs. I can't even get my head between my legs now, which is probably a good thing. The only school-administered vaccine I ever looked forward to was that lump of sugar which they introduced around 1962. For my younger readers, this was a pink-tinged sugar-cube impregnated with Albert Sabin's 'live, attenuated oral polio vaccine', whatever that means. It came too late for poor old Gary the Goalkeeper, I know that. I distinctly remember how brave I was when they gave me that sugar; I was quite proud of myself. Most of us looked forward to that more than the school milk. I always remember several crates of the stuff being dumped near the Head's office in the corridor, and it was my job as a house captain to ring the school bell to announce playtimes, lunchtimes etc. When the bell rang we were all handed a small bottle of milk in an attempt to strengthen our teeth and bones, which, on the surface, sounds great. Sadly, the milk was curdled in the summer and resembled a small-scale model of the iceberg that sunk the Titanic in winter. It was seldom just right, and, rather perversely, I am sure a lot of schoolkids cheered when

17

Margaret Thatcher, or Milk Snatcher as she was christened, put a stop to it.

Our teeth were a disaster in those days, just before fluoride was being introduced into our water supplies in the mid-60s. Brushing seemed to be sporadic or non-existent in Quarry Bonk, meaning that shopful's of sticky sweets and Tizer were consumed and hardly any of us bothered to wash the stuff off our choppers before bedtime, in spite of our parents' nagging. Consequently, by the age of eleven, most of us had been given a mouthful of fillings, but no one was that bothered as these were just milk teeth (or Tizer Teeth to be more accurate) and we had the chance to redeem ourselves, hygiene-wise, once the final set has replaced them. Only not many did.

My son, Jamie, who is 24, has one minor filling so far. My daughter, Laura, still doesn't have one, and she's 33. Most folks of my generation have a mouth so full of fillings that if they stray near to a magnet, their heads are wrenched off.

Our biggest dread, even worse than injections, was the ominous grey van that pulled noiselessly into the playground once a year and stayed there for a week. It had something of the Nazi death camps about it, and it made the blood run cold. If I was sat in class when a kid got back from an injection, I'd get very hot and dizzy, especially if he shouted across the classroom, 'It killed!' If I glanced out of the window and saw that grey van, the teacher would have to scoop me up from the floor and administer smelling salts. Once inside the Van from Hell we were knocked out with cocaine (I know people who'd pay good money for that now) or stunned with Laughing Gas, administered with an evil face-mask by Doctor Death, the Midlands Mengele. It took me many, many years to overcome my fear of the dentist, and I would like to credit, firstly, Mr Oliver of Dudley, and secondly, Kim Pickering from Kingswinford, with completely turning me around. It now genuinely holds no fear for me whatsoever, and I implore you lot with terrible gnashers to do something about it. It just doesn't hurt any more for a start. It's just the bloody noise

18

that's horrible, and personally, I can live with horrible noises. Trust me, just make that appointment now!

I vividly remember a couple of domestic incidents from this period that were truly horrific. In those days we all had a basic brick outhouse, not as yet converted to kitchens, which had a front and back door. If both were left open and there was a gust of wind, one or the other would slam shut with sickening force. One day we heard an ear-piercing scream from Mrs Brooks's house, a few doors away. We dashed round to see what had happened, and found her son, Clive, looking as white as a ghost, and bleeding from his hand. His index finger, meanwhile, was lying on the patio like a discarded McCain's oven-chip. My dad bundled him into the car and had the presence of mind to collect the finger and pack it in ice – for here was a man used to toolmaker-style injuries at work, who had built up a manly resistance to such things. They drove to the hospital, where it was successfully re-attached. It always looked wonky after that, but at least it still worked.

The twelve or so garages behind our council house had a very narrow gap between them, which we kids were always disappearing down to play hide-and-seek or retrieve balls. One day, David ran down the gap between our and the neighbour's garage and we heard a scream that easily matched Clive Brooks's scream on the Richter Scale. The reason for this was that a three-inch rusty nail was protruding from the neighbour's garage, and David, in his haste to find a cricket ball, didn't spot it, at least until it entered his knee and gouged out a chunk of flesh the size of…you've guessed it…a fat, greasy McCain's oven-chip. Curiously, there was little or no blood, but you could quite clearly see the bone beneath. Our mother took one look and passed out on the lawn. Mrs Brooks, returning the earlier favour, shovelled the whimpering child into an old pushchair and dashed to Doctor Fair's surgery in Lower High Street, while I did my best to revive Ruby by fanning her with a tea towel. Sadly, unlike the severed digit, the chunk of flesh was never recovered for some reason, so the good doctor had to stretch the skin across a gap the size of the Grand Canyon and just do her best. If you ever bump into David at one of his shows, convince him you're not a Freemason, and then ask him to roll his trouser leg up and show you. It is not for the faint-hearted.

Those amongst you with good memories will recall my small list of things I wasn't keen on, back at the beginning of this chapter, and the two that came directly after 'Amputations' were 'Love Letters' and 'Embarrassment'. I have only ever received one such letter (cue heart-felt cries of 'Oh, what a shame!' from the reader) and that was when I was around eleven years old. My mother heard the letterbox clank, so she went to see what it was, expecting a post card from Auntie Millie in Blackpool or whatever. It was, in fact, a love letter sent to me by one of two twin girls who lived just up the road from us. At the risk of embarrassing the poor woman, as she now is, (and why not, she embarrassed the hell our of me) it read:

I LOBE YOU SO MUCH. I LOBE YOU TO BITES.

My mother read it out to me, and I was mortified. I was so shy in those days, would you believe, that I would go bright red and hide my head inside my fair-isle jumper at any hint of girls or romance, and here was this badly-spelt epistle declaring undying love and enough hot kisses to make my body spontaneously combust. Janet or Julie, whichever one it was, I hope you realise what you did to me back then. Mind you, even that paled into insignificance in the Embarrassment Stakes compared to the incident in Mr Lewis's classroom one Friday afternoon. I was a notorious daydreamer, as you can imagine, and in those days, we didn't get changed for P.E. in a proper changing room. We would instead change in class, boys and girls mixed, and leave our effects on our seats. We would have our P.E. kit to hand in a small black duffel bag;

usually a plain white T shirt and blue shorts with a pair of black pumps that had elasticated tops rather than laces, which half of us couldn't tie properly. Then we'd proceed to the hall, if it was for gym, or outside to our grass playing fields for football, cricket, rounders or whatever.

I heard Mr Lewis give the instruction to get changed, so I immediately stripped off down to my vest and underpants and was just about to look for my pump bag when the teacher's voice, very low and conspiratorial, was heard close to my right ear.

'Geoffrey,' it said softly, 'why are you taking all your clothes off and currently resembling Mick McManus, the television wrestler, when everyone else is busy opening their maths homework books?'

I looked around for the first time, and he was not wrong. 25 children, their arithmetic books open and ready, were giggling behind their hands, and some were in hysterics. My face changed from sickly pale to deep crimson in seconds.

'I thought you said change for P.E.' I croaked, my lip quivering, as I looked around my desk for a convenient hole to swallow me up.

'No, Geoffrey,' smiled the kindly Welshman. 'I said, we'll spend half an hour going over our arithmetic test and *then* we'll get changed for P.E.'

Last on my small list of dislikes at the beginning of this chapter was Mrs 'W'. She may well still be alive, and her offspring certainly are, hence the pseudonym. In my final year I became a Yellow House captain and was handed a nice shiny shield-shaped badge with HOUSE CAPTAIN written on it, which I wore with pride. One day I was on sentry duty. Two of us had to stand outside the hall during morning assembly to prevent anyone walking in by mistake while the hymns and morning prayers were being conducted. You would get the odd late-comer arriving with a parent, for example, or a tradesman wanting to see the Head, and it was our duty to respectfully request that they waited in the vestibule until assembly was over. One day, a lady by the name of Mrs 'W' came steaming across the playground, putrid air snorting from each nostril like a rabid bull. Apparently, Mr Perry had dared to cane her awful son, Brett, earlier that week, and she was consequently both livid and rabid. This sounds almost Dickensian now, but in those days, and also during my grammar school days, the head was entitled to administer such punishments, and many teachers had a slipper in their drawer to wallop any kid that was playing up. I know I'm being somewhat controversial here, but it worked. I don't think the slipper, in particular, was particularly painful, but it was an embarrassment to the child, and one he or she wanted to avoid, so any hint that it might come out of the drawer resulted in much-improved behaviour. Parents of the time were completely aware of this slipper, or in the Headmaster's case, the cane, for more serious breaches of conduct, and they appeared, fairly unanimously I would say, to give this their blessing. In fact, I heard of many incidents where a child had been punished, and such was the shame of the parents, he (it was usually a he) would receive another punishment when he got home, for bringing the family into disrepute. Remember, these were times when it was looked down upon to even eat in the street, and these were council-house folk, mind, not the landed gentry. Nowadays, if a teacher even chastises a child for being lazy, the slobby parent is up at the school ranting about Human Rights and undermining the role of the teacher. And we wonder why law and order is crumbling.

Anyway, this fiend in human form was fast approaching my colleague and me, and my little weedy pipe-cleaner legs were trembling, for I knew of this woman's reputation.

'I want a word with that Headmaster NOW!' she barked. 'No one canes my Brett!'

'Not even if he's an obnoxious bully who terrifies most of the kids here, including me, and actually deserves to be

22

garrotted rather than caned?' I wisely thought to myself. Suddenly I found an ounce of courage from somewhere and said, 'I'm very sorry, but Mr Perry is still taking assembly. He should be finished in around ten minutes, if you'd like to wait in the vestibule.'

'I haven't got time to bloody wait, I'm seeing him NOW!' she spat, and began to barge past me. I could just imagine this woman interrupting 'All Things Bright and Beautiful' and screaming obscenities at the well-respected, statesman-like figure behind the oak lectern. By now I was terrified, and my colleague, who was not much use I have to say, suddenly seemed to be examining a passing ladybird with particular interest instead of backing me up. Then - and I'll never forget this - I found myself standing in front of her with my arms stretched out, and saying', 'I'm sorry. I can't let you in there. I have to do my duty.'

Miraculously, she stormed off, and I began to shake and quiver like an aspen, as P.G. Wodehouse used to say. I told Mr Perry about it afterwards and he put his arm around me and said, 'Well done, Geoffrey. That was brave of you. I won't even ask if you remained polite, because I know you would have done.'

It is true. In those days, my manners were immaculate, again, thanks to my parents who firmly believed in all that stuff.

Later that week, Mrs 'W' accosted my poor mother halfway up Quarry Bonk High Street and began poking her in the chest aggressively. 'Your boy barred me from seeing the Headmaster, and when I tried to walk round him, he flew at me, shouting and swearing, and his eyes were proper wild!'

La vendetta è un piatto che va mangiato freddo, Signora 'W', as my many Italian friends would say.

When I wasn't at school, I busied myself with a variety of healthy or intellectual pursuits, as most of us did in those days. None of us spent hours staring at mobile phones, worried about our status or the amount of 'likes' we receive on FaceBook. No one was obsessed with what Brenda had said about Cheryl's bitchy comment about her boyfriend, and that is because what we didn't know didn't hurt us, and the bloody awful mobile phone and all the social media sites were yet to be invented.

If I never see again those pictures of shirtless, muscle-bound, tattooed Narcissus-types staring into their phones, or the wistful, plastered-in-mahogany-make-up women sporting Groucho Marx eyebrows, with their hideous pumped-up pouts and their fake boobs that resemble two melons in a plastic Spar bag, it will be far too soon for me. Call me a curmudgeonly old git (and I am, I admit it), but I really think this phone obsession has destroyed an entire generation of teenagers. The i-phone is a more powerful drug than Heroin, and far more insidious, I'm convinced of it. It has rendered them all incapable of conversation and made them horribly self-obsessed and insecure. It's also spawned a generation of snowflake children who get mortally wounded by virtually everything, and enjoy taking offence, often on other people's behalf, even when the supposedly aggrieved party couldn't care less. And don't get me started on Virtue-Signalling, and the soppy University students who want to create safe spaces where visiting speakers are banned from speaking because the students don't agree with their points of view and it might upset the little dears. Isn't lively debate what university is all about? Incidentally, do you remember free speech? Cherish it folks, because it won't be with us much longer. George Orwell's gloomy predictions are coming true, bit by bit. I really do fear for the future of the planet unless this evil habit, namely the mobile phone with its internet facility, is better regulated or else falls out of favour. And we haven't even touched on perverts, paedophiles, the sexual grooming of

24

children and the radicalisation of the naïve and impressionable yet, all facilitated by this same tool, which should have been a force for good, but instead gave the evil ones that inhabit our world a brand-new lethal weapon to cause havoc with. I walk around Wollaston village each morning at 8am before starting work and watch the steady stream of cars on their way to Stourbridge and beyond. Without exaggeration, I would estimate that almost half of the drivers are not looking at the road, but down at their phones, and these are not just teenagers I'm talking about. Occasionally, a lady will be so transfixed by her phone that she hasn't noticed that the traffic jam ahead of her has cleared, or that she is now holding up a mile of cars behind her. Television was once called the Opium of the Masses. Now, sadly, the telephone has taken over that role. Never mind the awful new zombie drugs such as Spice. The i-phone is creating far more zombies than that ever could! Now excuse me while I dismantle my Ikea soap box using the Allen key provided and press on with this story.

When I was at home, David and I would spend hours laughing, writing nonsense poems, playing Subbuteo, kicking a ball about, riding bikes, and raiding our parents' wardrobes so that we could dress up in ridiculous costumes to make each other laugh. No, we were NOT budding transvestites, and I suppose I ought to add, 'not that there's anything wrong with budding transvestites', just in case one of the aforementioned snowflake students is reading this and decides to be aggrieved on behalf of the cross-dressing community.

David and I had a secret way of talking that only we understood, and in many ways, we were more like twins than kids with nearly a 4-year age gap. It was at this time that we forged our life-long bond and developed our senses of humour. David, in particular, loved nonsense poetry, and we used to write reams of the stuff in our prized comedy notebooks, one of which I still have. Here is a typical one of his masterpieces from that very early period that still makes me laugh.

> Perk yourself, Monster,
> Woblets 3 a packet,
> 40 men upon a rock,
> Eabstove's dire racket.
>
> Joe Gunne, less an arm,
> Many are his aspirin,
> Radiation Theory works,
> Only when he's gaspin',
>
> Zebra cutlets waft a draft,
> Who likes creosote?
> Discipline lacks all but logs,
> With Mrs Table-Boat.

Even his poem's titles would have me in hysterics. This young child would write epic poems, similar to Lewis Carroll's 'Hunting of the Snark', that had titles such as; 'The Doxology of Ulysses the Sheep' and 'Glandular Delights on the Amazon'. I still remember odd lines from these poems that would make us laugh until it actually hurt. Lines such as;

> 'Turple Crotchet, Turple Crotchet,
> how thou art a weedy plinth!'
> 'I am but what Flakes are.
> Thou art a mere Brook-egg!'

Or his huge list of people that featured in a poem about a surreal pageant or parade, six of whom, chosen at random, were;

'J. Johnson Grainger, Mortimer Grainger, 'Pantomime' Joe Higgins, the Grenadier Guards and Dartagnon, Jack 'The Bunny Rabbit' Flannion....'

These weird and wonderful pieces of gibberish sound almost Shakespearean in parts, and I vividly remember that the other kids on the estate thought we were both completely loony. They only laughed at 'proper' jokes, and if there wasn't a punchline, they didn't get it. They liked a joke to be like a simple pop song, with a clear structure; a verse followed by a chorus. Our humour, on the other hand, was, if anything, more similar to jazz, in that you either got it or you didn't. It was all about the juxtaposition of abstract words to create a comic effect. For us, telling jokes was like buying your humour off the peg. It was cheating. You didn't need to be a funny person, you just acquired a joke, retold it, and hopefully your friend would laugh, because society expected that of him, and then the recipient would retell it to *his* friend, *ad nauseam*. By contrast, we rarely told a joke. David would instead suggest a first line, such as, for example, 'Go up to a cowboy and hit him in the chin'. I would then add, 'dig a hole in his neck' and David would respond with, 'and then fill it in!' whereupon we would dissolve into uncontrollable laughter. Our mother would often look on with a puzzled expression, shake her head and carry on ironing. I daresay comedians Vic Reeves and Bob Mortimer had a very similar childhood, and of course, brother David and I understand their wavelength completely, though they would have been given short shrift on a Saturday night in the Labour Club. I always remember the stock response by middle-aged Quarry Bonkers to comedians that were too surreal for their taste. 'I cor loff at him, I cor. He's TOO saft!'

I am very lucky to have a brother that I get on with. There is no guarantee that this will automatically happen, and it must be a cause of great concern to parents. The only time that I can remember anything untoward was when he shoved me backwards over my pedal car in the garden (I can't remember why he chose to do this). David is, by nature, a stubborn fellow, and even at that tender age, he wasn't keen on saying sorry. He has to *want* to do things and he can't be cajoled into it. Unfortunately, for him at least, our wonderful mother could be just as stubborn, and in this instance, it was a case of the powerful force meeting the immoveable object, or whatever the exact expression is.

She asked him to apologize. He wouldn't. She got shirty. He still wouldn't. Livid now, and not wanting this little oik to get the better of her, she foolishly threatened to hold his head under the tap if he didn't. He definitely wouldn't. I could see things getting out of hand. He was hoisted up and placed in the huge Belfast sink. He still, resolutely, wouldn't. The tap came on. He definitely, defiantly and under no circumstances would offer an apology, even to avoid an untimely and watery death. (are you getting the idea that the powerful force was going to have to be far more powerful against this particular immoveable object if it wanted to see victory?) In the end, mom gave up, as David would have been filled up with water like a balloon via his right earhole with no apology in sight, and she'd have been looking at 15 years inside. Thankfully, nothing similar has happened since, and 'The Case of the Pedal Car' is now a footnote in history, but it does show us what a determined individual he is, does it not? Thankfully, he has harnessed that determination and used it in more productive areas ever since. Mind you, one day when he least expects it, I still intend to push him backwards over his BMW Z4.

I was a big reader back then, though I have to admit that I am now more of a sporadic, fitful one. I loved the Anthony Buckeridge 'Jennings' books, about a boarding school, even though my own upbringing couldn't have been more different. I also loved my Ladybird nature books, especially the 'Birds and Their Nests' editions. My friend at that time, Mally, used to go out bird-nesting and collecting eggs, but even then, that felt wrong to me. Which reminds me. I never understood that expression about teaching your grandmother to suck eggs. Mally used to blow them, not suck them. Am I misunderstanding something here? Anyway, the illustrations in these books inspired me and I was overawed by the artists' skills and still am. I saw some of the original Ladybird paintings at Fielding's Auctioneers in Stourbridge recently, and was sorely tempted to own a few, but the price tag suggested otherwise and I kept my paddle in my lap, so to speak. Another thing I'll probably regret in the fullness of time.

Our other big interest was Subbuteo, and for those who are not familiar, it was a table football game that comprised a large baize pitch and two teams of small plastic players, who were cemented into a half-sphere of plastic, a bit like the self-righting 'Kelly Man' plaything at the bottom of a budgerigar's cage that was nigh-on impossible to knock over. The players were positioned on the taut baize and flicked with the forefinger at the ball. We had a Subbuteo league on our estate, and each kid had his own team (I was Manchester City because I liked the pale blue top and claret and blue stripy socks). Fixture's sheets were xeroxed and distributed, and there was even, if I remember rightly, a small 'plasti-chrome' cup for the league winners. Lads would visit the away ground carrying their box of players, and an 'impartial' referee would often attend, though their knowledge of the rules was often suspect, and they were open to bribery and corruption. One lad, whose name I will omit to save his embarrassment, often made up the rules as he went along, and was known to get shirty to the point of threatened violence when anyone questioned him about it. One evening at my house, facing a penalty (which he pronounced PELUNTY) he suddenly shouted 'Blocks!' and positioned all ten of his players right in front of my striker who was standing behind the ball on the penalty spot, waiting to be flicked. I looked askance at the ref, who mumbled something incoherent because he didn't have the foggiest idea either, and, to cut a long story short, no goal ensued. Okay, I can't keep this inside any longer, it was Ian Genner who cheated me. Shame on you, man! I hope you've changed your ways in the last 53 years.

It was around this time that I decided I would like a pet. I have no idea how this went down with my parents at the time, but somehow, I managed to persuade them to get me a hamster. My dad set about building a home for this creature, and typically, he threw his heart and soul into it. Jennings's new apartment was a splendid affair. It was a 2-storey open plan 'space' with a set of wooden steps that led upstairs to his play area, dining room and sun terrace. Downstairs was a small bedroom and a gymnasium, where the hamster wheel was situated. The front of his palatial home was a large sheet of glass, so we could observe his comings and goings. This could be removed for when I cleaned the place, which never happened. Children promise the world to get hold of a pet, but as soon as they get one, all those promises go out of the window.

Dad was about to install central heating in the hamster house when I told him enough was enough already. There goes that Jewish thing again! I can't for the life of me remember the chronology of this, but at one stage I also had a tiny white mouse, which I took with me to visit Granny Bertha and Grandad Reuben, whether they wanted me to or not. I remember walking from our house to theirs, a good half a mile away, if not more, with this little mouse in my pocket or on my shoulder, as tame as a mouse could be.

The hamster, meanwhile, lived a happy life until one arctic winter, when I found him stiff and cold in his bed, and I blame myself. If only I'd allowed my dad to install the central heating system, this could have been prevented. With quivering lip, I took it inside and was planning a huge state funeral with all branches of the family attending and sandwiches at the Liberal Club afterwards, but instead my dad placed him in the pedal bin and assured me that this was what he would have wanted. Still sobbing gently, I took solace in my 'Reader's Digest Book of Small Animals', with the intention of selecting a hardier replacement, like maybe a badger. It was then that I came across the section on hamsters. It explained that, when a hamster gets too cold it hibernates, and this state can be mistaken for death. The animal, it continued, must be laid in bedding in a warm environment, where hopefully if will revive. I dashed back to the pedal bin, but in the interim, my mother had emptied half a ton of potato peelings and the dregs of a tin of Heinz Tomato Soup in there. I rummaged around and located the stiff little rodent, who was looking decidedly the worse for wear now, and covered in tomato sauce. I gently sponged him down and laid him on top of one of my socks, next to the three-bar gas fire with flame effect in the front room. Imagine my surprise when, some two hours later, he emerged from his slumbers, yawned a mighty yawn and immediately retreated into the cavity underneath the gas fire, never to be seen again.

My only other pet after that was supplied courtesy of the Rag and Bone Man, (not the tattooed, bearded singer of that *nom-de-plume*, but an actual Rag and Bone Man) who used to trawl around the estate on a horse and cart collecting unwanted clothing and so on. I saw him being given lots of rags, but I never spotted any bones, come to think of it. If a house had been particularly generous, the child would be offered a goldfish in a plastic bag full of water. It was hardly a hamster but it was better than nothing. I was particularly fascinated by the piece of string that hung from its belly on odd occasions, until dad patiently explained that it was, in fact, fish shit, and as to longevity, let's just say that my hamster's lifespan was Methuselah-like in comparison. Dad must have been inspired by my free goldfish though, because he came home from work with a tropical fish tank not long after and took up a new hobby that lasted several years. I now

31

know the difference between a Guppy and a Kissing Gourami. In fact, I made up a rather wonderful mini-sketch about them some time back, which went thus:

'I keep Kissing Gourami.'

'Well, stop doing that, you pervert!'

'No, it's a type of fish.'

'Oh right. Well I keep Burping Tuna fish, as it happens.'

'I've never heard of those, are they tropical?'

'No, I mean, I get terrible indigestion!'

Well, it's a work in progress.

Dad had a habit of bringing odd things home from work. At the time, I just took it all for granted and saw it as normal, but now I can't help but wonder where it all came from. He would emerge from the garage after a hard day's work bearing gifts for his children. I remember, for example, the end part of a periscope that the captain would look through, taken from a wartime submarine. He came home one night with a German Zither, a lovely, ornate musical instrument with mother-of-pearl inlays that I left in the coal cellar on a rainy night. It was worth considerably less after that. I had at least three saxophones and sold each one. There was an Edwardian shock machine that was supposed to be therapeutic. It was made of mahogany and had two wires coming from it which were attached to two metal and wood tubes which you held, and which administered electric shocks to your thumbs for reasons unknown. You were able to control the force of these shocks by means of another metal tube that fitted within a coil, and if I remember correctly, 'pushed fully in' was mild and 'pulled fully out' was severe. I pulled the tube out completely and asked David to try it, just for fun, or maybe it was retaliation for pedal car abuse. He is lucky to still be with us, is all I am saying about that unfortunate incident.

There were also assorted books, some of great antiquity, which I scribbled all over, old board games, several Tyrolean-looking accordions, hand-grenades (mostly de-activated), giant brass artillery shells (likewise), gas masks, war medals, and the odd stuffed creature, all of which went the way of last year's snow. How he came by these in a toolmaking factory in Old Hill remains one of the greatest mysteries of all time.

And talking, as we were, albeit briefly, of stuffed things, my friend Mally, the one who liked bird's egg collecting, was also a keen amateur taxidermist. He was forever filling his long-suffering mother's fridge full of dead and decaying things he'd found in Casson's Wood, and they didn't sit well alongside the marmalade and cheddar cheese. I was once offered one of his early efforts, an owl, if I recall, that had met its maker thanks to a disagreement with an Austin A40. I was willing to allow his bizarre and somewhat dishevelled effort to reside in my bedroom but this was vetoed by my mother who said it looked at her funny when she made the bed and gave her the creeps.

Money was tight, as it was for most people on the Birch Coppice estate but living in a council house did not have the stigma attached to it that it maybe has today. Quite simply, virtually everyone I knew lived in a council house, except Ian Genner (who cheated at Subbuteo; did I mention that?) and Mr and Mrs Glaze whose son Robert was eventually signed to Aston Villa. This was many years before Margaret Thatcher allowed people to buy their council properties, and naively, I don't think I realized that there were posh houses within a ten-mile radius with well-off people living in them, because I'd never noticed them. My mom was a good knitter, which saved us a lot of money, but it meant that I was always wearing chunky cardigans with big leather case-ball buttons, which, for the uninitiated, were around an inch wide and looked like small old-style footballs; the ones that were made up of rectangular leather panels, that Stanley Matthews used to kick around. I had knitted jumpers, knitted gloves, knitted underpants, bobble hats, water bottles, balaclavas - you name it, Ruby would knit it. Balaclavas were my worst nightmare.

We were all forced to wear them, and they were horrible and itchy. I have a theory about bank robbers. As far as I know, no infamous bank robbers came from Quarry Bonk, the reason being, we were so traumatized by having to wear balaclavas as children, that we couldn't face ever having to wear one again. In most cases, childhood deprivation leads to a life of crime, but in this case, the opposite was true, and it put us on the straight and narrow.

I hated balaclavas, but I admit that I was rather taken with a huge pair of brown leather gauntlets that I saw in one of the high street shops, mainly because they harked back to an earlier age of chivalry and knights in armour, and I loved all that. I drove my mother half-mad and eventually she allowed me to have them, once I'd politely refused a knitted pair. I was also obsessed with flintlock pistols, galleons and Treasure Island, my dad's favourite book. I got my first toy flintlock from Mrs Kendall's Toy Shop (of whom, more later), and I still have it. I quickly realised that the tiny toy gun was constructed along exactly the same lines as a real one, so one day I rammed the contents of a penny banger into it using the ramrod, added a ball-bearing that I found in dad's shed, and a cap from a cap gun which I placed in the 'pan', beneath the flintlock mechanism. I aimed it at my dad's newly-built garage, grimaced and nervously pulled the trigger. There was a deafening bang and the window caved in. I now own a real 1720s Balkan flintlock and I have no intention of ever trying to fire it.

One winter's day, while I was eating my cornflakes prior to walking to school, I was gazing dreamily out of the window that overlooked the garden, when I heard an almighty whooshing noise. Then, a big pile of sand on our patio that a builder was about to use, literally disappeared, followed shortly by a whole garden shed and a garage flying through the air, completely intact, and clearing Mrs Brooks's house with ease. I pinched myself to make sure this wasn't one of my bizarre dreams, but no, it happened exactly as I have

34

reported it. I abandoned the cereal and dashed out of the front door to see the garage sat in the road, bewildering the traffic. We'd experienced a rather powerful whirlwind or typhoon or whatever they call them. I duly described this incident to Mr Lewis in class, only to be subjected to outrageous ridicule from all present.

By the age of ten I had rested my trusty recorder in favour of a clarinet, a beautiful Boosey & Hawkes Emperor model made of ebony and nickel silver which mom and dad got me for Christmas, such was their devotion to me. I naively thought it was Santa's doing for a few years until I got wise, aged 33. I had just begun to have private lessons in a faraway, mysterious place called Wollaston, where I now live. It's actually around 5 miles away at most, but as a kid it seemed distant and faintly exotic. The music teacher was a Scottish disciplinarian by the name of Alexander Bryce, who was quite a bigshot in Clarinet World, as he was the man responsible for arranging most of the classical clarinet sheet music in Britain for the Oxford University Press, in conjunction with a Mr Bennoy who arranged the piano accompaniments. 'Arranged by Bennoy & Bryce', it said on all my sheet music, and Mr Bryce put me through my paces once a week in the drawing room of his comfortable detached house at No.42 or possibly No.43, Park Road. (This book is painstakingly researched, you have to admit. All I had to do was walk round the block to confirm the bloody number.) Dad would sit in another small sitting room reading National Geographic magazines while I stared at a million black dots on a music stand in the front room and tried to make sense of them. Mr Bryce sat next to me saying things like 'Och aye, that's a fine vibrato ye have there, laddie!' and other Scottish stuff. He had great hopes for me, that man. He wanted me to do the grades and join an orchestra. He said I was gifted and a natural, which I was, I suppose. I achieved grade 8 level by the time I was in my teens, by his reckoning at least, but I never actually wanted to sit the exams. For the first four or five years I loved having lessons, but as it all got more serious and intense, seven or so years down the line, the joy went out of it. Still, for the time being, I was enjoying the clarinet, and it definitely wasn't anything to do with Pushy Parent Syndrome. In fact, it was me doing all the pushing. They just coughed up money they hadn't got spare to encourage me, as most parents do. I've said thank you many times, but here it is in print. You were the best parents ever, by a Country Mile.

Meanwhile, David, who I had taught to play the recorder, was showing a prodigious talent for the instrument. I would have to watch him carefully. He was a bit *too* good! And can I just add that when I slammed the car door onto his hand that day, it was an accident. I could easily have severed all of his little digits in one go. I still shudder at what might have happened. Luckily, he made a full recovery. Mind you, I told him it was revenge for the Pedal Car Incident, just so he'd think twice in future.

Chapter 4

When the weather was good, we would be outside, riding bikes, kicking a ball around or playing an assortment of street games. Football, which I did eventually get slightly better at, was played on a grassy hill around the corner from our house. The slope of the pitch was at least 45 degrees, which meant that if someone passed the ball to a person downhill from himself, and that person didn't connect, the ball would be in Cradley Heath, two miles away, by the time we'd caught up with it. I suppose you could argue that it honed our passing skills.

We also played street games. Girls, of course, played hopscotch, a version of which was discovered in Pompeii and other ancient Roman sites. Boys played stretch, which involved standing facing each other on grass, and throwing a pen-knife into the ground, which the other lad had to reach with his foot without falling over. Anything other than that I could not tell you, as I only ever had the most rudimentary grasp of the game at the time. Perhaps I was too busy trying to avoid having my toes amputated to concentrate on the rules.

Some kids made fire cans; basically, old tin cans with holes punched in them, which were then filled with coal and set alight. A string wrapped around the tin and tied tight enabled you to swing it around your head at high speed, so that the centrifugal force kept the coals in position. Obviously, this was more spectacular at night, when the whizzing coals would create a lightshow, though most participants would end up in the Burns Unit when they tried to slow the thing down afterwards and the centrifugal force stopped working. The Burns Unit was even busier come Bonfire Night thanks to the questionable tradition of throwing a penny banger or a jumping jack at friends for a laugh.

Some lads collected newts and sticklebacks, though what they did with them afterwards I couldn't say. Incidentally, do sticklebacks still exist? I haven't heard them mentioned in 20 years. And before you mention Blue Peter, that was sticky-backed plastic, which is a different thing altogether.

Most days we'd hear the eerie sound of air raid sirens coming from the direction of Cradley Heath, which must have unnerved the older folks who'd been through the trauma of the second world war. Thankfully, in the 1960s they were just identical-sounding factory sirens announcing that the lunch break or the working day was over. On Saturdays, however, we heard a different sound coming from Cradley Heath, and it too used to float on the air for miles. It was the sound of the speedway, and Cradley had one of the best teams in England at that time. Just after teatime, one by one, people would vacate their houses and join forces, all heading for the same venue, as if hypnotised by the Pied Piper. They wore green-and white-striped scarves and bobble hats, and many would sport a little winged enamel badge that had extra bars attached beneath it to show how many years they'd been attending the stadium; thus, a veteran might have a badge that was 2 feet long. The fans also carried an A4 clipboard to hold their programme, usually hand-painted with Cradley Speedway designs, or the distinctive, if rather uninspired, green and white CH logo.

The races consisted of 13 heats, with two riders each from the home and away teams competing in a four-lap race. The bikes were fuelled by what was referred to as dope, rather than petrol, which produced a distinctive and not unpleasant smell. Speedway bikes had just one gear and no brakes, just to make life interesting. They raced on reddish-brown shale, and a rider would drop one leg to steady himself around the bends, an action they call 'broadsiding'. The bike's front wheel would follow the line of the bend, while the back of the bike swung wildly out towards the crowd members, who were showered in shale, but seemed to enjoy it. Crashes were commonplace, and sadly, a couple of riders died during my time there, but generally they'd get up, dust themselves off and be ready to do it all again in a few heats' time. After the main event there was an interval, during which you bought a hotdog and a cup of tea or Bovril, and then the novices heats began. We all loved those because the riders were rubbish and they dropped off a lot more than the first-team chaps. Even at an early age, maybe around 14 or so, I was entrepreneurial with my artistic skills. I began painting programme clipboards with action shots of riders on the back and selling them to people I knew. My dad would sometimes add a swanky battery-powered light at the top of the deluxe model, which was, I kid you not, a sought-after item. I also did a lot of sign-writing and artwork for the various shops in the high street. I did the sign for a turf accountant next to my junior school (I didn't even know that grass needed an accountant!), the Christmas window display for a newsagent in New Street, a couple of coal lorries and a few other odds and ends. I even designed myself a business card, which is reproduced in the photograph section.

All the kids on the estate loved to emulate their Speedway heroes, courtesy of cycle speedway. We would acquire an old frame, repaint it, straighten the forks (for reasons I am still vague about) by gently bashing them with a hammer, remove the brakes and have a fixed gear on the rear wheel. Some lads even secured a rolled-up fag packet to the back forks that faced inwards to touch the spokes, so that it made a noise like an engine when the wheel went around. Actually, I tried this recently and it doesn't sound anything like a bloody engine, I have to say. It sounds more like a rolled-up Woodbine's packet catching the spokes.

We'd hold meetings on 'The Table Top', a plateau near Netherton Reservoir, and create teams and leagues so we could race against each other and win trophies. I was in great demand during those times for making race jackets, which were a kind of vinyl bib with a design on the front and a number, from 1 to 7, on the back. I would design them, leaving my long-suffering mother to sew them together. I was always far more interested in the associated paraphernalia of any given sport or activity than the actual playing of it. You could also buy the authentic ultra-lightweight plastic, disposable speedway goggles from the Cradley Speedway stadium and wear them in conjunction with a dashing neckerchief, and, if you possessed a pair, leather gauntlets. I don't think there was a day during the period 1965-69 when my parents' backyard wasn't littered with bike parts, oil cans, filthy chains and Humbrol enamel tins. I bet they couldn't wait for me to turn my attention to loud electric guitars instead.

In those days we seemed to have lots of very small shops in Quarry Bonk that were once the front room of someone's house, and they sold the basic grocery items plus sweets and Tizer or Dandelion & Bird Muck, as we called it, for the kids. Cheese came in two forms, sharp or mild. No one had ever heard of Wensleydale, Parmesan, Red Leicester, Brie, or any of the other ones. It was hand-cut and wrapped in paper for you, as were the loose vegetables. Nothing was packaged, and our seas were in better condition and not full of plastic. If dad wanted a pint of beer at home, he took his jug to the outdoor of the local pub and they filled it for him. Either that or you signed up with Davenport's, whose slogan, in the form of a catchy little tune, was:

'Beer at home means Davenport's, that's the beer, lots of cheer. The finest hops with malt and yeast, turns a snack into a feast. Straight from breweries to your home. Why collect? We'll deliver. Soon you'll know why folks all say, beer at home means Davenports, cheers!'

We kids bought a Jubbly instead, which was a triangular fruit-flavoured iceberg full of E numbers that stained your face for days afterwards, or Tip-Tops, which were similar concoctions but in long plastic sleeves that we sucked until all the red or orange colour disappeared and we were left with a clear ice wand. Also popular were Sherbet Fountains, a tube full of sherbet powder with a liquorice straw that clogged up and became useless within seconds, Wagon Wheels, which actually tasted like I imagine a real Wagon Wheel would, and those funny little alien spaceships that were made from a form of almost inedible paper and had a fizzy powder inside instead of a real alien, which might have tasted a bit better. The bubble gum of choice was Bazooka Joe, which swelled up to the size of a small dinghy in your mouth and came with a small full-colour cartoon to read while your head was expanding. Those adept at bubble-blowing could usually achieve something similar in size to a hot-air balloon if they chewed three at once. I watched a girl I knew from Tenbury Wells do this many years ago, and then I popped it. It took her parents all day to get it off her face and hair, and, in spite of my easy-going charm and friendly nature, I was not popular with them for some time after that.

Our school was near the bottom of Quarry Bonk High Street, a few hundred yards before it disappeared around the corner and became Cradley Heath. The Labour and Liberal Clubs were opposite and down a bit, as far away as possible from the Conservative Club which was near the top end by the church. Not that anyone cared about the politics. Most folks went to all three, depending on their whim, or what was on that night (organ and drums duo, comedian, 'talented' vocalist, bingo, ballroom dancing even).

The high street, though not tortuous, is nevertheless a torturous affair (see what I did there?), being straight but very steep. In the 60s, it seemed to be largely made up of pubs, butcher's shops, wool shops, an ironmonger-cum-hardware store and, erm, more pubs. A bit higher than the school, and opposite the turning to Sheffield Street was Freddie Field's Barber Shop, the place where we all had to go for a haircut as there didn't appear to be any nearby competition. (currently called De Havilland Hair Art, and Freddie's old red and white sign is still there). Freddie was old-school and wore a grey nylon lab-coat affair with the instruments of his trade lined up in his breast pocket. He understood short back and sides and Brylcreem and that was about it. There was even a sign in his window that said, 'No Long Hair' which begs the question, what's a barber for if not to shorten hair when it gets too long?

You could ask for a Paul McCartney, it being the 60s, when that style was popular, and Fred would *pretend* he understood your request, and nod in all the right places, before ignoring it completely and wading in with the clippers to decimate the hair at the back and side of your head, leaving angry great weals in your scalp as he did so. Once finished, he would switch to the scissors to snip around frenetically on the top bit, before smothering Brylcreem all over your hair, brow, ears and neck. Then he'd sweep the loose hairs - the ones not stuck to your greasy head - right down your collar to save him the job of sweeping them up from his floor afterwards, thereby ensuring that you itched like crazy until your weekly bath night. Some poor unfortunates, usually the older men, even had their hair set on fire. The process was called singeing, and it involved Freddie lighting a small taper with his wall-mounted boiler's pilot light and whizzing it back and forth over the freshly-cut hair, melting the ends of each hair follicle into a tiny teardrop shape. The theory was that this bizarre process stopped you from catching a cold. It was never proven, but one thing was certain - It stopped the victims getting a girlfriend, once their head resembled the aftermath of an Australian bush-fire. Even worse than your actual haircut experience was the torment and humiliation you received upon arriving at school with a new hairstyle, come Monday morning. Nowadays, no one even mentions it unless you're an 80-year-old who's chosen to have a Mohican or dyed it bright green, but in those days the other schoolkids would whack you across the head in the playground and scream 'HAIRCUT!' at you. I used to dread it, almost as much as having to endure 'the bumps' on my birthday. It amazes me

42

how we all managed to avoid being rendered paraplegic by this vile tradition.

As Freddie removed your gown and your cash, he would ask one of two things, depending on if you were a minor or an adult. The child got, 'I thank you, John, would you like a penny chocolate, and shall I cross you over the road?' which was quite sweet, I think, even though every customer was referred to as John to save him from having to remember names. The men were of course asked, 'Anything for the weekend, John?' A sentence I never fully understood at the time, and one he never asked me, for some reason. Had he done so, I was going to ask for more penny chocolates.

Halfway up the street on the opposite side to Freddie's place was Mrs Kendall's toy shop, a formidable and unnerving place. I never understood why she ran a toy shop. A man who was good at art might wish to become a professional artist as I did, and a lady who, say, liked to knit might entertain the notion of opening her own wool shop one day, so what, in God's name, was an ogre who appeared to hate children, and for that matter, adults, doing in a toy shop, we all used to ask? My mother once went there to buy me an Airfix model, and she happened to be clutching a small bag of sweets from another establishment that she'd popped into a few minutes earlier. Mrs Kendall, on whom Giles surely based his surly grandmother cartoon, glowered at her and snarled, 'If you buy your sweets from somewhere else you can buy your bloody toys from there as well!' before turning her back on her and returning, troll-like, to the place under the bridge out the back of the shop where she lived.

On another occasion I nervously ventured in on my own, keen to buy a model Dalek, an exploding cigar, a stink bomb or some such novelty, and finding no one serving behind the counter, I rang the big brass bell, as instructed by the sign Sellotaped to it. Mrs Kendall appeared from the back room where she presumably whiled away her time by boiling the meat off children's severed heads to fill her sandwiches, and growled at me, informing me in no uncertain terms never to ring that bell again.

Chapter 5

Relatives are wonderful things and come in all shapes and sizes. You sort of inherit all these odd characters when you're a kid, and you're not really sure who they all are, but there's loads of them and most are bordering on eccentric, or at least, in our family they were. Take Aunty Millie, my Granny Bertha's sister. She had a habit of turning up at our house to borrow the club book. Now, if you are not familiar with these, they were thick, heavy catalogues full of just about every item known to man, from clothes and underwear to household goods, sports equipment, tents, shoes, settees, bikes, - you name it, and the idea was you ordered them from the club book agent – my mom in this case - and the item arrived at our house a few days later by post or courier van. The beauty of club books such as Grattan's, Kay's and similar was that you could choose a payment plan to suit your wallet. For example, you could buy yourself a nice orange four-man tent over 20 weeks at £2 per week, or a pair of nylon flared brown trousers at £1 per week over 12 weeks. This suited people on our estate, as money was often tight. My relative, David Nixon, who I call my cousin but he wasn't, was formerly, you will recall, the Angel of the Lord, and he once asked my mother if he could pay over 36 weeks for a pair of corduroy trousers, which would probably have worn out long before he'd finished paying for them. My brother whispered to me that he'd have been better off renting his trousers. He was already a promising comedian.

Aunty Millie was a nervy creature, and she obviously saw buying goods from a club book as a form of social embarrassment. She'd arrive at the house and make herself at home while mom made her a cup of tea, and speak in a perfectly normal voice, pitched at a normal volume. However, when it was time to explain to my mom the official reason for her state visit, her voice would shrink to a barely audible whisper that got even quieter as she said, 'I've come for the.... club book,' so that the last two words were just mouthed with no sound whatsoever. All this as she glanced this way and that, in case anyone hiding behind the arras like Polonius from Hamlet, was eavesdropping. I've seen people less reticent when asking for a Rampant Rabbit in a sex emporium. Incidentally, my brother David, not possessing the social graces to the extent that his elder brother did, never bothered to say hello to Aunty Millie when she arrived, which caused our mother to embarrass him by saying, 'Say hello to Aunty Millie, David.' I bet those of you who have been following his early career with interest can guess what happened next, if indeed 'nothing' counts as something happening.

I never ordered much from the Grattan's catalogue myself, but as a young boy I was fascinated by the ladies' underwear section and would spend many a happy hour perusing this when my mother was up in the high street, shopping. I also enjoyed the men's clothing section but for different reasons, I hasten to add. Both David and I loved to make fun of the Ansell's Bitter-Man-type models therein, with their massive sideburns, 1960's hairstyles, and roll-necked cardigans, their arms slung jauntily over a friend's shoulder as they pointed meaningfully at something in the far distance. These blokes were always pointing at stuff, or else fingering their manly chins, deep in thought. Their clothes, typically a cack-brown coloured, cardboard-like leather jacket or an Ansell's Bitter-Man chunky knit jumper worn with elasticated cream slacks, had small serial numbers plastered all over them so you knew which item you were ordering. What really amused me though, was the fact that, even while wearing just Y fronts in the underwear section, these blokes were still pointing at stuff, or clutching their manly chins, deep in thought, or else they had their arms around each other's shoulders. I make it a rule

46

not to get that matey with semi-naked men in locker rooms, but each to his own, I say. Live and let live!

I had a full complement of grandparents back then. My dad's parents were Frank and Elizabeth. Frank was, in every way, Tommy Trinder, a funny, sarcastic, woodbine-smoking, bushy-eyebrowed character who drank gallons of tea. In fact, we Tristrams are all sarcastic and all drink gallons of tea, and if I may digress just for a few seconds, I met a man recently at an event, and he happened to ask what my surname was. Upon learning that it was Tristram, he laughed and said, 'So you'll be a sarcastic bugger who drinks loads of tea then!' I swear this is absolutely true. Our reputation has travelled further than I thought. Elizabeth, sadly, was prone to depression. I don't think she was ever happy, not for one day of her miserable life, which God made a long one, just to spite her. She was in and out of mental hospitals for most of the time I knew her, and I felt desperately sorry for both my dad and my grandad, having to cope with that. She even had that awful electric shock therapy, like something from 'One Flew Over the Cuckoo's Nest' but none of it made much difference. If I'd known I'd have let her have a go on my Edwardian Shock machine for nothing, with the tube pulled straight out. It may well have cured her.

They had two sons, Leonard, the eldest, and Frank, who were like chalk and cheese. Dad was the family man who passed for grammar school but wasn't allowed to go because the family needed his wage packet to help out. Frank was Arthur Daley, the sheepskin-coat-wearing scrap dealer, the wag, the cad, the joker, the charlatan, the man who spent most of his schooldays on the Isle of Wight in a sanitorium, suffering from tuberculosis, and as a consequence, couldn't read or write until they taught him in prison, where he once resided at her Majesty's Pleasure for purloining a load of scrap metal that wasn't strictly his. Ironically, in spite of his complete lack of education, he was the one who made all the money, while my dad just earned his weekly packet and no

47

more. I quite liked Frank, I freely admit, but I'm pleased I got the right brother as my dad. Frank was street-wise and flash. He had a big house, a lot of old grandfather clocks and a spivvy second-hand Rolls Royce even, at one point. He taught his two children that money was the most important thing in life and he learnt far too late that it wasn't. His mother idolised this son who seldom bothered to visit her, and took for granted the loyal, true son that visited virtually every day. I have never, to this day, understood the tale of the prodigal son from the Bible. Perhaps I'm missing something or being a bit thick. Was Jesus telling us to welcome the errant Frank by killing the fatted calf and let faithful Len carry on eating fishfingers, or have I got the wrong end of the stick?

I was far closer to my mother's parents, Bertha and Reuben, who lived at the top of Quarry Bonk High Street, in Thorns Avenue, where, as you already know, I was born. Bertha was a funny, jovial ex-cleaner and ex-barmaid who enjoyed getting up and singing a few songs in her local, the Sun, or maybe the Blue Ball, now an Indian restaurant. She, like Reuben, had an authentic old Black Country accent, or at least, one of them. It changed town by town, and I can accurately guess where a person is from to within a few miles once I've heard them speak a few sentences. The Quarry Bonk accent, when it was spoken by men, was often a sort of bellow from the chest, rather than the nasal whine of Wolverhampton, and this is because many of them were chain-makers and had to shout to be heard above the constant clanking of hammers. Cradley Heath and Old Hill accents are full of biblical thees and thines, thanks to the plethora of Methodist chapels. Out Sedgley and Coseley way, they pronounce down as dow-en, and phone as pho-un, so that's a right give-away. I'm no expert on places such as Walsall, but further on towards Birmingham, it becomes nasal once more, but with odd quirks, such as the long 'A' sound with words such as laugh (larf) and bath (barth) which no self-respecting Black Countryman would sanction. If anything, broad Brummie

48

reminds me more of the Cockney barrow-boy accent than a pure Black Country accent. The perfect exponent of this is Professor Carl Chinn, the famous historian. As far as I'm concerned, he has the spot-on Brummie accent.

My own accent was fairly broad as a child, but gradually it was diluted by grammar school, and later art college, where I was mixing with people from all over the country for the first time, even though the college was just up the road in Wolverhampton. I must admit that I was always embarrassed about the Black Country accent and didn't care for it at all as a young man, but as I get older I have come full circle and I'm quite fond of it once more. I often wish I'd recorded Bertha speaking, because it really was an ancient dialect and sadly, it's fast disappearing, thanks to the influence of television. Now everyone who goes to university speaks with that faux Uni accent – the one where the sentence rises at the end as if they're asking you a question, and this was possibly learnt from watching endless episodes of 'Home and Away' and 'Neighbours' instead of studying. Those that don't have the Uni accent all sound like glottal-stopping Mancunians nowadays (none of them can pronounce the letter T if it's in the middle of a word), or else Imitation Londoners, who think the past tense of fink is fort. I am amazed that people from elsewhere confuse us with Brummies, (no offence to Brummies whatsoever, incidentally) when, to my ear, our accents are poles apart. I suppose Newcastle, Middlesbrough and Sunderland have the same problem. It all sounds the same to us lot down here but to them it definitely doesn't.

Anyway, just as an example, here are a few Bertha-style Quarry Bonkisms that I've strung into a small passage. I have written them phonetically, so say them exactly as they are written. It is pure Anglo Saxon.

Ow bist thay, me wench? Thist like one ez etten en throwed up bissn't thay? Ast thay got bally airk from them pig's feet thee et? Why dussn't thay goo-en sit theeself aht theer on that sate

in the shaird on we fode, ate a bitter fittle en power thisself
sum wek-tay. Thissle soon be right ez rain, yo be ruled be me!
Thiss-ed be better off bee-en sick but thee cossn't fetchet up,
cost thay?

Excuse the subject matter, if you can actually understand it,
but you get the drift, don't you? There's barely a recognisable
word amongst them. Anyone not living in our area who can
translate that accurately will win a prize. It's a night out with
me. The runner-up gets two nights. The old ones are the best
ones, eh?

Grandad Reuben was a gentle soul. He was a small, dapper
character with a soft voice. He liked his billiards and snooker,
and he liked to watch the boxing on his black and white
television. He was a dedicated gardener, like my other
grandad, and grew all his own vegetables. He would rise very
early each day, and potter about in his beloved vegetable
garden, digging, planting and befriending robins. Reuben was
wonderful with animals. He had a pet parrot called Cheeky
which he could hypnotise by stroking it gently. The bird
would then appear to fall asleep and flop over into grandad's
palm, as relaxed and peaceful as a parrot could be. I have a
pencil drawing that I did of Reuben, as he sat in the old
armchair in the kitchen, which is my oldest surviving sketch. I
must have been no more than 12 at the time. I've included it in
the photograph section.

David and I would often stay at my grandparents' house at
weekends. We loved it, and it gave my mom and dad a bit of
'freedom', which probably meant time to have sex. No
wonder she often looked a bit flushed when she came for me
on a Sunday teatime. And I always thought it was caused by
the arduous climb up the high street.

While we were there, I would forge bank notes with my 13-
colour biro. Mom says there would regularly be a production
line of pound notes, fivers, and tenners on Bertha's kitchen
table. I was convinced they were identical to the real thing,

and my idea was to spend them in the high street shops, in exchange for Airfix models, exploding cigars, flintlock pistols, leather gauntlets or whatever took my fancy. My mother patiently explained that this wasn't the best idea I'd ever had, and gently steered me away from my life of crime. I have been as honest as the day is long ever since, you'll be pleased to know. There is a picture of one of these forged banknotes in the photographic section, alongside my drawing of Reuben, two of the earliest drawings I have.

Bertha always seemed to be preparing food. She had giant pots on the stove, often full of pig's tails and trotters or home-made faggots, all bubbling away, while she chopped and prepared Reuben's vegetables to accompany them. I also remember wholesome stews with meat of some kind (best not to ask), pearl barley, lentils and carrots. David and I would be asked to pop the peapods and drop the peas into a dish for her. I'm sure a lot of children nowadays wouldn't know that peas begin in a pod. While all this was going on, her old radio, sat high on a shelf in the kitchen, entertained us with 'Round the Horn', 'The Billy Cotton Band Show', 'Jimmy Clitheroe' and 'Two-Way Family Favourites'. I always remember the requests on that programme coming from somewhere called BFPO in Luxembourg. I still have no idea what that means, but I'm guessing the BF stood for British Forces.

When Ruby arrived at Sunday teatime, there was always a programme called 'Sing Something Simple' on the radio, featuring the Mike Sammes Singers, and it was so bloody maudlin that it hastened our departure. The three of us would walk back down the high street together, ready for bed. Dad always had a car as far as I can recall, but we still walked a hell of a lot. Once home, it was a bath, followed by 'Sunday Night at the London Palladium', hopefully with the Beatles, who I loved and still do. Who in their right mind doesn't? At the end, they'd all stand on a circular revolving stage and wave at us as the host, Norman Vaughan I believe, said goodnight. In those days, every comedian had to have a catchphrase, and most were truly awful. His, I remember, was 'Swinging, Dodgy!' Hilarious, is it not?

This was a golden time for me, if I'd only realised it. I had recently passed my 11-Plus and was destined for Tipton Grammar School, which was all very exciting and nerve-wracking in equal measure. The 11-Plus is now a very controversial thing, so allow me to add my own thoughts to the debate.

I keep hearing about elite grammar schools and the unfairness of it all, and how all kids should be in a comprehensive. Grammar schools may well be elite institutions now, I don't honestly know, but in my time they were a way of getting a first-class education if you couldn't afford to pay for one. Almost everyone at my grammar school was working class and came from a similar background to me. If there were any privileged posh kids at my school, I can't remember them. Yes, I know it was Tipton and what did I expect, but I think it was a similar scenario at David's Dudley Grammar School, and also at Brierley Hill. These were all working class kids who were breaking the mould, escaping the factory life they would have been destined for if grammar schools hadn't been available, and becoming doctors, lawyers, artists, musicians, accountants... you name it. Suddenly, we could be anything. The controversial part in all this is the exam itself, which separated pupils from their classmates according to their academic brightness. Sadly, talent, brightness, whatever you wish to call it, is a fact of life. Some children are not academic, never will be, and all they want to do is get a job and leave the education system a.s.a.p. Then there's a sub-division of this sector who would dearly love to progress academically but are simply not good enough to do so. Add to this list those who not only don't want to learn, but they like to disrupt and belittle those who do. There are all sorts of people in this world, and they all have different goals. The 11-Plus passers were just given a chance to mix with like-minded types in the hope that it would encourage excellence, and there's nothing wrong with that. I still feel there are people out there who imagine that wealthy parents back in the 60s paid for the privilege of sending their child to a grammar school, when the opposite is the truth. They are confusing grammar schools, whose aim was to find our brightest kids, regardless of their background, and help them to be successful in their chosen subjects, with private schools, which any kid could attend as long as the parents had enough cash.

The only worry for me was the finality of that exam. I know many people whose educational lightbulb didn't come on at the age of 11. Some blossomed a few years later, by which time they thought they'd missed the boat. Conversely, some kids I went to grammar school with seemed to blossom bang on time for the exam, but you know what blossom does, don't you? A few days after it emerges, looking beautiful, the petals drop off and it's finished. Let's just say, there were some at my school who were no longer worthy of a place, just as there were kids who matured late who should have been selected. My friends, the late and much missed Tim Joplin and my oldest mate, Larry Homer, immediately spring to mind, of whom, much more later on.

Apparently, there was a safety net for the late developers in the form of another entrance exam, but sadly, once ensconced in their new secondary modern school, most seemed reluctant to move. The system was not perfect, but neither is life. I still prefer it to some communist, Marxist, we must all be exactly the same, Corbyn and McDonnell Hell. People are, by nature, similar to plants. There are mighty oaks, pretty flowers, hardy shrubs, grass and weeds, and all species in between, and those who were intended to grow will, regardless of where they're planted.

My mom and dad did not have the artistic talents that David and I were blessed with, other than maybe my dad's perfectionism gene. I really don't know where these talents came from, but what our parents did was allow us to be just

53

what we wanted to be, and though it was not discussed in detail as far as I remember, my theory regarding their liberal attitude is that, when my dad passed for grammar school, his parents didn't want him to go, because they couldn't afford the uniform and needed another wage packet, and I can understand that. There was also a lot of nonsense about, 'My friend didn't pass so I'm not going either.' This is such tosh and should never get in the way of something so important. It's not as if they were leaving a wife and a home to go to sea for ten years, for goodness sake. See your mate when you get home from school at teatime is my advice.

It is my belief that dad was proud of us for passing, and though his own dreams had been tragically stamped on and destroyed, he was damned sure those of his children would not be. Mom and dad might not have had the talent for art, music or English that we both had, but it was their encouragement and support that made us what we are.

Right ho! This is getting far too maudlin, so let's get back to the comedic stuff, before I shed a few tears. (and I've just realised that my previous sentence sums up my whole attitude to life, which is in itself quite poignant!)

So... (as every sentence begins nowadays if you're under 30), the school uniform was duly purchased, namely a black blazer with an embroidered badge, a black cap with an enamelled metal badge sewn onto it (highly unusual, and it came sharp and fetched blood if someone whacked you with his rolled-up cap in the playground), grey short trousers (no long ones till year 2) and a maroon tie (nasty knitted thing), all with name labels sewn in.

It was around this time that my family did something rather bold and interesting, by our standards at least. We bought a caravan in rural Tenbury Wells.

Chapter 6

The New Inn Caravan Park, opposite the old pub of that name in a country lane a few miles from Tenbury Wells' town centre, was in its infancy when we arrived. There were just four other vans on the field. Granny Bertha had a couple of friends called May and Tom who owned a caravan opposite the Peacock, an ancient Inn on the main road into Tenbury. They'd obviously been talking to her about spending weekends and holidays in that lovely part of the world, and this must have spoken to Bertha's depths, especially as she'd spent many a happy summer hop-picking in the countryside, often accompanied by a youthful Ruby. It was all reminiscent of 'The Darling Buds of May', or in this case, 'The Darling Buds of May and Tom', and Bertha was all for it. Now here's an interesting fact. Bertha had never flown in an aeroplane, never been abroad, never been on a ship, never been to the seaside, and didn't own a phone or a fridge. She kept her food in a cool pantry that was a step down from the floor level in the rest of her house. Meat was kept under a sieve-like affair to keep the flies away. She had coal delivered in sacks to her house, from a coal lorry. And this was 1965, not 1865. That's how much we have changed in that relatively short space of time, folks.

Ruby's cousin, Albert, worked for a company by the name of Dunsley's, in Kinver, South Staffordshire, that sold new and second-hand caravans, and it was he that fixed them up with the nice two-tone blue 6 berth (or should that be 6 Bertha?) van that dad's similarly two-toned blue Austin Cambridge Shooting Brake (Registration No.5551 UK), was towing into the almost empty field.

The van was powered by Calor gas and had very Victorian-looking gas mantles to illuminate the interior, rather than lightbulbs. There was a cosy living area with a dividing wall that hid a big, fold-down double bed, and there were two further single beds down that end of the van. At the kitchen end there was another small bedroom containing two bunks for David and me. The lavatory was a chemical one that had to be emptied into special drains scattered around the site, that also had a hosepipe, so it could be cleaned afterwards. A delightful job, methinks! I tried it myself once and blasted half a gallon of fresh sewage into my face. We called our lavatory the Chemi-Karzi, because anyone who volunteered to clean the thing was potentially committing suicide. There was also a toilet block a minute's walk away, to which whistling, overly-cheerful men in vests, carrying rolled-up towels and shavers strode purposefully each morning in order to perform their ablutions. All around us were farmer's fields full of pheasants, lapwings and assorted flora and fauna, and it was all jolly pleasant, I have to say.

My parents and grandparents had an arrangement that was mutually beneficial. Neither Bertha nor Reuben could drive a car, and Len and Ruby couldn't afford a caravan. Now, we all had an idyllic country home where we could spend weekends and summer holidays, whenever we liked.

We spent our time walking, exploring, fishing, going to the little cinema in Tenbury, bird-watching, and in my case, drawing. It was heaven on earth. It was so idyllic it could be the inspiration for a cosy Sunday night drama series – a bit like the Durrells but without all the swarthy Greek chaps. On an evening, we'd walk over to the New Inn, which was usually full of farmers and, as the site eventually became more populated, caravan people. Within a few years there were probably more folks from the Black Country than locals. It was not unusual to see the odd sheep in the bar, fraternising with the drinkers, and border collies were ten a penny. Everywhere you walked, you fell over one. At closing time, they would often round us up and lead us back to our field. Okay, I'm being silly now. There were also a couple of ferrets in the back yard, and horses in the field behind the pub. The Inn and site were run by Mona and Ray, who had proper Farmer Giles accents, and a daughter called Dilys, who still had the remnants of a Bazooka Joe bubble gum explosion in her hairdo. There was a farmer with a very high-pitched voice who drank there called Charlie, who would regularly arrive in the bar, not with currency, but with dead rabbits slung over his shoulder and a shotgun by his side. He'd shout up a pint of cider or two, and then slap a rabbit on the counter as payment. Quite how much cider constituted a rabbit, I don't know, but by closing time, which was a fluid affair in terms of chronological accuracy, he was at least three rabbits to the wind, as I believe the old saying goes. He would then stagger out and drive his tractor home, taking the racing line around the bends. The local bobby might have had something to say about that, had he not been propping up the bar in the lounge.

On a Saturday evening, Bertha would be standing on a low table, her stage, belting out 'Ramona', or 'Are you Lonesome Tonight?', by Elvis Presley, with its recitation bit in the middle. Often, if she'd downed a few too many Guinnesses, she'd mistakenly sing, 'the stage is there, and I'm standing bare', but no one seemed to notice apart from embarrassed family members. When I look back at the old photos, some of which are reproduced in this book, I am struck by how lovely my mother looked, and how smart my dad was, with his swept-back, brylcreemed hair and his blazer with the embroidered Artillery badge on the breast pocket. He had been stationed in Salisbury Plain when he was called up for National Service and rode motorbikes ahead of convoys, amongst other duties, long before anyone had heard of Novichok. It all sounds very glamorous.

Then, when last orders were finally called, we staggered out into the cold, dark night, my mother cuddling David in a slightly squiffy way, thanks to two sherries and a half of Guinness with a sweetener in it, and Bertha, seriously kaylied, (a Black Country expression) hanging onto Reuben for dear life, with Len leading the way with his torch across a pitch-black field. Bats would dive-bomb us every inch of the way, but I didn't mind that. It was the great big, fat moths I hated. We had to open the van door and dash in before a battalion of them fluttered in behind us, all aiming for the solitary gas mantle we'd left on. To this day I am petrified of fat moths.

It was all so very cosy, and sentimental as hell for me now. We'd get undressed and scurry off to our bunks, and mom would wish us 'night night'. Then, after what seemed like ten minutes, Grandad was making cups of tea for us all at 6.30am, just because he was up and about, and the dawn chorus was going full throttle.

Bertha would soon be outside in the sunshine at her small Formica fold-away table, peeling and chopping things, and quiet, lovely, gentle Reuben would be smiling and just taking it all in. Dad would often take David and me into Tenbury, for a change of scenery. We'd visit the toyshop, and maybe buy comics, or Airfix model bi-planes and vintage cars. Then we'd go fishing along the banks of the Teme, and catch huge chub, which we always put back. There is an old joke about chub, which dad used to tell us. To prepare one, you remove the innards, season it with salt and pepper and a squirt of lemon juice, wrap it in tin foil and then chuck it in the pedal bin. They were awful to eat, apparently, which is just as well, as I wasn't the sort of child who could kill anything or watch it being killed. I didn't mind giving them a bit of a sore lip though. I think my moral values need a bit of work, if I'm honest.

Sometimes, we'd visit neighbouring pubs like the Trapnel or the Peacock for a meal. The country lanes were very rural and narrow, often with only enough room for one car. Bertha would always sit in the back with myself, David and Reuben (it's just dawned on me that 6 was far too many people for a car!) and if a passing place was a bit tight, she'd ask us to move over a little in our seats to help the other car get by. This never failed to amuse the rest of us, but she never quite understood that her gesture made absolutely no difference to the situation. I also remember that our dad seemed to be obsessed with 'Tenbury's Disappearing Puddles.' He was forever pointing them out to us with great excitement, and shouting to his back-seat passengers, 'Look, quick, watch this one, it'll disappear in a minute!' The larger main roads around Tenbury looked as if they were infested with these massive pools of water, but as we approached them, they would simply vanish. They were mirages of course – a trick of the light, but Tenbury seemed to have more than anywhere else in Britain.

Occasionally we'd go to the Royal cinema in the high street, not far from the river bridge. I distinctly remember seeing 'Goldfinger' there, and I was enthralled by it. I saw a B-film 'Batman' there too, which must have been from the 1940s, as it was in black and white, and the Batmobile was just an old Ford gangster-style vehicle like they used in Humphrey Bogart movies. Sometimes we'd venture further afield, to places like Ludlow, and I'd get myself photographed sat astride the big cannon in front of the castle, like all kids did. The memories of those days are so powerful and poignant now, I can barely type because my eyes have filled with tears. What a softie I am becoming. Just give me a second to reach for the tissues.

Right, I'm back! We went on to enjoy many an idyllic summer there, and that was when summers lasted forever and it never seemed to rain. It was now 1965, and soon I would be heading for Tipton Grammar School, and a whole new chapter of my life.

In those days, children from Quarry Bonk were sent to the Secondary Modern schools in Coppice Lane. There was one school for boys and another for girls, both located in the same long street, one at either end. if you were fortunate enough to have passed for grammar school, it was usually a choice of either Brierley Hill, Dudley, where Sue Lawley was educated, or Tipton, which was much further away, and involved coach travel. On our first day, I had to walk from my house to the end of Woodland Avenue and wait for the Parkes's Coach to arrive. It was a nerve-wracking time, as this mysterious town, Tipton, which I'd never even visited before, was seven miles away on the other side of Dudley, and we were used to walking just a few yards to school each day. Luckily, I was with several other kids from my old school that I knew well, which helped. We all congregated on the small patch of grass by the public phone box, and suddenly, the big grey coach arrived, driven by a man who looked like a clown before the clown make-up was applied. His name was Roger. If Max Wall ever needed a stunt double, Roger would have been the man they'd have chosen, had he been capable of performing stunts, which he wasn't. His brain seemed capable of only two functions, namely sucking Polo mints to extinction one after the other till his teeth went rotten and fell out, and shouting 'Sit down!' As far as I can recall, he wore the same tatty black blazer, blue jumper and black greasy trousers for seven years.

We clambered aboard and sat down, the newcomers at the front, the old hands in the middle and the smattering of sixth formers at the back. We all looked perfect in our brand-new uniforms, and we were chatting in over-excited fashion for most of the trip, which, on average, took at least three quarters of an hour. We clutched out duffel bags, blue with a white plastic trim, that held our snacks, sandwiches and flasks, all lovingly prepared by our mothers. Roger, who looked as if he'd survived a full-frontal lobotomy, drove in silence, occasionally shouting, 'Sit down on the coach!' and glaring at us. He pronounced the word 'coach' as would an army sergeant major on the parade ground.

When we finally fetched up at the gates of Tipton Grammar, we filed off and stood around looking lost. A teacher led us to our form rooms, and we looked around us, wide-eyed, excited and petrified in equal measure. It was all so big and scary compared to Quarry Bonk Junior School. Huge playgrounds and playing fields, a Science and Art block, an Air Training Corps building, a swimming pool, quadrangles with small lawns in the middle and a massive - to my eyes at least - assembly hall. We had all heard tales of bullying that was on par with Tom Brown's School days, with its fagging system and frightening prefects.

And do you know what? It was all true.

Chapter 7

The first-year intake of 1965 was separated into four classes, based on academic ability, but quite how they knew that already was a bit of a mystery. I was in the 'A' stream, naturally, because I am borderline genius material, as you are aware. We also had a 'B', 'C' and 'D' stream. I was in a class with a few people from Quarry Bonk; namely, Dennis Williams, Stephen Knight, Robin Wilding and Margaret Parsons. If I have missed anyone out, it's because my memory is awful, and I apologize. There were also a few more from my old school in the other classes. I seem to remember that David Nixon (The Angel of the Lord), Peter Fisher and David Coley were in the 'B' stream.

The 'A' streamers did Latin, German, and French, and for some reason, the lower streams did Spanish instead of French, and I seem to remember that Latin wasn't a part of their curriculum either. This was either because the powers that be imagined the more bookish, academic ones would holiday in Cannes one day and the other lot would end up having package holidays in Benidorm. You see, even when we'd made it to grammar school, the social engineering didn't stop. They also stream the kids in secondary modern schools and comprehensives, so don't ever imagine everything is equal in those places. It ain't.

At first, we studied around half a million subjects a week, and after the second year these were considerably reduced, and we were able to choose subjects that suited us...in theory.

I liked the lessons, generally speaking, and I was coping, but unlike my brother David, who was flipping good at everything, I was only good at the subjects I liked, which is why I was hopeless at Maths, Biology, Physics and Chemistry. I just didn't see what they were for. I know there is a square on the hypotenuse, but it didn't affect my daily life one iota. I could vaguely understand why it might be useful to know how long it took Peter to dig a hole three yards long, by one yard wide and two deep, for example, if he'd murdered his Maths teacher and needed to bury him in a hurry, but when things got more abstract, I was lost. And the three sciences might as well have been in Swahili as far as I was concerned. I suffered the first of many, many 'classical' migraines during a Physics lesson, and I know that wasn't random - it was actually caused by my Physics intolerance. For those who are not aware of this insidious, evil curse – migraine I mean, not Physics, though that is too, a classical migraine begins with terrible, frightening eye distortion, namely blurred vision and zig-zags of bright light that last around 20 minutes, followed by the mother of all headaches, which lasts all day and night, often accompanied by vomiting. Sounds great doesn't it? And I endured this, on average, once a fortnight all through my school years, usually, though not always on Saturdays when my weekly routine was interrupted. It is often referred to as 'The Weekend Headache' for that reason. It can be caused by certain foods, drinks, strong sunlight, having a lie-in, Tony Blackburn or a Science lesson. This lasted until I was around 20 and then disappeared, re-emerging when I was a 50-something, but thankfully in a more sporadic and watered-down form; often just the eye distortion without the headache. People in the exclusive Migraine Club HATE when others who just have a headache call it a migraine. We are Migraine Snobs. A real one puts you in bed with all light banished and a bucket by your side. It feels as if you are dying a slow death from a brain haemorrhage, and for once, I am not exaggerating.

As to languages, I was, shall we say, okay. Not rubbish, not the best. I just wish I'd paid attention now that I adore languages but my tired old brain won't help me to learn them nowadays. I can speak German a little, as I went to night school many years later to continue studying it, but if I try to learn Italian, my favourite language, the German words flood out of my brain for good in order to let the new Italian ones in. I can still muddle my way through in basic French, and Latin is the closed book it's always been. All I could ever say was 'Marcus is talking to the sailors in the temple' and sadly, I don't have conversations like that nowadays, though I know a few lads who do like meeting sailors in ruined temples, so I've heard.

Our Latin teacher was called Cecil Cartwright, and he was one of those who would definitely talk to sailors in a temple. He was an old-school privately-educated homosexual and must have hated being stuck in grotty Tipton. He was a classics scholar with a degree from a posh university but was treated as a redundant laughing stock by the crueller element of the pupils who couldn't see the point of learning a dead language, and consequently tormented him in every lesson. He eventually drank himself to sleep most nights in a Kingswinford pub and died, perhaps even committed suicide. All very tragic. We had some fairly eccentric teachers, in hindsight. There was a Biology teacher called Crispin Xerxes Ridge (we spent many years trying to work out what CXR could possibly stand for), and he was as tall and spindly as a baby giraffe. Our P.E. teacher, a Mr Jones, sent his kids out onto a freezing cold football pitch, got them started, and then sneaked back to his room to cook sausages on a small primus stove. Another teacher, who shall remain nameless, seemed extremely infatuated with me for some reason and invited me into his office on several occasions to talk with real enthusiasm about removing my trousers and slippering my naked backside. I didn't know whether to laugh, or cry for help. We were so naïve in those days that we never realised the man was almost certainly a paedophile. We just thought he was an oddball. Another teacher, also nameless, was a confirmed bachelor (not a euphemism for gay in this context by the way) that lived with his elderly mother, who continued to cook and wash and clean for him. This continued well into late middle-age. When she died, he immediately got married, though how he found a wife so quickly was a mystery. Thailand maybe? Grattan's catalogue perhaps? The man was nothing if not practical.

My favourite lesson, of course, was Art. My teacher was a fairly strict character by the name of Peter Trafford. He had a mop of untameable blonde hair like David Hockney, with a bit of Boris Johnson thrown in, and we got on famously from Day 1. In fact, we are still good friends now, with me in my 60s and Pete in his 80s. I think he was rather pleased to get a talented kid to work on for a change, and I was likewise thrilled to have a really good teacher who could push me a bit, having been at a junior school where the staff were 'Jack of all trades' people that - lovely as they all were - couldn't even draw as well as I could.

My least-favourite lesson was Swimming. I HATED it, and I still cannot swim today, I'm ashamed to say. The problem was, - well, where do I begin? Firstly, the swimming pool was located in a modern block just to the side of the hall, and quite a distance from the quadrangles where the classrooms were situated. We had to vacate the classroom after a lesson had finished, dash down the corridors and get changed in a hell of a hurry in communal changing rooms, at a time in our lives when we were all developing and shy, which meant baring our all to strangers. I always remember how different we all were down below, so to speak. Some would be ultra-coy and slip their trunks on beneath towels, while others, such as a chap called Hickinbottom, would parade himself around the room with his huge member encircled with what looked for all the world like a giant ginger eagle's nest. Then there was the swimming itself. I was frightened of the water for a start, and I couldn't stand it going up my nose. For some reason, my nose doesn't seem to block off the water supply. It just floods up there into my brain and chokes me, and the idea of going to the bottom of a pool and retrieving a brick fills me with a nameless fear. All that noise and splashing terrified me. I used to hide up the corner with the two or three lads who were extremely effeminate and play with the foam rubber thing that keeps you afloat. It was not dignified. I was only talking to my wife, Susan, about these lads the other day, and we were in agreement. In those naïve days, we never seemed to use the word homosexual, or realise that people, even at that age, might be that way inclined. The boys who kept out of the way in the pool did the same on the sports pitch. I liked football and played it. I was just crap at it, whereas they *hated* it, and preferred to hang out with the girls on the tennis courts, giggling, chatting, and not actually taking part in any form of sport. I know one lad who, when the pupils were asked to form a line of boys and a line of girls, always joined the girl's line without thinking twice. I find this very interesting, in that, there are two distinct types of gay man; one effeminate, as my fellow non-swimming pupils were, and one indistinguishable from heterosexuals in terms of public behaviour and mannerisms. There are also boys who feel they should have been born a female of course, but that's a different scenario altogether. I have always felt great sympathy for all three categories, not because I share their sexual desires; I don't – I am extremely heterosexual, as it happens, but I was a shy, gentle-natured and rather sensitive artistic soul in those days who was constantly feeling under pressure to 'fit in', and so must these lads have been, only far more so of course. It can't have been easy for them, living a lie for so long. And yet no one, as far as I can remember, ever said that these kids were queer, or gay, or whatever, back in the 60s, that I can recall. The effeminate types might have been labelled as sissies, but that didn't mean quite the same thing to me. I didn't associate it with preferring men to women, and as a matter of fact, they seemed far more relaxed and at home in female company, as I mentioned earlier. All very confusing!

Anyway, after I'd endured half an hour of hell in the water, we had to dash back to the changing rooms and, indignity of indignities, have a communal shower, before dashing to our next lesson, soaking wet beneath our uniform so as not to be late, and thoroughly miserable. Did the teachers never think that little boys might be shy about communal bathing? Did they not imagine that Hickinbottom and his well-developed cronies might just laugh at the little prawn-like, downy-haired members that others possessed, and make them feel ashamed and suicidal? These kids couldn't hide behind their towels in the shower. They were exposed and vulnerable. Maybe the teachers would have been more understanding had they been asked to shower together too, and while we're on this subject, I'm sure the girls had the same trouble as us. There'd have been those with a giant 'boobs 'n' pubes' combo sat next to those that had none. Those formative years could scar kids for life. It's about time we introduced cubicles as standard, in all schools.

I'd been at Tipton for two years when the bottom nearly fell out of my world. It was time to reduce our subjects by half, and for some inexplicable reason, Art was axed from my curriculum and I was down to do Latin instead. I went home that evening, in tears of frustration and livid. I had a word with Mr Trafford, as I called him then, and he was dismayed too. As I said earlier, I was a shy, gentle soul in those days, but I could not let this happen. I arranged to see the headmaster, Mr G.S. Smith, who was a formidable character in a black gown and mortar board. I explained that, if he cut off my head, he would see the word ARTIST running through me, like a stick of Blackpool rock. My intention was to become a professional painter – there was no alternative, and this could scupper my chances before I reached the age of 14. Peter Trafford came with me to back me up, bless him, but G.S. Smith was having none of it.

'Do you really think we can rearrange the curriculum just for you?' he growled.

'Yes, sir, I do,' I replied, displaying another bout of that very occasional courage that I had treated Mrs 'W' to, two years previously. 'I want to be an artist when I have finished my education. It's the only thing that's important to me, and if I can't take Art here, I will leave and find another school.'

I can still remember that Headmaster's study, and his face when I delivered that killer line. How dare this weedy young upstart talk to G.S. Smith, Oxford and Cantab. with such arrogance? He glanced over at Mr Trafford, looking for a fresh opinion.

'Young Tristram is one of the best artists we've had here for several years, sir,' he said. 'The aim of this school is surely to do our best for each child, and not being able to take Art would destroy him.'

Later that week, I heard that I was being allowed to take Art after all, but how many kids end up bitter and twisted because they don't possess my big mouth and steely determination?

Mentally, I was sharp, quick-witted and sarcastic. I also drank lots of tea. Physically, however, I was weak and fretful. I mentioned earlier that bullying was rife, and the prefects were power-mad and like something from Tom Brown's Schooldays. I never stayed school dinners, as I was a bit fussy in those days about that I ate, and I didn't like the smell of rancid cabbage coming from the dining room. I took sandwiches, and they were eaten in The Sandwich Room, strangely enough. This daily occurrence was presided over by a prefect from the 6th form, who insisted we say grace before eating a cheese cob and a packet of Hula Hoops. Out in the playground, older boys regularly bullied the younger ones in all manner of ways. They were made to perform humiliating tasks, threatened with physical violence – all the things I could never do to anyone. I would not be able to live with myself. I witnessed an awful lot of bullying, but never thought it would come from people close to me. We were all from another area, and we were doing our best to integrate with the Tiptonites. I had made friends with many of them, and they were, by and large, lovely people. Danny Sims, for example, was a hero, because he was our best footballer and a very nice chap to boot. Tim Saxon lived just down the road from the school, with his elder brother whom he called Bluto and his gorgeous sister whom he called Potters, sadly no longer with us. He is now my accountant. Barry Stanton, who also lived a few minutes away, became a friend, as did Dennis Hodgetts, now a director of the Kawasaki Centre in Cradley Heath, who I regularly created artwork for, many years later. Incidentally, he met his wife, Lynn, at school, and by year 2 they were an item. Neither has ever been with anyone else as far as I know, and they're still married. What I never expected was hostility from my own people, the Quarry Bonkers. In one of the most hurtful and unforgettable periods of my young life, a couple of them that I'd always been friendly with began to control and bully me. We are all given the same advice by adults about telling someone about it right away, but bullies are clever, and they immediately make it very clear that, if anyone finds out, the punishment will be 50 times worse. You must suffer in silence, not tell your parents, or you will wish you had never been born. I will always remember that I was shoved up against a wall one day in the playground with a fist in my face, and one of them snarled, 'We have been lenient with you so far...' I honestly cannot remember the rest of his sentence. The first half was enough. At that time, being the shy artistic type, I kept a diary in my bedroom, and I distinctly remember writing in it about what a misery my young life was becoming. (I also remember a very funny earlier entry that said the Beatles were playing at the Plaza Ballroom in Cradley Heath but mom wouldn't let me go because of the Teddy Boys.)

The worst thing was the betrayal of my own people; lads I'd been through Junior School with, without a hint of what was to come, and I couldn't tell anyone. I am not going to name anyone, because now we have all grown up and we still know each other and get on well. We are different people. I have forgiven, but not forgotten, as you can see by my real need to get it down on paper. I was in turmoil and couldn't see an end to my ghastly predicament. Each day was pure misery, as I haunted the lonelier areas of the playground, trying to avoid these people. I had many friends though, and one, Barry Stanton, knew something was the matter. (You can spot Barry in the black and white picture section in the Year 2 class photograph, 4th from the left. I am 4th from the right, with Tim Saxon 7th, and Dennis Williams in-between Mr Easom's legs. I look forward to the court case!) Eventually I confessed to Barry, and he was furious. He was extremely highly-strung and could be aggressive. He definitely had anger problems, but he also had an abstract sense of humour and liked music, so we bonded through those mutual interests. He was an extrovert, a fashionable chap who liked the girls, a soul fan, quick-witted, confident and quite creative. He was also a very spoilt, only child (as opposed to an unspoilt one, of which there are many, before you rant at me and tear my book to shreds). Once he'd heard my tale of woe, he became extremely angry and wanted to sort things out for me, but I begged him to forget what I'd foolishly blurted out, or else my life would quickly take a turn for the worst. So far, they'd not actually hit me, just threatened to a fair bit. Bullies can spot a weak child to prey upon, just as lions pick out the easiest gazelle to chase. Barry duly took no notice of my pleas, and one breaktime, he approached one of the offenders and gave him a simple ultimatum. If either of them touched his new friend, or was nasty to him in any way, he would beat the living shit out of them. Those who had witnessed Barry's frenzied fights in the playground knew he meant it. Physically, he wasn't much to look at, but when one of his rages took over, it was not wise to get in his way. He had destroyed bigger, more powerfully built lads, and he had a hair-trigger temper.

From that day, the bullying ended, and I, for one, was immensely grateful to Barry Stanton for that. He would come to my rescue again in dramatic fashion several years later, in a local pub, of which, more anon.

A lot of my generation found the general bullying culture abhorrent, and we swore that when we became prefects, we would not treat the younger lads the same way that we had been treated. I can honestly say that we changed the system. Whether it remained that way after we left, I couldn't say.

Things got better quickly after Barry intervened. I was doing okay at school but I wasn't all that studious. I liked being the class buffoon too much, I suppose. I was clever enough to think I didn't need to revise, which of course I did, and I only ever skimmed the surface with most subjects, rather than dig deep, and this applied to Music, Art and English too. One teacher said to me, 'Tristram, you are a *dilettante*, that's your problem,' and this intrigued me. I looked the word up in the dictionary and I was annoyed to learn that it meant a dabbler with a butterfly mind that flits from one thing to another without ever mastering anything. What hurt was that he was absolutely right. I didn't seem to have that vital work ethic, and I felt I was fizzling out early after a promising start. I was also becoming very temperamental at home, and my mother was constantly reminding me that I'd been 'an adorable child until I went to that bloody grammar school'. Looking back, I now realise what that was all about. Hormones obviously had a lot to do with it, but the real reason was that, in my head, I was a better artist than in reality. Every piece of work I created was nowhere near as good as I'd seen it in my mind, because my technical skills were lagging way behind my imagination. I was prone to melodramatically tearing pictures into pieces in disgust and becoming frustrated, a bit like a violinist who hears the complex tune in his head, but constantly makes a complete hash of actually playing it. The only solution was applying myself and putting in the hours in order to discover and perfect my real style, but at Tipton, there were far too many distractions.

71

I was still having clarinet lessons, and whenever we had a prize-giving or a concert night, I was wheeled out to play a classical clarinet piece, accompanied my Mr Reynolds the music teacher, who apparently went to the Royal Academy of Music with Rick Wakeman. My mom and dad would attend these events, and dad, who was a nervous listener where David and I were concerned, apparently held his breath throughout my performances and only started breathing again once it had finished and the audience was applauding. Knowing this, I always played something that wasn't an hour long, for fear of losing him. David, meanwhile, was now having private classical guitar lessons with Mr Bryce, and had won the Staffordshire Schools Recorder Prize at Dudley Town Hall. He was awarded 99 out of a 100 by the judge, so David, being David, wandered over to her and asked why he hadn't been given full marks. She told him it was because he slouched onto the stage with an over-confident look and his tie undone, played a flawless piece of Bach and flounced off again. She docked him 1 point for his attitude. If she was waiting to hear 'sorry' she'd have waited a long time. When he got home, I heard Roob threatening to put him in the sink again.

We also had regular school discos, and I took it upon myself to design the posters for these events, which became, shall we say, legendary, or maybe a better word is infamous, as I took the opportunity to caricature and even ridicule the teachers. A few years later I took it a tad too far when I painted the posters for the School pantomime, but for now, I'll just tease you with that snippet.

Chapter 8

I sat my 'O' level exams and did, well, okay-ish, but not great by any stretch of the imagination. I had 6 passes, with very average grades, even in Art, Music and English, but here's an interesting fact. Did you know that different areas and schools sat completely different exams, even though they were all called 'A' levels, 'O' levels or CSEs? There were various exam boards, each with vastly different standards and levels of difficulty. The Joint Matriculation Board, which my school used, was renowned for being the tough one, whereas others were far easier to pass. This will always sound like sour grapes, given my poor results, but it's true. Don't you think this makes a mockery of the system? Surely, there should have been one board with one set of standards, so that every 'O' level that was dished out to our children was identical to the rest. That said, I did the bare minimum to scrape by, so that's no excuse.

I managed to stay in the 'A' stream throughout school but my dilettante streak remained a problem. I wasn't taking anything too seriously and enjoyed being the class comedian. The word 'immature' sums it up nicely. I also seemed to have lost my drive.

In the outside world, skinheads were suddenly everywhere, like a contagion, all dressed in their hoisted-up Levi's Stay-Pressed trousers and red braces, Ben Sherman shirts, Crombies, red socks and Doc Marten boots. We held school discos in the main hall, and groups of skinheads stood at one end, with the long-haired progressive rock types at the other, being entertained by a disco and a live band (often French teacher, Mr Kent's son's outfit, The Light Fantastic) that catered equally for neither faction. It was pathetic really. Back in Quarry Bonk, there was a disco at the British Legion every week, called 'The Screaming Apple'. Gangs of lads from our town talked with enthusiasm about fighting gangs of lads from other towns, something I will never, ever understand. The disco blared out Tamla classics such as 'Third Finger Left Hand' by Martha and the Vandellas, and 'Band of Gold' by Freda Payne. Barry Stanton introduced me to 'The Harlem Shuffle' by Bob and Earl, and 'I Heard it Through the Grapevine' by Marvin Gaye. I actually love those songs now, but back then, it all felt a bit too tribal for me, and something deep inside me was trying to get out. I began digging around and discovering songs that were very different to all that reggae and soul stuff that the skinheads professed to like, and it excited me. I had a few friends from Quarry Bonk that didn't follow the herd blindly and these people interested me for that reason. Their hair was longer, their clothing was less like a military uniform, their attitude was not that of the brainless pack animal, and I found myself gradually drifting away from the peer pressure of the teenagers on my estate and crossing into enemy lines, having briefly dabbled with cropped hair, red socks and checked shirts, in a half-hearted attempt to try and fit in. One of these new friends lent me an Island Records sampler album called 'Nice Enough to Eat' and it opened my eyes. It was new and exciting, and I felt I'd discovered something for myself, rather than had it foisted upon me. There were bands on that album with strange, exotic names like King Crimson, Jethro Tull, Blodwyn Pig, Spooky Tooth and Quintessence, but one track, by a band called Free, really grabbed me. It was called 'Woman' and it was raw, powerful and earthy, and what I thought rock music ought to sound like. There were also more thoughtful, acoustic songs by people such as Nick Drake, and I loved it all. From then onwards, I defected to the opposition, and I decided I was going to learn to play the guitar. Around this time I got friendly with a chap called Kenny Stevens, who had long blond hair and an occasional beard. Kenny was from my grammar school but a year older than me, and he was the nearest thing you could get to John Lennon in Tipton. He was a rabid Beatles fan, as was I, and he played guitar well and wrote songs. I begged him to teach me guitar and he begrudgingly showed me a few things. He also drew me chord diagrams, known to guitarists as Bar Charts, which showed me where to put my fingers. It was only when I applied this to a real guitar that I realised he was having fun with me and had created charts which were only suitable for a person that had at least eight fingers on his left hand. Nevertheless, it was enough to get me seriously interested, and I subsequently bought my first electric guitar at the age of 16. I honestly can't remember the make, but it was soon sold and replaced by a lovely Antoria Honeyburst Les Paul, which was my pride and joy; the first of many nice guitars that I owned. I also bought a copy of Free's third album, 'Fire and Water'. It was the first album I ever bought, but sadly I didn't have a record player. I would cuddle that album and stare lovingly at it for several months, until my dad finally got me a stereogram, a long, faux-teak affair with a moulded plastic lid and integral speakers. I was in Heaven. I locked myself in the front room every night after school and taught myself to play guitar like Paul Kossoff, by playing along to that album over and over again until I virtually wore the grooves off it. It is fair to say that I learnt to play lead guitar in spite of Ken's help, not because of it. I was also determined to be better than him at it.

Someone who actually did teach me a lot was Larry Homer. I'd been to see Blodwyn Pig, featuring Mick Abrahams, who'd also been in Jethro Tull, at an ex-cinema venue in Cradley Heath High Street, and I got talking to this exotic, hippy-like creature wearing an Oxford boating blazer, loon pants and blue and silver stack-heeled boots that had stars on them. This enchanting ensemble was capped by a hairdo of tight frizzy curls that formed a perfect triangle on his head. Facially, he resembled a handsome dead Pharoah. They say opposites attract, and we did. He was a hippy trippy, progressive rock and folk lover who played guitar and had a sitar at home because George Harrison had one. He liked bands I'd never even heard of, like Frank Zappa and the Mothers of Invention, and The Incredible String Band. He'd been to many festivals and had many girlfriends. I hadn't, and I hadn't, (if you exclude me sitting in the dark at Elaine Shakespeare's house one Saturday when her parents had gone out and not knowing what to do next). I was a studious classical clarinettist who painted pictures and went to a grammar school. He was a car mechanic who'd left a grotty secondary modern school as soon as he could so he could earn a few quid. And we clicked instantly. We arranged to meet up, and from then on, he was either at my house, showing me how to play guitar like Hendrix, or I was at his, nagging him about using proper technique, i.e. using four fingers to play lead like a jazz musician instead of three like Eric Clapton. Larry's playing was intuitive, emotive, wild and soulful. Mine was considered, technical, anal, and proper, which just about sums up the rest of our lives as well. In a nutshell, I taught him chromatic scales and he taught me passion. Hopefully, we're now both more rounded as a result.

At this time, our school was going through a massive transition. It was becoming a Comprehensive school, like many others in the UK. I remember feeling very disappointed with this, as did my friends. It just didn't feel special anymore. You can call me what you will, but it suddenly felt bog-standard, and we were all deflated. The magic, if you could ever describe a school in Tipton as magical, was gone. Tipton Grammar School was becoming Alexandra High School, but I was to remain there for two more years, in the 6th form, to sit my 'A' levels, which were to be Art, Music and English.

Suddenly we were 'grown-ups', and we had our own common room. A few lads decided that, because hairs had begun sprouting out of their chins, they simply *had* to grow a beard, even if it looked like someone had stuck a piece of ginger wire wool on their jaw in the dark. Hair got longer, whether it suited us or not, and usually, it didn't. The extra-boring ones would insist on regurgitating every line from the previous night's Monty Python programme, *ad nauseam*. The humour was abstract, the way David and I liked humour to be, but now that too was being used in exactly the same way that jokes were previously used, so that people with no humour of their own could once more buy their comedy off the peg. Some days in the common room, halfway through the umpteenth re-telling of 'The Dead Parrot Sketch', I felt a very real urge to scream.

One spotty Herbert in our 6th form bored our pants off by banging on and on about his awful new 'Grand Funk Railroad' album, which he'd purchased for the sole reason that they were officially the loudest band on Planet Earth (did he not realise that it was just the volume control on his record player that determined how loud they would be?). Another would give us a blow-by-blow account of the recent Emerson, Lake and Palmer concert, and waxed lyrical about how Keith Emerson, at the end of the show, stabbed his Moog synthesiser with a dagger (yawn). I'm afraid this is what happens when 17-year-old Science students are allowed to go to rock concerts.

The Maths students informed us that a new Maths teacher was arriving. He was Max 'Maths' Thomas, no more than 24 years old, blond curly hair, glasses, nervy, intense. He wanted to form a music club in the 6th form common room, where all the Yes, Genesis, Emerson, Lake and Palmer, Moody Blues, Led Zeppelin and Black Sabbath fans could bore each other shitless by making the rest of us listen to 20-minute-long album tracks over a machine coffee and a Twix, and all after school too, meaning Roger the Polo-sucking Zombie had long gone home in the coach and it was seven long miles back to Quarry Bonk. At least Steven Knight and a few others owned scooters covered in regulation Mod-mirrors, so a lift was a possibility, if you didn't value your life. Not long afterwards, the first student-owned Minis would gradually begin to appear in the school car park, with lifts offered in exchange for petrol money. Robin Wilding ran a professional taxi service in all but name, and eventually became a bank manager.

Max presided over these soirees, which occasionally featured me playing electric guitar and him singing Bob Dylan whilst strumming an acoustic. All very hip for a Maths teacher in those days. He told me that he was in a band, back in Birmingham where he lived, and they were about to make a demo record. He asked if I would play bass guitar and lead guitar on it, as they currently didn't have either. I imagined them all being teachers in tweed jackets and leather elbow patches, singing 'Kumbaya' and banging tambourines, but I said yes anyway, just for the experience.

I was picked up from Woodland Avenue by a chap with a beard named Lol Mason. (by which I mean the chap was named Lol Mason. His beard didn't have a name as far as I know). I liked him a lot. He was fairly posh by my standards, and his dad, a well-known BBC type, had written Dick Barton for the radio, and he also created and wrote the Archers. How's that for a C.V.? When I got to the Zella studios in Brum, I met Steve Broughton from Harborne, who I also liked a lot. (None of them, other than Max, was a teacher, by the way, so my initial vision of them was completely wrong.) Steve reminded me of Michael J. Fox. Smallish, good-looking, and a great front man for a band. They played a few acoustic songs for me that were extremely classy in a Paul Simon kind of way, with clever lyrics and spot-on vocal harmonies. I played acoustic lead guitar on a couple and bass on another, if I remember correctly. It was a long time ago, and thanks entirely to them, my memory of the evening was a bit foggy. They plied me with white wine during and after the session and made me feel very welcome, not to mention very drunk. At the end of the evening, Lol, who shouldn't have been driving, dropped me off at the end of Woodland Avenue (where I caught the school coach each morning), because he was already lost and didn't want to get even loster. I walked home in pouring rain, ricocheting off every fence I passed and giggling like an idiot. I eventually fell through a privet hedge and lay there, upside down, my feet silhouetted against a full moon. I will always remember that view and the rain running *up* my legs rather than down. The cheap Spanish plonk was more powerful than I had imagined. That was my first of many nights recording with, fraternising with, drinking cheap wine with, or designing album sleeves for, a band that would eventually call themselves City Boy, and go on to have several top ten singles including their biggest hit, '5705', best-selling albums, and massive USA stadium tours under their belts. Eventually, years later, when City Boy split up, Lol would do it all again with a band called The Maisonettes. Sadly, they never recorded Kumbaya.

During my time in the 6th form I became good friends with Dennis Williams, who lived not far from me. A group of us, a mixture of Tipton and Quarry Bonk lads, would go out to the Tipton pubs, drink Guinness and laugh a lot. One evening we'd stayed over in Tipton and walked to a nearby pub, where we sat in the corner, chatting. Barry Stanton, who had left school by then, was there with us that night too. Most of us, as I have already mentioned, had longish hair, as was the style back then, and I was wearing a rather fetching boating blazer, with light and dark blue stripes. Unknown to me, a small group of local skinheads, maybe three or four in total, were stood at the bar, drinking and swearing. One, a small, nasty-looking weasel of a youth, had taken exception to the way I was dressed, or my longish hair, or my smarmy face, or something. I will never know exactly what upset him. We weren't even making a noise, or being flamboyant, or anything to excite a skinhead thug; we were just talking. The next thing I recall was a wet feeling on my cheek. I turned around, thinking someone had maybe spilled his drink, and I was confronted by this angry weasel, who had decided to show his dislike of me by spitting on my face as I chatted to my friends. Then, to add injury to insult, he punched me in the ear, which began to throb quite a bit, let me tell you. If I'm honest, I didn't have a clue what to do next, other than panic, as I am not the pugilistic type, though I can knock you senseless with a well-chosen word. Suddenly, Barry Stanton stood up and strode towards the bar, drawing this chap's attention from me, for which I was eternally grateful. The Weasel, as shall now refer to him, followed Barry, who asked the barman to eject this foul cretin, as he'd hit someone he didn't even know, for no reason whatsoever. The barman suddenly realised he'd got some glasses to dry in the bar and disappeared. Meanwhile, the Weasel began punching Barry from behind. Barry turned around, still being whacked. I saw his face turn into the Hulk's face, and I knew we were in for fireworks. Barry shouted to the entire pub, 'I am going out into the street with this c**t, and I am going to break his nose and leave him crying for his mother in the gutter'. He exited stage right, followed by a Weasel in hot pursuit. The room went deathly quiet, like a Wild West bar-room when the aggrieved stranger walks in, six-guns at his side, and the frightened honky-tonk piano player stops playing. The three remaining skinheads seemed to go a bit quiet, but surprisingly, they did nothing. Seconds later, Barry stormed back into the pub and shouted, with tremulous voice, 'Go and take a look at the tough boy now, folks.' He then returned to our table, shaking like a leaf, his face bright red. 'Let's get out of here,' he said to us, and we did, sharpish, watched by a crowd of silent, fascinated drinkers.

Outside it was carnage. The Weasel lay in the rain-soaked gutter, his face busted to pieces and blood everywhere. He was groaning pathetically, but somehow, I fell just short of feeling sorry for him. We walked down the main road at a business-like pace and disappeared around the corner before the skinheads decided to call for reinforcements.

Several years later, when I'd passed my test, I was heading home from seeing old schoolfriends in Tipton in my old Mini, on a foggy November night. I pulled up at the Zebra crossing at Roman Mosaic, near Burnt Tree Island, to allow a pedestrian to cross the road. It was the Weasel. My heart began to pound. There was not a soul to be seen, just him and me. I felt my right foot beginning to accelerate as he reached the middle of the road. I slowly let the clutch out till I could feel the bite. Then I regained my senses, pushed the clutch back in and watched him walk into the fog and disappear.

Chapter 9

We went down in history as the worst set of 6th formers that Tipton Grammar School had ever tried to educate. Not that we were bad people, far from it, but a series of, shall we say, unfortunate events helped to seal our fate.

The first was 'The 446 Affair'. For reasons lost in the mists of time, we had adopted Jerusalem as our 6th form hymn. It was a stirring piece, for starters, and I argued that if it was good enough for the W.I., it was good enough for us. The hymn was number 446 in our school hymn books, and every time it was chosen for morning assembly, the pupils sat in the last two rows of seats in the main hall felt a very palpable frisson of excitement curse through their veins. Normally, we would sing along in that awful, half-hearted, very quiet or-else completely mimed way that wedding guests employ when they can't sing in tune and don't want to stand out like a sore thumb in the church. However, when the Tipton Grammar School Sixth Form Singers spotted that 446 was one of the numbers on the hymn-board next to G.S. Smith's oak lectern, they were transformed instantly from those whispering, atonal, self-conscious wedding guests into the Welsh Male Voice Choir.

Mr Reynolds, sat at his grand piano next to the stage, would play the introductory chords, so, in theory, we knew what key it was in, and then, all hell would break loose. The headmaster and the teachers, lined up on stage, knew damn well we were taking the mickey, but they couldn't really say much about it. After all, we were singing our hearts out in an enthusiastic way, and there was nothing wrong with that. The best bit, from our perspective at least, was watching the faces of the staff. Some had wry smiles, others buried their faces in their hands, some were stony faced and rather red about the gills, while others, particularly G.S. Smith, were apoplectic with rage, and yet, remarkably, nothing was said. I suppose it was just knowing how to broach the subject. What made it even worse was the fact that the other 800 or so pupils were all turning to watch us perform instead of facing the front.

Then, thanks to an idiot by the name of Trevor Withers, who should have known better as his parents were devout Salvation Army members, the joke was taken a step too far, and we nearly all got expelled.

Before I explain what happened, I'll provide a brief insight into this lad's character. This buffoon took 'A' level music with me, and noticing that our History of Music teacher was quite deaf (this, by the way, was not Mr Reynolds, a superb musician who took us for the practical aspects of the subject, but another chap who looked and sounded like the late Derek Nimmo), Trevor took to occasionally saying random words out loud in class at just the right level of sound to render them undetectable – words such as 'Bollocks!', or 'Fuck off!'. He had honed this dubious skill to a fine art, and what made it even more amusing/nerve-wracking was that there were only two of us taking 'A' level Music that year, so classes were intimate affairs consisting of just the three of us. So cocky had Withers become that he was regularly answering questions thus:

'Was it Domenico Scarlatti, sir? Fuck off!

And our partially deaf teacher was not picking it up. Trevor had perfected the knack of controlling the volume of his voice with such accuracy that the word died just two inches before it got to the man's ear.

The next part of this tale is so absurd that I can't expect you to believe it, but I swear it is true, and perfectly illustrates what a complete cretin Trevor was. One day he handed this half-deaf music teacher a piece of homework, as did I, and in the mid-morning break, he told me, with great pride, that he had employed the same basic premise, i.e. the slipped-in, quietly spoken swearword, when writing his homework essay. In other words, he had actually - follow this - added these written words randomly to his text. I stared at him with incredulity.

'So, let me get this clear,' I said. 'You have written an essay on Bach and added swearwords to it, here and there and throughout, and this won't be detected because the man is deaf?'

'Yes!' replied Trevor, pleased with himself.

I tried to form a sentence, but none would come. I let it go.

The following day, Trevor was summoned to the teacher's office for what I would describe as a frank exchange of views. Had it been me, Heaven forbid, I would have been clever enough to have explained to this teacher that I had a rare form of Written Tourette's Syndrome. That said, I would also have been clever enough not to have bloody done it in the first place. Now, given what you know about this imbecile, read on.

One day, this Withers idiot took it upon himself to pop along to the main hall and borrow the huge cardboard box full of hymn books. He took it who-knows-where for a few hours and carefully removed every page 446 from the books, before replacing the box. After that he dropped all manner of hints about what might happen the next time 446 came up but refused to explain himself. Mercifully, the hymn did not rear its head for the best part of a year, thanks, almost certainly, to our rowdy rendition of it. It had become the *persona non grata* of the hymn world. Then, one dreadful day in the summer, there it was again, flagged up on the board. The nerves were jangling on the back two rows as Mr Reynolds gave us the famous intro. 800 schoolkids flicked through their hymn books in search of the number, but it could not be found. There was a panic amongst the lower ranks, and Withers was now near hysterical with restrained laughter. His face was a deep shade of purple and it looked as if he were exploding from within. The 6th form lads, who didn't need a visual prompt from a hymn book as they knew the song inside out, roared forth with a particularly stirring rendition, as the rest of the school stood in puzzled silence, looking about them for an explanation. I honestly thought that G.S. Smith was going to have a coronary. I didn't know where to look.

We were all put on probation after that, and had our prefect's badges confiscated, even though it was the idiot Trevor's fault. We feared that we'd be the only group of male 6th form prefects in the history of the school that had ALL lost their prefectship, if indeed there is such a word. Incidentally, the girls had nothing to do with it, I must make that clear, before I get angry letters. We lads had to be on our very best behaviour before the head would even consider reinstating us. Oh, the shame of it all! Then came the school panto, which really put the lid on it, and I'm afraid that was *my* fault.

I can't remember why, or how, or when, but we mooted an idea to the powers-that-be about writing our own pantomime that year and acting in it. Maybe G.S. Smith saw this as us trying to redeem ourselves for the 446 incident. I don't know, but whatever the reasoning was, we were given the green light.

Lord knows why it fell to me to write the script – I'm guessing that it was because I was a comedy genius and the only real choice – but off I went, and the lads then chipped in with some great suggestions. I eventually delivered my script, and we chose parts for everyone, male and female, and set about rehearsing, if rehearsing is the right word. Once all this was ready for public consumption, I designed the posters, which were duly taped on windows all over the school. I think my only mistake, up to this point, was taking a little vendetta too seriously. With hindsight, we should have let it go, but we didn't. There was a teacher by the name of Mr Kent (those of you that are paying attention will remember his name mentioned in regard to the school discos), and this Mr Kent, for reasons lost in the mists of time, was not well liked by some of us. He had a thick mop of grey hair and a pair of huge grey sideburns, which we all took an irrational dislike to, as opposed to the completely rational dislike we had for the rest of him. These distinctive features made him an easy target for a talented caricaturist such as myself, and I had already used these pictures of him on my disco posters, due to the fact that his son's band often performed at them. It is fair to say that, thanks to my handiwork, virtually every pupil in the school was familiar with the cartoon and knew who it was meant to represent.

What I did was immature and unforgivable, but it was funny at the time. My pantomime poster featured said teacher as one of the panto characters, so you'd have, for example, a cartoon of Dennis Williams with, say, Widow Wankey written beneath it, and Nobby Smith with, say, Dick-wit Whittington beneath it, and Mr Kent with Mr Kent written beneath it, only I had deliberately begun to misspell it as Mr KU, with the U crossed out, before then spelling it correctly. It didn't take a genius to work out what KU would have spelled, had it not then been corrected.

On the day of the end-of-term panto, the hall was full of pupils, all looking forward to their afternoon treat. The teachers were fully expecting a bit of gentle ribbing, but let's just say that some of it went a tad too far, especially when we made constant reference to Mr Kent, each time beginning to pronounce it the KU way, before hastily correcting ourselves, just as my poster had done. We must have said it 15 times. The panto itself was very funny, I remember. Half the teachers loved it, and the other half did not, so it was a bit like Brexit in a way. Two who did not were, guess who...Mr Kent, and G.S. Smith. I think Peter Trafford liked it, as I saw him falling about the place laughing, bless him.

The next day I was summoned to the Head's office, and his face was like thunder. He did not beat about the bush.

'You meant that Mr Kent was a c**t, didn't you, Tristram?' he growled. I have never before or since heard a Headmaster swear like that. I was quite shocked.

Suddenly, I remembered my last private audience with him, when I was a 14-year-old who didn't want to take Latin. I gulped audibly.

'No sir!' I insisted.

'Do you think I am a complete idiot, Tristram?'

'Not a complete one, no sir.'

Okay, I made that last line up, but you get the point. It's too painful a reminiscence to spend any more time on. Suffice it to say that we all had to knuckle down and concentrate. We had tons of revision, and 'A' level exams to do. This last part was where it all got serious, and I needed to man up.

Chapter 10

I was approaching my 18th birthday now, and the dreaded exams were upon us. The results would determine my future, as in, art college or potential factory fodder, so I should have been ultra-conscientious, but sadly, I still wasn't. It didn't seem to sink in how important it all was, and I continued to muck around and be the dilettante.

If I did revise, it certainly wasn't a lot. A Joint Matriculation Board 'A' level was a stinker. For example, Music involved a 3-hour written exam, a playing exam, where you would have to play the instrument of your choice and also a piano, the rudiments of which we had to learn from scratch. Then there was a History of Music paper, again three hours. In short, we had to demonstrate our skills in composition, creating chord progressions and melodies, reading from music, playing an instrument to a high standard and knowing who bloody Domenico Scarlatti was. There are BA (Hons) degrees that are easier than that nowadays, trust me! Then there was Art, my chosen subject. We had a 3-hour life-drawing exam, a 3-hour painting exam and a 3-hour History of Art exam. English comprised a 3-hour Language paper and a 3-hour Literature paper. We had to know Hamlet off-by-heart, line by line, plus loads of other stuff such as Jane Austen's 'Persuasion'. To this day I can still quote 'Hamlet' in huge chunks, and I know what every little bit of it means, thanks to Miss Titley, our devoted and passionate English teacher, bless her.

So, as you might have gathered, it was not a pushover. I remember swatting up on the History of Art fairly well, and the practical exams in Art and Music held no fear for me. Thanks to the aforementioned Miss Titley, I was quite sound on the English stuff, but by the time I'd ploughed through all this, I'd had enough, and it was the Music exam revision that suffered. The reason was, though I liked and respected Mr Reynolds, the half-deaf Derek Nimmo chap bored the living shit out of me. He was about as inspirational as a carpet sample. My brain wouldn't take any more information; it was full, and quite frankly, I couldn't give a damn about Domenico Scarlatti and his bloody dates, or who his royal patron was in Vienna, or any of the rest of it. I've always been a musician and an artist who performs and creates, not someone who writes about other folks doing it. Those who can, do. Those who can't, prattle on about it and criticize the ones who can.

The exams arrived, and I for one, hated them. Nowadays I'd be fine, but at school they terrified me.

First up was Art. I sailed through the two practical exams, and now all I had left was the dreaded History of Art 3-hour one to get through. Never mind. I had swatted up on the things we covered in class, and I was reasonably confident. The questions were in a little A5 white booklet, so I opened it to the first page and began to nervously scan it. There was nothing I knew about there, but this didn't worry me unduly, as Peter Trafford had explained to us that different schools tackled different subjects, so we should expect to find the odd section we knew absolutely nothing about. I moved down to the second section. Peter walked past my desk in the hall and smiled at me. He strolled on. Section 2 meant nothing to me either. Never mind. I turned the page. Hmm! Nothing I knew about there either. Then I found a question I did know about. The Pre-Raphaelites. I began writing and was quite pleased with my efforts. Then I moved on to the next page, and once more, it was like a closed book to me. I hadn't studied the Abstract Expressionists, so there was no way I could take a stab at it. I quickly scanned the last inside page, nervous now, as this was the very last half-page of text in the booklet. There were just two questions here, and I knew nothing whatsoever about either subject. The questions had ended abruptly halfway down the final inside page, and I still needed to answer three more. I began to panic. I clutched nervously at my groin, like I needed the toilet, and frantically tapped my feet. I squirmed around in my chair and rubbed the skin off my fevered brow. This wasn't going at all well. I don't know if you are familiar with that sketch from 'The Young Ones', where Rick is answering an exam paper question about Crop Rotation in the 14th Century. He initially looks enthusiastic, and confident that he can wax lyrical on the subject. He picks up his pen and mouths the words he is writing on his exam sheet.

'Okay, let's see now, crop rotation in the 14th century was...erm...'

And then 'all his golden words are spent' (as Hamlet says to Horatio, with regard to the fabulous fop, Osric.)

Well, that was like me in the History of Art exam. I sat there, mortified, until ten minutes before the time was up, when Peter strolled round again and spotted his star pupil in torment. He gave me a frown I'll never forget, and discretely turned the page over to reveal the very back page of the booklet, where the questions about all the subjects I had studied in class for the last two years were waiting to be answered. Peter looked at his watch, sighed a very heavy sigh, and strolled on. A few minutes later, it was all over. My life flashed before my eyes, and I could see my wonderful career - the one I'd begged G.S. Smith to let me embark upon - crumbling to dust in front of my eyes.

Next up was Music. As with the practical art exams, I sailed through the various sections of the paper that involved playing, composing and so on. Then came The History of Music 3-hour paper. 'O, my prophetic soul' I thought to myself (Hamlet again, when he discovers it was his uncle who killed his father), can this dreaded exam be History repeating itself, or at least History of Art repeating itself, in terms of disastrous consequences? Erm, yes it can, and it was. I sat in that hall and the panic set in more and more with every question I read. This wasn't a case of looking for the topics we'd gone over in class and missing them because they were hidden away on the last page. This was more a case of, I didn't know a thing because I hadn't listened to the boring Derek Nimmo git once in two years and I didn't revise AT ALL. I was in deep trouble and I knew it. I glanced over at Trevor and he gave me a hollow look that said it all. He hadn't listened to a word or revised either. At least he was writing *something*, even if it was just 'Bollocks!' and 'Fuck off!'.

There was only one thing to do. I raised my hand and attracted the invigilator's attention. She came over to see what was up.

'I'm really sorry,' I croaked, 'I'm having a migraine. I have to go home.'

I stood up and feigned wobbliness as I walked to the door. I may have even bounced theatrically off the door frame to demonstrate how my eyes were not functioning properly. I crawled out of the school, onto Alexandra Road, flagged down a Dudley-bound bus and legged it home.

A few days after that I sat the various English exams, and did okay, as opposed to really well. My schooldays were all but over, but what happened to me next was, because of my gross stupidity, now out of my control.

In the period between the end of our exams and leaving school, quite a few interesting things happened to me. It was a worrying time, thanks to my awful performance, but I had applied to Wolverhampton College of Art and been given an interview. Peter Trafford was a bit angry about my idiocy but reckoned that the art college would be lenient with my presumably mediocre exam grade once they'd interviewed me and seen my work and listened to my excuses. It had been a 3-part exam, so hopefully the first two parts would compensate for the disastrous 3rd one. They still required me to pass two 'A' levels though, which was a worry.

On the home front, I was still playing the guitar and seeing Larry a lot. I'd also got myself involved in a band or two in my spare time. I dabbled with a couple of friends, Tim Yorke and Geoff Toye, and we played at a community centre in Blackheath, my first ever live gig. Geoff was a likeable, crazy lad who had fairly rich parents. They lived in a very big posh house with a huge garden, and they had a wine cellar. Geoff was a bit of a loose cannon and drove round in a converted old ambulance that he stored his musical gear in. One day he informed me that his parents had gone on holiday to their other place in Scotland, and he intended to have a party while they were away. He invited every hippy in the vicinity and they all descended on the house, Larry included. It was chaos. There were people all over the garden, trampling the flowers, riding the Toye's pet donkey (yes, you heard me correctly) and raiding the wine cellar. One woman whacked her unfaithful boyfriend over the head with a very rare and expensive antique chair and broke it – the chair, not the head, thankfully. Larry, who was drunk, noticed that a disliked rival guitarist, Arthur Jackson, had left his bike in the entry and somewhat vindictively smashed it up with a chopper he'd found in the shed (no, it wasn't a chopper bike, before you ask), and couples were freely fornicating in the many bedrooms. You can imagine what Mr and Mrs Toye's reaction to this was when they returned. You can mend a chair, maybe, but to discover that a cellar full of rare wines has been reduced to, well, nothing, takes some rectifying.

I had a school friend by the name of Steve Webb who played the bass guitar after a fashion (as bass players went, he was an excellent angler), and I knew a chap who lived in Kingswinford who was a good drummer, so we used to rehearse in his mom and dad's large garage. I was then introduced to a good-looking chap called Rob Lake with a lion's mane of hair, and a good voice that could handle Free songs, so we were complete. I had found my own Paul Rodgers. The first time I met Rob at the garage, he bought with him a lovely Gretsch 'Country Gent' guitar, which had a problem with its electrics. He asked me if I'd take a look at it for him. Lord knows why he thought I'd know anything about electrics, but I agreed to have a dabble, so after the rehearsal, he handed this very expensive guitar to me in a tatty triangular cardboard box, and I headed for the bus stop. I waited ages for a bus to Brierley Hill but none came. I didn't wear a watch in those days and we'd been so engrossed in playing that we didn't realise how late it was. Consequently, the last bus had gone. I didn't have enough money for a taxi so I resignedly began walking home, a distance of at least 6 miles, I would guess. I hadn't got far when a police panda car pulled up alongside me.

'Jump in,' said the officer in the passenger seat, so I did.

'What have you got there?' he asked.

'It's a guitar, a very expensive one, actually,' I answered.

'Is it yours?' he asked.

'No, it's my mate's,' I replied.

'What's your mate's name?' asked the other cop.

'Erm, I don't know,' I said. I couldn't for the life of me remember, as we'd only met for the first time that evening. I duly explained this to the officer.

'And this chap lends you a very expensive guitar in a shitty cardboard box, even though you only met for the first time tonight and you can't remember his name?'

'Yes!' I said, chirpily.

'You've stolen it,' suggested the first officer.

'I haven't,' I insisted, somewhat hurt by this slur on my character.

'What sort is it?' asked the driver.

'I can't remember,' I said. I couldn't.

'It gets better by the minute. Can you play the guitar?' asked his partner.

'Yes,' I said. 'Do you want me to?'

'Yes please,' he said, so I got it out of the box and played a spirited version of Colonel Bogey for him.

'Are you taking the piss?' he asked, somewhat curtly.

'Of course not,' I assured him. I tried my best to change the subject. 'Would you mind if I had a lift home, 'I continued, 'I'm struggling to carry this thing.'

'Piss off,' they both said in unison, so I did. I staggered off into the cold night, lugging the huge semi-acoustic guitar. Then it started raining, and it gradually turned the cardboard box into sludge, like a biscuit that's been dipped in a mug of tea and left there too long. What seemed like hours afterwards I was still plodding along the main road from Kingswinford to Quarry Bonk, and I was soaking wet. The bright orange Country Gent was clearly visible now, and it just had a few clumps of soggy biscuit clinging to it where the box used to be. My only hope at this juncture was if Dennis Williams drove by in his newly acquired second-hand mustard-coloured Mini Clubman on the way home from seeing his girlfriend, Susan, who lived in Tipton.

Just as the thought entered my mind, blow me down if the mustard Clubman didn't pull up alongside me. I opened the passenger door and slumped inside with a world-weary sigh, carefully pulling the Gretsch between my legs and trying not to scratch it.

'Thank God you're here,' I groaned, exhausted, as I turned to the driver.

'Who the fuck are you?' he growled. It was not Dennis Williams. It was a bloke who was about to join the night shift at Round Oak Steel Works. I shot out, sharpish, mumbling apologies.

An hour later I crawled up my parents' steps, let myself in and went to bed. Miraculously, the Gretsch suffered no serious ill effects from its ordeal. I never mended the electrics.

It was around this time that another drama occurred, also involving a musical instrument. My beloved Boosey & Hawkes Emperor clarinet, the one my parents got me for Christmas, had been stolen from school. We were all deeply

94

upset, especially after I'd had all those expensive classical lessons. I was spending most of my time playing the guitar at the time, as I figured it was easier to get a girlfriend playing in a rock band with a sexy Les Paul than it was playing 'Stranger on the Shore' with a B flat clarinet. That said, the loss of it hurt. Incredibly, I was to be reunited with it in the most unforeseen and frankly amazing fashion some ten years later, but for now I will press on. You can read about that when the time comes. It's a tale to look forward to.

School was drawing to a close, and we were all nervously looking forward to the next chapter in our young lives. Dennis fancied a career in the army, or maybe teaching, and I was, by the grace of God and my exam results, headed for art college. Our head boy, Steve Nicklin, was a sciences whizz-kid, Phil Jones wanted to be a doctor, Jeremy Weston wanted to be a silversmith, Tim Saxon wanted to be an accountant like his older brother (well someone's got to do it!) and Lord knows what the rest fancied doing. I never asked.

To keep us amused, once the exams were over, we were sent on a few socialising trips. I remember going to Ingestre Hall, Staffordshire, a stately home with residential facilities. We scared each other silly with ghost stories and played Black Sabbath's album all weekend; the one with the creepy lady in the churchyard on the cover. The village idiot Trevor Withers took his chunky black felt-tip and drew a huge knob on a Victorian oil portrait. The boy needed locking up.

We also went Youth Hostelling in Stow-on-the-Wold, in the Cotswolds. After a 17-mile cross-country trek Dennis and I found a lovely pub in the town, and, finding the bar too crowded with other trekking Tiptonites and locals, we opted for a tiny little snug room at the back instead. We settled into a couple of cosy chairs and thought about what we could order from the food menu. It was at this juncture that the landlord arrived and told us to vacate his living room or he would call the police.

Not all of my friends stayed on for the 6th form. Ken Stevens, who was a year older than me, had left at the end of the 5th year, but we were still in regular contact thanks to our shared love of guitar playing. His final day at Tipton is noteworthy. He often sported a beard, as you already know, though this was not allowed according to the school rules. He was stood in an area of the playground that we called Smokers' Corner, for obvious reasons, sucking on a Benson & Hedges as usual, when, unexpectedly, Miss Tompkins, the girls' P.E. teacher pounced upon him, demanding he extinguish the cigarette immediately, a request he politely refused. Not realising that Ken was due to leave forever in around an hour anyway, she then berated him about his illegal beard. Those with him on that day then heard him say, after a brief moment of thought:

'Tell you what, Miss. You shave *your* beard off, and I'll shave mine off.' What made this particularly cruel was that Miss Tomkins was actually rather hirsute in the chin region.

He then slipped through a hole in the wire fence and strolled along the canal into the sunset, never to be seen by her again.

On a more sombre note, we learnt that Mr Perry, our beloved headmaster from Quarry Bonk Junior School had died, and his will stated that he wanted certain ex-pupils to carry his coffin to the church if they were willing. I was one, and David Raybould, who I think went on to become a surgeon in America, was another. Sadly, I can't remember who else was there.

Our local pub in Tipton was the Shrubbery, and we chose that venue to say goodbye to each other. In what's oft referred to as a 'drink-fuelled' lunchtime session, we closed another chapter of our lives. Dennis had a cheese cob to accompany his many pints of Guinness, and while he visited the lavatory to create room for more, I placed a round beermat in it, which

I have to say, fitted perfectly. It was a testament to how much beer he'd consumed that he ate it without complaint.

Then I went my way and they went theirs, and it was all very maudlin. The next four years were, I would say without hesitation, the best ones of my life, and extremely eventful.

Chapter 11

My exam results confirmed my worst suspicions. I had passed but with very mediocre grades. I felt a lot of guilt about this, and then something happened to me. It had finally dawned on me that my attitude could easily have cost me a place at college and a bright future. I also felt that I'd let my parents down. Almost overnight, I became conscientious and hard-working. I vowed that, from that day forth, I would apply myself to my chosen subject and do my best, rather than the bare minimum required to get by, and this I did. That attitude has stayed with me for my whole life since the beginning of college.

Sadly, my parents and grandparents sold the caravan, as David and I were now more interested in seeing local friends than heading off to Tenbury every weekend, and so another golden chapter ended and a new one was about to begin. David was halfway through his stint at Dudley Grammar School and doing well. Unlike me, he even did well in subjects he didn't like. He would have been around 15 when I left Tipton, and would go on to pass around 200 'O' levels, 45 'A' levels and score at least 3,000 goals for the school football team. The little devil was seriously academic, and sporty too.

I was granted an interview at Wolverhampton College of Art, which was, I'll have you know, considered one of the best art colleges outside of London in those days. My interview went well and I was, thank the Lord, accepted and due to start after the summer break. It was now 1972. Time flies when you're having fun!

The first day was interesting, to say the least. I had to cadge a lift from my dad as far as Cradley Heath, where I'd get a 244 bus to Dudley. I'd then walk across town to the Saracen's Head pub and transfer to a 58 bus to Wolverhampton, where I would again walk across town to the Art Gallery in Lichfield Street. The Foundation Department, in those days, was situated in the same building, but our entrance was at the back.

We all assembled, registered, met out tutors, John Aubrey, Bob Rose, Ed Brettell and John Brierley, and were allocated a studio space. There was a brief session that dealt with the rules and regulations, followed by a few minutes spent introducing ourselves to our new colleagues, and then we were thrown in at the deep end. We were shown into the life drawing room, where a naked woman was waiting for us. She was lying on a trestle table that had been covered with a white cotton sheet, and there were chairs positioned around her so that we could draw her from a variety of angles. Any thoughts of this being a sexual experience were quickly dashed when I saw Andrea the life model. She was all of four feet high with a hooked nose and pebble glasses, but what made her truly unique was her breasts. It is fair to say that some women have small breasts, some have medium-sized ones and some have large ones. Andrea's were conservatively around a ton and a half each. My first impression was that I'd accidentally wandered into an autopsy, a bit like in 'Silent Witness' on TV, where a circus dwarf's life had been tragically cut short by two giant Edam cheeses that must have dropped on her from a great height. We all glanced at each other nervously. John Aubrey, head of department, an affable Welshman with a giant grin, told us to sketch this vision in pencil, changing seats after an hour and beginning again from a different angle. This was as different from Tipton Grammar as you could get, I remember thinking. I looked around the room and studied the inmates. There was a chap who resembled Peter Sutcliffe, the Yorkshire Ripper, a nice-looking girl with curly hair and a sexy black T shirt with no bra beneath it, a couple of lads who looked as if they were supposed to be attending a seminar on banking and somehow ended up in the wrong building, a few drippy birds with floor-length skirts, Pre-Raphaelite hairdos and assorted beads, an earth mother with arms fatter than my legs, a chap that looked like Groucho Marx and a joke hippy chap with a silly leather headband and freckles who called everyone 'man'. Nice! I wonder what they were thinking of me. It was all a bit nerve-wracking too, if I'm honest, because we were all used to being the best artists in our classes at school, and now we'd been thrown together in a small room and were about to see how we measured up to each other in The Big Playground. Was I going to be the most useless artist by a mile, or the best, or arguably most depressing of all, average?

We began sketching, and my hand was full of nerves. I looked around me and the nerves soon passed. I was doing okay. One thing I learned early on was that those who looked like artists weren't necessarily able to draw like them. I was already breaking down the opposition into categories. Some talked the talk, like the Headband Hippy, but were woeful. The ones who'd come for the banking seminar were actually half-decent. Earth Mother was already ignoring the brief and drawing flowers from memory because she was no good at figures. The sexy one with no bra could have been drawing a stick man for all I knew. I was focused on something else.

Every other week we'd get a male life model, who sat in a chair without a stitch on. We'd encircle him and start drawing, and then - and I'm talking in veiled language here - he appeared to become flattered by the attention. All around the room, students were reaching for their Staedtler erasers and rubbing out, and then making 'it' a bit bigger. Ten minutes later, lo and behold, he'd change shape again. Out would come the erasers, and more vigorous rubbing out would ensue. It was deeply embarrassing. Then this chap would realise that things were getting out of control down below and he'd try desperately to reel himself in. Maybe he'd imagine he was watching a dreary nil-nil draw on a rainy day at the Molineux. Whatever turns you off, I suppose! Consequently, he would, erm, shrink a bit, and then out came the erasers again, as more adjustments were made. By the end of the session, the man would have had more rubbers on the end of his willy than Casanova.

Art college was not all about naked people, however. The idea of a Foundation course is that you get a small taster menu before you get to decide which main meal you'd like. We did photography, sculpture, woodwork, soft materials, ceramics, painting, drawing, Abstract Art, 3D design, Impressionism, Pointillism, typography, even caricature, you name it. Students who arrived thinking they wanted to be a fine artist often left wanting to be a photographer, and vice versa. Then, after a year spent working out what you did and didn't like, you did a 3-year BA(Hons) degree in your chosen subject. After that, you left and worked in B&Q, or became a teacher, or forgot about Art and married a rich bloke, or worked in the library.

Okay, it sounds cynical, but there was and still is a high fall-out rate, and only the strong survive. There's no room for folks who merely play at it. Art is as competitive as football, and the folks you regard as friends will be trying to take your job when they leave college. The other thing people don't seem to understand about Art is that it's not all about painting a picture and putting it in a frame in the hope that you can sell it. Some do that, obviously, but Art is also product design, graphic design, illustration, cartoons, animation, advertising, packaging, murals, interior design, the design of everyday household objects, theatre design, architecture and fashion design. Every supermarket is, in effect, an art gallery full of our work. Imagine a magazine, or a whiskey label, or a crisp packet without its distinctive design – just plain white. What a dreary world that would be. Then there's TV and cinema films, theatre sets, postage stamps, jigsaws, handbags, children's books. They're all created by people like me. Art is a very small word for a very big subject.

The biggest culture shock was the freedom. You could come and go when it pleased you, dress how you wanted and act the fool in class sometimes, and the lecturers didn't seem to mind, and this was where a lot of students got themselves into trouble. Discipline was transferred from the teachers to the students themselves, and this is where some came unstuck. Thankfully, I had learnt my lesson at grammar school, and now I was Mr Conscientious, but I saw many fall foul of the new 'relaxed' system, which in reality was not relaxed at all. John Aubrey was a very nice man, but if a student failed to be self-motivated and produce the work on time and to a good standard, he or she would be invited for a chat, and if that didn't have the desired effect, they were out on their ear, and the art school dance was over.

Back at home, I was still rehearsing with Rob Lake and Webby at John the drummer's house in Kingswinford. One evening, Rob was a bit late. He had to travel by bus from West Bromwich, and it was a tad unreliable. In the meantime, we decided to get his microphone up and running, so we could begin as soon as he showed up. I was standing with my beloved Les Paul around my neck next to the mic stand, and I remember reaching out for it to see if it was working. What happened next was one of the worst moments of my young life. A massive electric shock gripped my body and began in earnest to boil my brain. It felt as if I had been plunged deep into a boiling-hot swimming pool and fifty men were beating me senseless with lump hammers. I remember my addled brain thinking, 'Oh well. I am dying. Just like Jimi Hendrix.' And then I was gone. The shock had flung my right arm around the back of my body and dislocated it. I apparently fell to the floor with my eyes in the back of my head and smashed my Les Paul into the concrete floor. I had 6 clearly defined string cuts running across my cheek, maybe where my boiling head had collided with the guitar en-route to the ground.

The next thing I was aware of, presumably a while later, was the faces of three band members, sobbing with shock and relief, as I became conscious once more, and the sound of an ambulance's siren wailing. John had wrenched the plug from the wall, once he had eventually located it. It was hiding behind the amplifiers and the lads were, understandably, all too frightened to touch it. Meanwhile, my brain continued to fry. I was taken to Corbett's Hospital, near Stourbridge, where I was seen by a doctor who told me I'd been more than lucky. A guitarist by the name of Les Harvey, from the band Stone the Crows, had recently died on stage of exactly the same thing, and miraculously, I survived. Maybe the rubber soles on my Bumpers saved me. I will never know. And for those of you who don't know what Bumpers are, they are those black and white ankle-high baseball boots which are now more often known as 'Converse All-Stars'.

I was sent home and told I must go to bed and rest. My parents were worried sick, as you can imagine. The next day I didn't feel too bad, but my arm was sore after the dislocation. I decided to go to college, against the doctor's advice, mainly so that I could show off about what had happened to me. I told Kate, the girl with no bra who had become a good friend, and she was fussing around me like a mother hen, which is exactly what I wanted. Mid-afternoon, however, I suddenly began to feel ill with flu-like symptoms, and I decided to go home early. By now it was raining, and I'd taken a hat with me in case this happened. I caught the bus to the Saracen's Head, staggered off it feeling like death warmed up, into what was now a full-on rain storm. A gust of wind blew my hat off my head, and instinctively reaching to grab it, my arm dislocated again and I fainted. A taxi driver found me lying in a puddle, shaking, and kindly took me home. I went straight to bed but I was boiling hot and then shivering, as if I had a fever, and then I had an awful nightmare and woke up screaming. The next morning, I was hallucinating, and when my mother asked if I was well enough for her to go shopping, I began to shake with panic and I dreaded being on my own. She did eventually go out, once she thought I'd be okay, but while she was gone I

103

saw a devil-like figure in the mirror and other vile visions I'd rather forget, thank you. It took a day or so of this and several more nightmares before it calmed down and I was 'normal' again (I use the term loosely). My shoulder was prone to dislocation for several years after that, and the pain would be excruciating when it happened. I have heard about delayed shock, but I had no idea what it entailed. I would not recommend electrocution as a hobby. What surprised me was how different a small shock feels to a large one. They are utterly different. Maybe this was revenge for playing that trick on David with the Edwardian shock machine.

Strangely, I was to receive another shock when I was around 30. I'll tease you with that snippet for now, but that tale is, in my not-so-humble opinion, one of the funniest anecdotes from my repertoire, so don't hand this paperback to the charity shop just yet.

I loved college, but the daily commute was a pain and I didn't know how to drive at the time. Four buses per day plus a considerable walk can grind you down, but it was all made bearable by the strange characters that I encountered on and around public transport. The 58 Dudley-to-Wolverhampton bus had a Caribbean driver by the name of Jimmy, and I christened him Jimmy Triplicate because of his habit of saying everything three times. It was never two or four, but always three. I'd sit at the front when the bus wasn't crowded and chat to him each day. I'd say, 'How are you, Jimmy?' and he'd reply, 'Not bad, not bad, not bad.' Every single comment he made was in triplicate, without exception, but I could tell by his facial tics that this affliction was disturbing him. It was almost yet another form of Tourette's Syndrome, and he could not stop. Then, one day, I said something to him, and he replied, 'I know what you mean Geoff, I know what you mean, Geoff.'

I waited for the third one, but nothing came. I observed his tortured face in the mirror as we travelled in silence. He was struggling to hold onto the third sentence, to try and break his debilitating habit, but it was clearly taking its toll. All through Sedgley he drove, his face contorted and his mouth opening and closing with nothing coming out. We sailed through Fighting Cocks *en route* for the Mander Centre, and still he was trying to keep his demons at bay. We eventually pulled up outside the shopping centre, and he opened the doors to let me off. I smiled at him and alighted from the bus. 'I know what you mean, Geoff,' he blurted out, and then, suddenly, he appeared to deflate like a punctured balloon. He was a spent force - thoroughly defeated and miserable.

A male passenger on that same bus would get on from Monday to Thursday, as regular as clockwork. I called him Arthur, for reasons that hopefully will become obvious. On Fridays, he would not show, but strangely, a woman that looked uncannily like him would sit where he always sat, only this woman was not his twin sister. She had a 5 o'clock shadow and a deep voice. I called her Martha.

Another customer would travel in silence, but suddenly scream, 'BUST IT CLEAN OPEN!' with ear-shattering volume, and then resume his silence as if nothing had happened. It would scare passengers to death if he sat just behind them. Possessing, as I do, the inquisitive mind of an artist, I was fascinated and horrified in equal measure by what he yelled. Was he referring to a safe, perhaps, or, heaven forbid, the head of his wife?

The 244 from Dudley to Cradley Heath also had its regular oddballs. One evening I was sat halfway down a completely empty bus, minding my own business, when a small Asian man got on, and sat immediately behind me. I thought this strange, as he could have chosen anywhere to sit. A few moments later, I felt his hot breath in my ear, as he whispered sweet nothings to me in Urdu, Punjabi, or whatever it was; I am no expert. Then, to my absolute horror, he began to tickle my ear with his finger. I turned around and gave him what I fondly imagined was my best Clint Eastwood death-stare but was in reality probably more akin to a weedy come-hither look, before resuming my forward position. A few seconds later, the Punjabi sweet-nothings and ear-tickling started again. At this juncture I decided it was a good idea to leave the bus and wait for the next one, but to my horror, the little Asian chap seemed to be either following me or coincidentally getting off at the stop I had elected to leave at. This took me into deep waters. I didn't want the randy little bugger following me down the road. I stood by the doors, and he did too. He kept gazing over at me like he was deeply in love, but I was desperate not to make eye contact. The driver opened the door, and, with a sudden burst of inspiration ... (I have a favourite motto, by the way, which is 'Out of Desperation Cometh Inspiration') ... I affected one of those 'No, after *you, I insist!'* gestures with regal, somewhat camp sweep of the hand and a sweet smile. The Asian, who must have thought his luck was in, stepped off the bus but I stayed on. 'Drive off bloody QUICK!' I hissed to the driver, 'He's a bloody pervert!' To his credit, he did just that.

There was one character that chilled my blood. She was always waiting for a bus on Stafford Street, by the Polytechnic, and to this day I have never seen a more frightening creature. She was around 35 years old, at a guess, with a weird, pixie-like face, but this was not your good-natured Disney-style pixie. She was a fiendish devil-pixie from a nightmare painting by Richard Dadd, if you know who he is (or even if you don't). For the uninitiated, he was a Victorian artist who went mad and killed his father with a carving knife, but because he was certified insane he was not hanged, but allowed to spend the rest of his life in a mental asylum, where he painted exquisite pictures of weird goblins and creepy fairy folk. Check out 'Bacchanalian Scene' (1862). She was a bit like that but MUCH scarier. She had a strange angular face which was painted deathly white, like a clown's. Her cheekbones made Romilly Weeks's look like Billy Bunter's (look, I can't keep explaining who all these folks are), and her ears were long, pointed Mr Spock ears. The eyes were not human, but long, angled, severe slits that housed centres that were pure black, like a rat's, with no discernible irises. She wore a blue school-type blazer, a black skirt and wellingtons, of all things, and on her head was a blue-striped turban with a jewel in the centre. She would stare intensely, as if in a trance, and if she turned her head to look at you it made the blood run cold, because I swear it creaked as it slowly twisted around, like something from the original Exorcist movie. I curse myself that I did not take a sneaky photograph of this nightmare creature at the time. Then I could have included it in this book, so you wouldn't accuse me of exaggeration.

Foundation year flew by far too quickly, and it was magical. My new-found professionalism was paying dividends. I worked hard and got noticed. I loved my lecturers and we became friends too, but it would be some time before I found my artistic 'voice', as we writers and artists say. I was dabbling in various techniques and getting frustrated as usual, but at least I was beginning to see where I was going. It was fairly obvious that Fine Art was not for me. Had I been born a hundred years or more earlier, then I would certainly have fitted into that scene, but I was, without trying to sound grand, a craftsman painter in the making, not someone who was into conceptual art and enjoyed hanging the entrails of a dead badger from the stairwell and then writing a 200-page po-faced thesis to explain why this was artistically legitimate. That said, I actually came up with the 'Unmade Bed' concept well before Tracy Emin, but sadly, by the time I got home at night the bed fairies had made it look all neat again. Spiritually, I came from a tradition of fine painting. I loved Leonardo, Michelangelo, Holbein, Vermeer, and Co. I admired Victorian realists such as Arthur Hughes, Millais and Waterhouse, and 20th century illustrators such as Norman Rockwell. Let me assure you that all that would have been knocked out of me straight away on the mysterious 7th floor of the Faculty of Art building on the ring road. To get anywhere in this world, to make my mark and earn money, I needed to be an illustrator, and maybe a cartoonist as well, so that's where I set my sights.

I had applied for the BA(Hons) course at the main art college, which was, and still is, a fairly grim-looking 7-story block of flats situated on the ring road, immediately next to the Molineux, the famous Wolverhampton Wanderers' ground. I will always remember my interview. I was sat in a small office on the 3rd floor being grilled by three tutors as they examined my portfolio. The main chap looked like Oliver Reed, with a black beard and a black leather jacket that he wore over his shoulders at all times, like a cape. I was dying to inform him that the dangly bits each side were intended for his arms, just in case he wasn't aware of that, but he looked a bit gruff and I didn't want to upset him.

I don't know if you're familiar with art college interviews, but they could be a bit quirky, especially in those days. My initial reaction was that these blokes were a bunch of dickheads, but I suppose they were trying to see how creative I was under pressure. Artists need to be quite adept at arguing and standing up for their output. The tutors presumably wanted to see what I was made of, and if I could handle myself. Either that or I'd been right first time. They were a bunch of dickheads.

Halfway through looking at my work, which, in fairness, they were well impressed with, the Gruff One suddenly piped up with, 'Mr Tristram, how would you make a hole in the River Thames?' apropos of absolutely nothing that had gone before. I pondered this for a second and replied, 'I'd chuck *you* into it.'

I was fully expecting to be shown the door at that point, but they all laughed and one of them added that it was a good idea, something the Gruff One made a mental note of, judging by the look he gave him. A few very odd questions later, they shook my hand, congratulated me and said I was being accepted on the course. I was so thrilled, I rocketed home on the bus to inform my parents. Incidentally, David and I took to calling them Roob and Len as a sort of joke, and it stuck, so if it's okay with you and not too disrespectful, we'll call them that from now on. Our kids now do that to us, and I can't really say anything about it, can I, even though I long to be called dad every now and again.

Roob and Len were delighted of course, and even better, in those days we were actually paid to attend college by the local authority, as opposed to nowadays, when kids get themselves into thousands of pounds' worth of debt to study a useless degree in Sociology or Sports Science or Medieval Drainage Systems or whatever; subjects they will almost certainly never need in their real jobs afterwards. I am stubbornly old-fashioned about this. I believe your subject at University should be part and parcel of the career you chose afterwards, or at least, that is what you should be aiming for. I fully understand the counter-arguments, but I know so many people who took subjects such as a BA (Hons) in 'The Ethics of Cultural Appropriation' and ended up being a Carpet Warehouse Deputy Manager, or whatever. To their credit, they would never dream of going to fancy dress party dressed as a Mexican, but they now have a £30,000 debt to pay off, all because their parents wanted to show off about having an offspring with a degree.

Anyway, I was being given the princely sum of £5 a week to become a trained artist. I intended to spend most of that on women and booze, and just waste the rest.

Chapter 12

Around this time I had abandoned the Kingswinford band, possibly due to the fact that visiting that garage always resulted in me experiencing flashbacks about being fried alive by a million-volts. I was now rehearsing with a new outfit by the name of Fallen Angel with Rob Lake, my big buddy Larry Homer and a new drummer by the name of Mick Spedding, who reckoned he was related to the famous guitarist, Chris Spedding. Our new bassist was an affable lad called Trevor Gadd, which rhymes. In hindsight, 'a clever lad called Trevor Gadd' would have worked better, but he wasn't, particularly, and I can't lie for the sake of a neat bit of poetry. That said, he wasn't thick either. Just of normal intelligence I'd say, so let's move on before I dig an even deeper hole. I always remember that he had one of those 8-track cassette-player monstrosities welded underneath his glove compartment that was the size of a skip. He only had a small car, and each cassette was bigger than a suitcase, so if he had his entire collection of tapes with him he couldn't fit me in as well and I had to be strapped to the roof rack.

We played a couple of gigs, namely Dudley Technical College and some well-known club in Nottingham, and then we packed it in. Larry kept hold of Rob, who quickly morphed from a Paul Rodgers (of Free) look- and sound-alike into the new Peter Gabriel. Meanwhile, Kenny Stevens, Tipton's answer to John Lennon, invited me to join his 'pubs and clubs' pop band, Tobias, as a lead guitarist, alongside George James, who had a beautiful voice, ideally suited for Beatles songs and much else, Steve McLoughlin on bass, who looked as if he'd unwisely taken tips on sideburn management from Noddy Holder, and a succession of drummers, depending on what day of the week it was. The original one was Phil

Cunniffe, a nice lad whose nose had its own post code. He was another chap who wouldn't have looked out of place in Slade, with his feather-cut hairdo. Then came a chap who's name I can never remember, which is either down to my awful memory or the fact that he left no impression on me whatsoever, or both, and finally a hell of a good drummer by the name of Ian Hart, who was the Wolverhampton Chief of Police's son, which meant we never got pulled over for speeding, or rather, when we did we got away with it. More about these characters anon. Ken, Clocky and George owned an old blue Ford transit van which had an extra row of seats added to accommodate the band. Behind this was a plywood barrier, and behind that was the gear. The band, unlike previous ones I'd dabbled with, were very busy, and we had one or two gigs each weekend, in and around the Midlands area. We played charts songs that we liked, and lots of Beatles, as we were all big fans, and George was a dead-ringer, vocally, for McCartney. We'd also play Bowie, Rock and Roll standards, the odd Free song, The Stones, The Faces and so on. Nothing too cheesy in other words. Venues ranged from pubs to the larger social and political clubs. We were actually not bad at all, but we loved to muck around, sometimes with disastrous results.

One of our regular venues was Boulton Court Sports and Social Club, Tipton. One evening, Ken was rummaging backstage and found a feather duster in the janitor's locker. It was the kind of thing another Ken, Ken Dodd, used as his 'tickling stick'. Ken thought it would be a great idea to tickle Phil the drummer with it as he played, so halfway through the very first song, he produced the tickling stick and wiggled it about in Phil's face. A second later, Phil had stopped drumming and was writhing in agony on the floor. The feathery bit had a sharp bamboo pole running through it, and Ken had poked this in Phil's eye. That gig lasted all of 20 seconds before it was abandoned.

111

We had a roadie by the name of Farouk, an amiable, stockily-built Asian lad, who would often volunteer to get the band fish and chips in the break, as most of us didn't get time to eat before we set off for the gig. At one venue, Farouk came onto the stage and began taking orders while we were still halfway through a song. He returned early from the chip shop, which meant eating the stuff on stage as we played. To facilitate this, we played a rambling rock and roll number by Chuck Berry. I played an extended guitar solo so that Ken could eat his roe and chips, and he returned the favour for me. It was far more difficult for Phil, so Farouk hand-fed him as he drummed. To allow Clocky to eat his cod and chips, Phil then played a drum solo. We were nothing if not considerate.

Each gig had its memorable moments. At a club near Cannock, we arrived rather late, so Ian Hart hastily assembled his drumkit as we plugged in our amps and tuned guitars in a mad panic. We had just learnt a Bad Company song called 'Can't Get Enough', which begins with a count-in followed by two loud cracks on the drums and four massive, macho power-chords from me. It promised to be a dramatic start to our set, and it would have been, had Ian's drum kit not fallen to pieces after his first bash. It transpired that, in his haste, he'd forgotten to screw all the bits together.

At another Cannock venue we were confronted by a scary man with tattoos all over his face who asked, 'Can you play 'Whole lotta Love'?' (the Led Zeppelin classic, for those who are not from this planet.)

Ken answered, 'No, sorry, we know it but we've never played it before.' The tattooed man then snarled, 'Play it!'

On-cue, the opening chords of 'Whole lotta Love' growled forth from my Les Paul, followed by George handling the Robert Plant vocals with assured virtuosity. So far, so good. We continued in confident fashion until we reached the weird bit in the middle, full of sound effects, orgasmic moans and odd noises. Again, somehow, we improvised this section with aplomb, with George howling, and Ken and I rubbing our guitars up and down the microphone stands or placing them against the amps to achieve feedback and distortion. Out on the dancefloor, the Tattooed Terror and his cronies were leaping about with gay abandon, like they were high on illegal substances at Glastonbury. Then we hit a sizeable snag. Suddenly, all the weird stuff ends, and Robert Plant pulls it back together with the words, 'Woman, you need ...' whereupon Jimmy Page belts out two crash chords, before Plant sings...LOVE!' Then the main riff of the song begins once more and all is fine and dandy till the end. The only thing was, neither Ken or I had the faintest idea what those crucial two chords were. I glanced over at Ken, who seemed to be struggling with some complex mathematical equation in his head. He was scratching his chin for all he was worth, fully aware that an audience would only wait so long. George, sensing what the problem was with his two guitarists, began to improvise. He repeated his earlier line and jazzed it up a bit.

'I said, let me tell you now, woo-oo-oo-oo-man, you-oo-oo-oo need, I said you-oo need...'
Still nothing came from either guitar. It was getting desperate now. The Tattooed Terror had stopped dancing and was eyeing George as a cat would a pigeon. Then, sensing that nothing was forthcoming from Ken or me in the near future, George did his level best to sing the two power chords, the problem being, human beings are not equipped to sing chords, and can only manage one note at a time. The result was 'BOOM BOOM', sung in a vocal tone that was meant to assimilate a distorted Les Paul, but actually sounded exactly like Basil Brush shouting through a loudhailer at an anti-foxhunting rally. The crowd fell about laughing at us. Mr Tattoo had the look of a man who had been seriously contemplating butchering us all but had then reluctantly decided against it. We all breathed a huge sigh of relief and pressed on with the rest of our set. As we packed away the gear at the end of the night, we even contemplated adding this

113

new tune to our song-list. Then Ken suddenly exclaimed, 'It's D major, A major.' Better late than never I suppose.

There were many memorable incidents, not least of which was the night when we got slung out of the Adam's Best Butter Sports and Social Club in Stoke-on-Trent for stealing toilet rolls from the ladies' loo, when England was suffering from a national toilet roll shortage (incredible, yet true). But the one that topped them all was the evening we played at a club in West Bromwich and were told by a very officious committee member that we were far too loud. Ken begrudgingly turned everything down a tad and proceeded, but this was still nowhere near quiet enough for this gentleman. He stormed up to the stage and asked us, in no uncertain terms, to reduce the sound further. Ken, being Ken, he then elected to mime the entire next song without a note being played, which of course infuriated the committee man, who then demanded that we turn it back up a bit, which we duly did, to number 10 on our 100-watt Marshall amps. For a split second, the Labour Club thought they had mistakenly booked Grand Funk Railroad, and now the committee man was apoplectic with rage, which was made worse by the motorcycle fraternity at the back of the hall who liked the noise, and were calling him nasty names for spoiling their fun.

Then, without warning, all hell broke loose. I saw a chair fly through the air, and I saw fists fly, so I warned the lads. Quite soon, a full-scale bar-room brawl was in progress, and stray chairs were whizzing past the stage. It was all very well for the band on the Titanic to carry on, but they weren't in West Bromwich and in danger of a chair knocking their head off. We scarpered backstage and let them all get on with it.

We had many crazy evenings with Tobias, but even for us, starting a riot was a first.

College life, meanwhile, was wonderful. I had some old Foundation friends with me, my mate Kate for one, and a lot of new characters that I liked a lot too. We all sat in a room on the 3rd floor, and unlike the Foundation department, which had

114

the feel of a traditional, Victorian art college, we now had desks that made the place feel more like a university classroom. Four desks were arranged in a unit, so that there were two people opposite and a person next to you, and to maintain a bit of privacy, we had small divider panels that effectively created an 'L' shaped noticeboard for each desk, which enabled us to pin up our ideas and picture references. It also prevented us from pulling stupid faces at each other when we should have been deep in concentration.

We were able to wander around the studio rooms freely, chatting to colleagues and seeing what they were up to, and often their different approach to a brief would provide inspiration. We all fed from each other, creatively speaking, and I genuinely feel that this raised the standards.

The college was arranged thus: The lower ground floor was the photographic department, the ground floor was print, compositing and bookbinding, the 1st floor was ladies' underwear - sorry, I'm getting confused with Beattie's now – I meant the exhibition space and refectory, the 2nd floor was the library and offices, the 3rd floor was graphic design, where I lived, and also silkscreen printing and etching. The lecturers there had a reputation for being especially *louche*, which is why I referred to them as the Jazz/Booze Set, a name that stuck, I am pleased to report. The 4th floor was 3D design, i.e. woods, metals and plastics, the 5th floor was ceramics, and finally, the top two floors were fine art and sculpture, also known as The Astral Plane, another one of my creations.

I was on the Graphics course, though I was never really a Graphic Designer. I was always an illustrator, but there wasn't an Illustration course available in Wolverhampton so they dumped me in with the designers, a bit like putting a rabbit in a hutch with guinea pigs. They're a different species but they co-habit okay and seldom fight.

I had many friends, including Dylan Waldron, who still sends me Christmas cards, Ted Stephenson, a kindly

Northerner with a Rod Stewart hairdo, Phil Sanders, a Black Country lad who now lives in America, Judy Moss, a buxom good-time girl, Kate of course, and Nigel Sutherland, a complete loony from the South Coast. There were loads more in my class, but I don't want this to become a telephone directory, so you'll be told about people on a need to know basis, i.e. if they did something memorable that deserves a mention.

Back at home in Quarry Bonk, I had begun to frequent a small rock club by the name of JB's, in King Street, Dudley, that had a reputation for great live music. The club was a tiny, rough and ready, converted primary school behind the Pathfinder clothing store, and it hosted most of the great names in rock music over a 40-year period. Bands such as U2, The Pretenders, The Police, The Stranglers, Squeeze, Nick Lowe, The Boomtown Rats, Judas Priest, Paul Carack, UB40, Dire Straits, The Manic Street Preachers, Annie Lennox and Dave Stewart, Ian Dury, Elvis Costello, Steve Marriot, The Cure, The Wonder Stuff, Blur... I could go on, and on, and on. They all played there either on their way to fame and fortune, or else on the way back, as was the case with Steve Marriot of the Small Faces.

It was here that I met Susan Bate, a Black-Country wench who was propping up the bar one night as I approached it in search of lager. We chatted briefly, and she dropped a Wigwam into my drink in a playful act of flirtation. I must make it clear that it wasn't an actual wigwam, which would have been difficult for many reasons that I don't have the mental strength to go into now. It was actually a small nibbly thing, akin to a Hula-Hoop, and I, being eternally optimistic, saw this as an invitation; a green light to proceed, so I did. We have been together now for 44 years, and I think she found me sexy and attractive for the first two of those, which is better than nothing. I was attracted to her, not because of her dazzling intellect, because she hasn't got one, but because she was extremely pretty and also the only woman in Netherton

116

without a tattoo. I suppose, in hindsight, I could have widened my search to include Cradley Heath, Dudley, Stourbridge and Wolverhampton, but I was young and naïve. Besides, she keeps me grounded, which is to say she has never been even mildly impressed by anything I've ever done and offers zero enthusiasm and encouragement. I like that in a woman.

I was duly introduced to her parents and was a regular visitor to their little flat in Darby End, Netherton. One night, Larry called to see me about something band-related while I was there, and when Susan's mother, Nancy, opened the front door and saw Larry, she actually screamed.

College nightlife revolved around the Molineux pub, situated a hundred yards or so from the college itself. In many ways, though I was an active member of the group in the daytime, I was never really a part of their night-time gang. I seldom ventured out to Wolverhampton in the evening, as I now had a steady girlfriend and was playing most weekends with the band. I was always ribbed for being boring in this regard, but in truth, I found the average art student's lifestyle fairly dull. All they ever did was get drunk, play darts, eat unspeakable shit and occasionally end up in the Lafayette Nightclub, trying in vain to secure a sexual partner for the night. The morning after their sordid nights out, they would regale me with tales of madness. One evening, Dylan, an avid Guinness fan, wandered upstairs in the Molineux pub to find the lavatory, and having opened an old brewery loading door by mistake, found himself walking through it and into the sky, whence he quickly fell to earth he knew not where. Pissed and concussed in equal measure, his life was saved by the statuesque Amazon warrior, art student Susan Eden-Allen, who flung him over her broad shoulders and dropped him off at the hospital on her way home. Dylan awoke to ask the doctor, 'Where am I?' in classic fashion.

He also nearly came to grief on a college-sponsored canal trip in Kinver. Again, thanks to Guinness, his nemesis, he fell into the lock by the Vine pub and saw his life flash before

117

him. It didn't help that he was wearing a pair of cowboy boots which filled with water and anchored him to the bed of the canal. Again, the Gods were on his side that night, and he somehow survived. The only person who was thirstier than Dyl was his fiery Irish-Brummie redheaded gal, Susan Hilcox, another art college inmate. Was everyone name Sue in those days, I wonder? Those two, like us, are happily married and living quietly in the Leicestershire countryside in a cute little cottage. Dylan is still a professional artist, as am I.

Thanks to Tony Messenger, our Head of Department (the Gruff-looking one with the leather jacket thrown over his shoulders), we had loads of visits from famous artists. Unknown to us students, Tony had in fact been the spearhead of the new Art Movement in London back in the 60s, and quite a pin-up in his youth. He was friends with the likes of Peter Blake, a famous pop artist who designed the Sergeant Pepper's album sleeve for the Beatles, Alan Aldridge, who illustrated their songbook, Gerald Scarfe, the cartoonist, David Hockney, who is of course the world's most famous living artist, and many more. His wife, Helen, who I never met, was a well-known actress and also designed costumes for David Bowie in his Ziggy Stardust phase. Don Bessant, the thirsty printmaker on the 3rd floor was another Messenger import, and back in his native London on weekends, he was dating actress Julie Christie, but none of us naïve art students had the faintest inkling about the celebrities running our department!

It was because of Tony's connections that our college was punching above its weight, and we were able to get superstars like Blake, Aldridge and Scarfe to talk to us plebeians for relatively smallish fees.

One day, Scarfe came to chat to us about his work and I went down to the Molineux for a basic pub lunch, as did Messenger, Scarfe and his wife, before the afternoon session began. Not that I was fraternising with them you understand. I was just there, in the same pub and sharing a couple of large tables with them, Dylan and a few others. When I arrived back at the college, my friends ribbed me about my star-studded lunch date.

'How was lunch with Jane Asher?' asked Ted Stephenson, enviously. Jane Asher was Paul McCartney's ex-girlfriend, before he swapped her for Linda, in case you didn't know.

I knew exactly who Jane Asher was, I just didn't realise I'd been sat next to her in the Molineux for an hour. Unknown to me, she was now Scarfe's wife. In the afternoon, Scarfe invited questions, so I asked, 'How much do you earn?'

He told me to mind my own bloody business.

As we entered our second year, so a new 1st year were settling in just down the corridor in our old room. I soon made friends with a few of them, including Robin Greenwell, who went on to run a very successful design studio, Denise Serphentine (lovely surname don't you think?) who did likewise, and a young lad by the name of Mike Timmins who was one of the few artists at the college that I was really scared of. By this, I mean that he was extremely good, and looked to be *en route* to becoming a top airbrush illustrator. He was also a gentle soul. Dylan, the Homer brothers (two nice lads from other departments within the Faculty of Art) and I took him under our wing when we found him looking lost one playtime and asked the lecturers if we could keep him. We regularly went for lunch together over at the main refectory and laughed ourselves silly. Just like the caravan years, these were golden times, but sadly, we only seem to recognise this once they have gone, as Joni Mitchell once told us in 'Big Yellow Taxi'.

If I may be permitted to leap a few years into the future for just a moment, one day, a few years after I'd left college, I wandered into the room on the 3rd floor where Mike Timmins was based, and commented on the postcard he had pinned up on his noticeboard. It was a picture of 'The Tennis Girl', a famous photograph, taken by another friend of mine, Martin Elliot, from Halesowen. You probably remember this image well. It was a shot of a girl in tennis gear from the back, taken on a clay court. She is lifting her short tennis skirt to reveal a bare buttock. That photograph made Martin a small fortune in royalties, thanks to Athena selling a squillion posters and postcards of it. It was even featured on Minder, the TV show, in Dennis Waterman's bedsit. The shot was actually taken at Edgbaston Tennis Club, and he asked his then-girlfriend, Fiona, to pose for it. I sat down next to Mike and I was waxing lyrical about this girl's lovely backside, as we red-blooded males tend to do. Usually, Mike would be the first to chip in with some enthusiasm, but on this occasion, he was strangely muted. His eyes seemed to be darting about nervously. I sensed that something was wrong and stopped speaking. Mike reached for a post-it note and began writing on it. I was intrigued. It said:

'She's on the other side of this noticeboard. Shut up!'

Fiona, the model for the famous 'Tennis Girl', had enrolled on the Graphics course. I wanted the ground to swallow me up.

I lost both my grandads in fairly quick succession. I was in our kitchen with David one Saturday morning back in 1971 when an ashen-faced man called, and informed us that my dad's dad, another Leonard, had suffered a massive heart attack and died instantly. My dad worked on Saturday mornings, and was yet to arrive home.

My beloved Reuben succumbed to lung cancer when I was 20, caused by those filter-less cigarettes such as Woodbines, Senior Service, and Craven 'A', the ones that promised not to 'affect your throat' in their advertisements. I will always remember that poor, skeletal, yellow-skinned man that could barely whisper, and how we lied to him that he'd soon be back up and about, tending his garden in the sunshine. So far cigarettes have killed my great grandads, my grandads and my dad. They have killed Susan's grandad and her dad, Derek. How many more should we watch die before we get the message? They are evil, and vaping is even worse. I just love

120

walking through a town when someone blowing more steam than the Flying Scotsman walks past and shares with me his pre-breathed, sickly sweet Poundland air freshener cloud.

Around this time, I was experiencing the odd nightmare, which was troubling. I would wake up shaking and nervy, and I somehow knew it was a recurring dream, but didn't know what it was about, which sounds like a contradiction, I know. It wouldn't happen every day, or even every week or month, but nevertheless it wouldn't go away, and even after I was married to Susan at the age of 24, it persisted, albeit intermittently. When I eventually realised what was causing this to happen, it was quite a shock, but more of that later.

The band was still intact, but we had experienced a personnel change. Out went Clocky, to join a heavy rock outfit called Possessed, and in came my brother David on bass guitar. At first I was not wholly in favour of this, because, it meant my kid brother, still only barely 16, would now be socialising with me and the others, and...well, I was a bit protective and didn't really want him hearing what we 'grown-ups' talked about. We were best friends in our home environment, but now he'd be a party to what happened at night with me and my band-mates, and having already read about some of the things we endured at Tobias gigs, I'm sure you'd agree with my reticence. The others outvoted me, however, and David joined us. I need not have worried, and quite soon he became an indispensable member of our little happy troupe. He was also (no offence to past members), ten times the musician that they had been, and he vastly improved our sound. That said, his first outing, at Blackheath Sports and Social Club, was so nerve-wracking for him that he faced the wrong way for the whole evening.

I would often bump into Clocky and his friends from Possessed at JB's, and we'd ask each other how things were going. One evening I was talking to Vernon Pereira, their singer, and he told me they were playing in Wales the

121

following evening. I wished him well and then sidled off to talk to Larry. I received a phone call from George, our singer, two days after that to say that Possessed's transit van had veered off the motorway in Wales and struck a parked oil tanker. They think their roadie-cum-driver fell asleep. The equipment was shunted forwards by the impact and it killed several of the band, including Vernon. I won't say how he died, as it is too horrific to repeat. Clocky got off relatively lightly, if you count multiple broken bones and months of rehab as lightly. Suddenly an acute awareness of the frailty of our lives hit home for a second time. Had my electric shock killed me, everything would have changed from that point onwards. No promising career in Art, no marriage to Susan, no children; the catalogue goes on and on and the net widens by the second to include more and more people who are affected in some way, or even worse, were denied a life of their own as a result of my passing. It's truly mind-boggling how one death affects everything in the future, but of course, we only know what might have been, and how history might have been rewritten, if that death is prevented, as mine was.

By way of contrast to my good fortune, one minute I was drinking by the bar at JB's with Vernon, and the next he was lying lifeless and mutilated on a Welsh mortuary slab, his young hopes and dreams wiped out.

Most of the people on my course were destined to become designers, rather than illustrators, a subject I have already touched upon, but we were expected to be at least proficient in all the aspects of design, such as typography, photography, page-design and illustration. I would call myself a proficient, pedestrian designer, rather than an inspired one, whereas I think Dylan just ignored most of the briefs he was handed and carried on drawing, usually in pencil, with a large pair of imaginary blinkers strapped to his face, a bit like an imaginary horse, so he didn't get distracted by irritating college lecturers who kept insisting that he at least attempted to vaguely follow the curriculum. He has since vastly added to his artistic repertoire and paints, usually calm, serene, unhurried, restful still-life subjects, which reflect his gentle, placid nature. He too endured unspeakable sorrow later in life, due to his younger brother, Russell, who was also a student on our course after we had left, and then became a professional graphic designer, being killed by a London bus driver as he cycled across the London bridge on his way to work.

Money was always tight, in spite of our generous £5 a week from the government, so we constantly looked for ways to supplement our income. We had a print technician by the name of Wilf who owned a holiday home in the shadow of Harlech Castle, and being rightly proud of this, he commissioned me to produce a very detailed, photographic pencil drawing of said place, having previously done his research and shortlisted the students who might have been not only 'up for it' but 'up *to* it.' As legendary football coach, Brian Clough, once modestly explained, when summing up his talents, 'I might not be the best manager in the world, but I'm in the top one'. In fairness, Dylan was equally good at that pencil style but I probably clinched the commission by being a completely useless businessman as well. Wilf, when gently probed about the remuneration for this time-consuming task, assured me in gloriously vague fashion that I would be 'looked after'. I duly began working on this drawing, based on his supplied photographs, usually at weekends, perched on Susan's bed. I'm sure she was enthralled by having to watch me scribbling for hours on end and ignoring her, come to think of it. You can see visual proof of all this in the photographic section, by the way.

I finished the drawing and took it to college in my portfolio, first showing my tutor, John Lowe, who said, 'Excellent, he should be well-pleased with that!' This was what I wanted to hear. I delivered the picture to Wilf's print room and it is fair to say that he was similarly impressed with it and began to wax lyrical about precisely what frame would suit it and where it should be sited in his bungalow. Then he reached into his pocket and pulled out a fiver and offered it to me like he was parting with the Ko-i-noor diamond.

'But, erm...' I spluttered.

'No, don't be silly,' he interjected. 'You've earned it!'

One of the stranger tales to emanate from the F.A.D. (The Faculty of Art and Design, though now I've been forced to explain the acronym I might as well have just given you the full title in the first place) was about Mrs 'M', the Soft Materials Lecturer. This department was housed on the 5th floor alongside the 3D design people, and it was where you went if you wanted to make something from, as the name suggests, soft materials, such as cloth, foam rubber, leather, plastic, wool and so on. There were a lot of fashion students who frequented the place, as well as 3D Design students, who specialised in furniture and household item design. I liked going there because Mrs Marsden, to use her full name, was a lovely, funny, sociable lady who was almost a surrogate mother to the students. She'd always got the kettle on and the biscuit barrel to hand, so we'd flop down on a pile of foam rubber and chill out for ten minutes with a cup of tea and laugh ourselves silly. I first met her when we were given a soft materials project, and I chose to make a faux leopard-skin waiter's jacket. Okay, pause for a moment. I can hear what you're thinking. I am not Lily Savage. Roxy Music's first album had just been released and I was mad for it. It's just a shame that they went on to become mainstream, because that first album was totally original in concept, as was 'Mental Notes' by the New Zealand band, Split Enz, who later morphed into the more mainstream but still wonderful Crowded House. Both decided they'd had enough of the denim shirted, long-haired blues band image, and offered us a really interesting alternative with great, inventive, original music too. Anyway, I digress. Bryan Ferry, then virtually unknown, remember, designed the sleeve and the music as a throwback to the era of 50's glamour, as seen through a weird, distorted mirror, and he wore a waiter's jacket, i.e. those bolero-style short coats, but in a shiny leopard skin, so naturally, I wanted to make one. Damn! I've just read all that back and it's hardly a defence is it? Anyway, on with the story, which is far too good to dither about with the way I'm doing. So, it was fairly obvious to anyone with acute observational skills - and being an art college there should have been a fair few - that Mrs 'M' wore a wig. One day, sat on our foam rubber mountain with two mugs of tea, she explained to me why this was. One night she was having trouble sleeping, unlike her husband who was snoring away next to her. She saw a bright light in the sky and dashed to the bedroom window to see what had happened. The light got brighter and brighter, and then receded and disappeared, so she went back to bed. The next morning, her face was itching. She went to the bathroom and looked at herself in the mirror, to discover that her face was very red. Over the course of the week, her hair began to fall out, until she was forced to buy a wig. She saw the doctor, who sent her for tests, as her skin looked burnt. The test came back, and here we need a bit of creepy music as a soundtrack. The results stated: 'Almost certainly some form or radiation burn, but we have not seen anything similar before.' Gradually, the itching subsided, but the hair never returned, so she continued to wear the wigs. But that was not the end of the matter. She also noticed that she was having strange thoughts and premonitions. One day she suddenly said to her husband, 'Let's pop to West Bromwich and see the Town hall burning down!' Assuming his wife had had one too many Proseccos with her lunch, he ignored her, until the next day's Express & Star newspaper reported a fire at the town hall that needed three fire engines. More incidents followed. She was becoming psychic and predicting all manner of things. One day, Ken Sambrooks, the photography technician, visited her, and she advised him to put a load of

125

money on a specific horse riding in the Grand National, though she did not know the runners or riders. She merely plucked the name from her mind. Ken ignored the tip and the next day, discovered that he was unwise to do so, as the horse had won by a mile. Reports of these psychic incidents soon spread around the college. Eventually, our beloved Mrs 'M' retired, and we never saw her again.

Not all the staff were lecturers. We also had technicians, such as Wilf, the cut-price art buyer, Stuart, the jovial print compositor, Ron Astle, who ran the materials' store and Bill Kimpton who set up exhibitions. I was always amused by Astle and Kimpton being 'mere' technicians, because they were two extremely talented individuals. Ron, when not dispensing tracing paper and masking tape from his tiny storeroom, ran the BBC jazz orchestra, whilst Bill, whose day-job was to hang other people's artwork on the wall, was renowned as one of the top cartoonists in Britain, taught by the famous Norman Thelwell, and in my humble opinion, a match for him, though in fairness, he did 'borrow' Thelwell's cartoon style.

I, in turn, stole most of my cartoon style from Kimpton, and I now produce cartoon greetings cards for Rainbow, his old company, though I am not fit to shine his shoes as a cartoonist. It always makes me smile that all our lecturers would never show us their own work or sit down and demonstrate how to draw or paint, as I do now on the rare occasions when a college invites me to pop in for a day. I may have been at art college for four years, but, in effect, I taught myself through practise and copying others – people such as Bill for cartoons, Disney too, of course, Norman Rockwell for illustration, Vermeer and Holbein for fine art, and so on. People always ask, 'Self-taught or did you go to college?' and I always reply, both. The college just gave me a place where I could try to perfect my skills in peace. They didn't actually teach me a fat lot, and remember, I was drawing since the age of four, a long time before art college.

As with all good things, the time flew by too quickly. It is not my intention to bore you rigid with a day-by-day report on every single painting and drawing, event, lecture, lunch and anecdote, because I was still only 20, going on 21, and I have a lot more fertile ground to cover before this book is finished. Let's just say that, before we knew it, our final year was looming, and we had to prepare our 'dip shows', as they were often called. The expression comes from the word 'Diploma'. When I first applied for the course, we were to be 'Diploma of Art and Design' students, but to our delight, the qualification was upgraded to a full Bachelor of Arts just as we arrived. This was a much posher-sounding certificate to flash around, and maybe it was God's conciliatory gesture for degrading my grammar school to a comprehensive.

In our final year we had a big degree show to stage, featuring the best of our work from the three years we'd been there, and there was also a very important final showpiece project to embark upon. Last but not least, we had to write and illustrate a thesis on our chosen topic for the related studies department. I chose the life and work of Charles Lutwidge Dodgson, a.k.a. Lewis Carroll.

Before all that, however, was the summer holiday. Students vacated their halls of residence and disappeared back whence they came, which for my year meant, Sweden, Scotland, Yorkshire, London, the South Coast, the Midlands, and, in my case, Quarry Bonk. Each year I'd found myself holiday jobs, and they deserve special mention.

One summer I spent weeks loading hundreds of tyres onto a van every day until every bone in my body ached. One thing you probably won't appreciate is that the smell of one or two tyres is neither here nor there, but if you are in a room with ten thousand of them, it chokes you. Rubber stinks!

During another summer break, I worked in a factory that made insulation for buildings. The tradition for all places offering summer jobs was to give the students the worst, smelliest, nastiest jobs that no one else wanted to do, so Rob Lake and I were tasked with gluing sheets of featherlight corrugated plastic together. If you imagine a wafer biscuit without the chocolate covering, made up of several layers of lightweight wafer sections, that was pretty much what they looked like. We had to put them through a roller into a glue bath in order to coat both sides, and then assemble them into this giant wafer thing that was something or other to do with insulation, but don't ask me what. All I know is, it stank of glue which took your breath away, and we were completely sozzled by mid-afternoon and slurring our words. Nowadays, we all know about the dangers of glue-sniffing, but back in the 1970s no one gave a damn, especially if it was only a pair of disposable long-haired students doing it.

Another place had me painting large square-section metal poles green. Don't ask why. The foreman took me outside, showed me the poles and said, 'do you know how to paint neatly, son?' I replied that this was my speciality, and he took this wrongly, like I was being sarcastic. I grabbed a plastic chair and sat down beside the poles, ready to begin. He came over again and said, 'What are you doing?' I answered, slightly puzzled, 'with regard to what?' and it was clear by his attitude that he was getting annoyed with me before I'd even begun work. 'All the men here paint standing up', he said, 'so you will too.'

I reasoned that the poles were on small stands, on the floor, so it was silly to be standing up, breaking my back trying to paint something that was 9 inches from the ground.

'I repeat,' he repeated, 'you will stand up, because the men who work here are told they have to,'

'Then why don't you inform all of the men that they can sit down?' I asked, perplexed by his logic.

'What's your fucking horrible name?' he snarled. I will always remember his exact phraseology.

'Tristram,' I replied, and this seemed to send him over the brink, into the abyss. He fired me on the spot and stormed off. As I collected my effects (flask, sandwiches, Twix, new

Musical Express) and was reluctantly about to head for home with not a penny earned, one of the men hinted at what might have upset him.

'His surname is Tristram too', he said, grinning. 'so maybe he thought you were still taking the piss!'

I shudder to think that this idiot and I might have been related, but thankfully our paths have never crossed since.

I moved on to a place called Dudley & Dowell Iron Founders in Old Hill, which specialised in flanges, whatever they were. I was asked to report to the stores, where my old school friend, Dennis Williams, was also doing holiday work. He'd worked there before, so he explained what my duties were. I know you will presume I am exaggerating here, but this is exactly how it happened. Dennis showed me around a warehouse that was full of flanges, which are a bit like clay pigeons, if you know what they look like. If you don't, the best way to describe them is, a bit like a small flange. If you've ever seen a pipework company digging up your road in order to mend or lay sewage or water pipes, flanges are the things that they use to join two pipes together. They come in all shapes and sizes with multiple diameters, according to the size of pipe they are joining, and that, ladies and gentlemen, is probably more than you will ever need to know about flanges. Oh yes, and they have holes around them so you can bolt them together.

'What we stores people have to do,' continued Dennis, 'is wait for an order to arrive, and then we collect the flanges from this warehouse and pack them in one of these wooden boxes with a copy of the paperwork, nail down the lid, stamp it with this stamp thingy and put them over there, to await collection.

This was fine. I understood it. I could do it either standing or seated. Dennis assured me that it was a very easy-going place with no officious managers or foremen. He asked me to follow him to the restroom for a cup of tea before we began.

129

In the restroom, there was another student, sat doing a crossword in the corner, and two gents sat together by the sink. One, I noticed, was knitting.

'Who's she?' he asked of Dennis.

I looked around but there were no females present. Then it dawned on me that he meant me.

'This is Geoff,' replied Dennis, winking at me as if to say, 'I'll explain all this later.'

We made a cup of tea and sat down. Dennis suggested a game of cards. I don't know about you, but when it's your first day in a new job, don't you feel that you should be sort-of respectful and enthusiastic and straining at the leash to get stuck in? I know I do, even if this euphoric feeling passed by mid-afternoon. Here was Dennis inviting me to a card school, which was a bit of a worry, and who were the two blokes by the sink, and why was one of them busy knitting a jumper? Were these flange-packers (no euphemism intended) experiencing the lull before the flange-packing storm and making the most of it, or what?

I nervously played a few hands of cards, which seriously messed with my mind, I can tell you. The two gents, and please don't accuse me of stereotyping here, were as queer as 9-bob notes. Gerald was a veritable mincing machine. He was part Larry Grayson, part Kenneth Williams, part Dick Emery and part every-cliched-cartoon-gay-you've-ever-seen-in-a-70's-Carry-On-film. Gordon was just as mincy but somewhat quieter. Gerald called every man he gossiped about 'she' or 'her' and his camp hand gestures were making me giddy. Then a foreman walked in unexpectedly. I found myself standing to attention in a frenzied panic, knocking all the teacups over and virtually saluting him, all at the same time. He just waved me back to my seat, saying,

'As you were chaps! No need to rush. Finish your game. There's a box of 8-inch flanges needed for Wednesbury, in your own time.'

He handed Dennis the paperwork and disappeared.

And this was how it was, every single day for four weeks. It is no exaggeration to say that some days we did absolutely bugger all. Most days, we might pack one box, maybe two, and then retire to the restroom. I never saw the two elderly gays do ANYTHING. Quite why they needed a couple of extra hands was beyond me. There wasn't enough for the old gents to do, let alone Dennis and me, or the other student chap. To this day, I am mystified, and can only explain it by saying, maybe it was a tax scam or something, not that I understand what that means or how it might work. Anyway, they paid us both on a Friday, and it financed our first ever foreign holiday, to Malta, with Larry and his then girlfriend, Joanne.

I eventually found out what the nightmares were all about too. One morning I awoke and managed to grab onto the tail-end of my dream, something I'd never managed to do before. In it, I was walking to catch the coach at the end of Woodland Avenue, on my way to my History of Music 'A' level exam, knowing I had not revised anything. I walked into the exam hall and sat panicking at my desk, sweat pouring from my brow. I was crying and whimpering. It was then that I would usually wake up, often yelling aloud and soaking wet, much to the consternation of whoever was within earshot at the time. Then, miraculously, once I'd finally identified the reason for my bad dreams, they stopped forever. Ever since then, I have changed from Hardened Sceptic to Firm Believer on the subject of Dreams and their Meanings. I was riddled with guilt, a very conscientious person that pretended he was Jack-the-Lad to fit in with his peers, and this was self-punishment for letting myself down so shamefully and feigning illness to boot. The mind is a wonderful thing, and I know I am right about this analysis. Ever since, I have striven to be true to myself, and to try the hardest I can at everything I do.

131

Nowadays, if I've been commissioned to paint a picture, I apply my own standards, even if the customer expects far less. When they lift the illustration's dustsheet I want them to say, 'Wow! That's far better than I was expecting.' If it's only as good as they expected, I can tell immediately, and I am not at all happy. All I ever did at Tipton was cheat myself, like a fat lady who pretends she is on a diet but sneaks a chocolate when no one is looking.

We were back at college again after a very enjoyable summer, and still having fun in spite of the ramped-up pressure. We had a new intake, so I thought it would be fun to play them up a bit. I printed a few notices that said:

'Due to the new influx of students, it is now necessary to pre-book the cubicle toilets on the 2nd floor. This can be done at the ground floor office.

I then signed them, and printed underneath, Tony Messenger, Head of Graphic Design'. Nothing more was heard about it, and I began to think my joke was a damp squib, when one day, as I entered the college in the morning, I overheard a young Chinese lad asking the receptionist about booking a lavatory (only he pronounced it Ravatory) for around 1.30pm, which I presumed was when his daily motion was due.

It was, however, true that we had to book silk-screen printing presses, due to the limited numbers and high demand, especially from 3rd years preparing their final show material. The best way to secure a press during that intense and busy period, I discovered, was to be an attractive female with large breasts and a short skirt. Easier said than done in my case, sadly. Things were very different in the mid-70s I'm afraid. Nowadays, a lecturer can be sacked for having sex with the students. In those days, I'm convinced that they could be disciplined for *not* doing so. I won't name names for obvious reasons, but it was a free-for-all for some of them. I'm just pleased that independent adjudicators judged our degree shows.

The final part of the final year was indeed a bit pressurised. I coped well because I was ahead of the game and confident in my abilities, but some struggled, especially a few of the girls, I seem to remember, for whatever reason. One of them got so wound up and emotional about the final show, her brain went loopy to such an extent that she forgot how to use a ruler and had to ask me how to measure something for her. Interestingly, if ever I am under terrible pressure or stress nowadays, I forget pin-numbers, but I am 64 now so it's more understandable. People blow fuses, just like houses do.

For those who are not familiar with how degrees are marked, the best result is a 1st class honours degree, of course, but only the chosen few get those. Second best is the 2:1, followed by a 2:2 and then a 3. Anything lower than that isn't worth talking about; it basically means that you managed to spell your name correctly on the exam sheet. It was at this late stage of the game that students turned their thoughts to these marks, and what they would mean in terms of future jobs, personal pride and the threat of a bollocking from parents who'd wasted a small fortune trying to educate their offspring. Thanks to my newfound work ethic, for once I was fine, and fairly confident, but some were undoubtedly feeling pretty much the same emotions that I'd felt at Tipton four years previously, and that is no fun whatsoever.

On the day we were to receive our results, most of the lads went off to West Park to play football or mini-golf, just to take our minds off things. I don't know what the girls did. I have to say that the way the college elected to give us our results was nothing short of cruel. There was a large noticeboard situated by the lifts on the first floor, and the results were pinned to this for all to see. You can imagine us all gathered around it, some yelling with delight and hugging their friends, others wandering away dazed, some in tears of

133

happiness, others with tears of sorrow...it was, I always thought, a bit like a public hanging, and not all that sympathetically managed. Happily, I got exactly what I'd realistically hoped for, a 2:1. Only one student got a 1st, and he was a fairly intense and serious-minded young photography student who travelled extensively through some exotic countries, where he snapped rustic-looking sun-parched Arabs and beautiful young Syrian girls with intense stares – the kind of stuff you see on the covers of National Geographic.

Soon, it was to be all over, and I can honestly say that, eventful as my life has been, I will always remember Wolverhampton College of Art as the best of all times. I may have been touched up on a bus, electrocuted to near-death and been in the middle of a bar-room brawl, but I've also never laughed as much and met so many memorable people as I did between 1972 and 1976.

We celebrated the final shows with a marathon drinking session in the Vine pub, where we all got truly maudlin, not to mention legless. The summer was the hottest on record, People were kissing and cuddling, hugging, shaking hands and saying their goodbyes. I sat with Phil Sanders, Dylan and few others, drinking lager and reminiscing, when a gorgeous blonde from our course sashayed by on the way to the bar.

'Do you know,' said Phil sadly, 'there's only me and you who haven't had sex with her in our year.'

I smiled a sad smile and drained my glass.

'It's just you, Phil,' I replied.

Okay, it was a lie, but it was quite a funny line at the time. Besides, Susan might actually read one of my books one day if she's *really* bored, so I need to cover myself.

I wandered back to the college to collect a few things, and was heading for the lift and home when Tony Messenger appeared from his office.

'So it's goodbye, Tristram,' he smiled. 'What next for you, love?' (he called everyone 'love'.)

134

'I want to be an illustrator,' I replied, 'so I suppose that means trawling around London with a portfolio, trying to find an agent.'

Tony dug into his black leather jacket and produced a bunch of keys.

'You'll need somewhere to stay then,' he said. 'These are the spare keys to my house in Notting Hill. You can fix up a string of appointments and stay there for a week. In three weeks' time I'll be on holiday at my place in Wales so the house is free. Look after it, make sure you lock up and feed Dolly the cat as instructed. She's 23, bless her. Look after everything, and don't lose my bloody keys. I trust you, don't let me down!'

I was flabbergasted. 'Thank you very much,' I croaked.

'No problem, Tristram.'

'Erm, Tony,' I added. 'My name is Geoffrey.'

'Well blow me down, love,' he smiled. 'I never knew that!'

Chapter 13

I arrived at Messenger's house in Notting Hill with my battered suitcase. It was one of those typical magnificent white London-style four-storey places with railings and a separate set of steps that lead down to a floor beneath the street level. Inside, there were book cases full of posh first editions and trendy red leather Chesterfield settees. A David Hockney painting graced one wall and there was a framed Peter Blake picture of 'Liberty Blake in a Kimono', still waiting to find a home, propped against another. This place was where the artistic elite in London gathered for drinks and chatted about forthcoming exhibitions, darling. I went exploring. I found what I presumed was to be my bedroom (he'd left a comprehensive list of things I needed to do and where to find stuff) and there were loads of other rooms besides. Down in the basement, an American by the name of Jerry was renting the rooms, so I wasn't allowed down there. I was to contact him if I had any problems, though it turned out, the only problem I had was Jerry.

I'd fixed up several appointments with Illustrator's agents, and each day I would set off with my portfolio, catch a tube and emerge, blinking in the sunlight like a mole. I saw a couple of agents who said I was good but not quite ready yet. This was fair comment, but I needed someone who would have faith and realise that the best way for me to progress was to get some real-life commissions under my belt. Maybe not the front cover of the Times Colour Supplement right away, but some relatively minor jobs that were less high profile, just to get me off the mark.

I returned, exhausted, to Tony's home each night and settled down in front of his telly to distract me from the disappointments of the day. As soon as it was turned on, I heard an angry-sounding knock at the door. It was Jerry, who informed me that the TV was far too loud. It wasn't, trust me, but I apologised and turned it down. ten minutes later, Jerry was back again, complaining about the noise, so I reluctantly switched it off and read a book instead. That bloke had missed his vocation. He should have been a committee member of a West Bromwich Labour Club.

The next day, I turned the TV on and pulled my armchair right up against it, so I could hear without much volume. Again, Jerry knocked the door and complained. This man was beginning to annoy me. Either I had suddenly become seriously deaf or he had ears like a pipistrelle bat. I was currently half an inch from the screen and straining to catch what folks were saying. Predictably, within seconds Jerry was at the door. I switched the set off and left it that way for the rest of the week. I thought seriously about committing Jerricide and wondered if the judge would be lenient, given that my victim would try the patience of a saint. I also wondered if Jerry ever asked Tony to turn the TV down. I'd have loved to have been a fly on the wall when that happened.

I fed the ancient cat, Dolly, as instructed. She was no trouble in the daytime, but she wailed like some unearthly banshee at night. Going to bed was interesting, though, in that, the woman in the house opposite would undress in front of her window with the curtains wide open. She slept naked and wasn't ashamed to let everyone to the rear of her house know about it. I didn't sleep well in strange environments and would often spend the night tossing and turning after the free strip show had finished, though I recall that it was more tossing than turning.

I next went to Piccadilly to see Artist Partners in Ham Yard, a small cul-de-sac in the middle of that vibrant area. The boss was Dominic Rodi, who I knew vaguely. He was an old boy of Wolverhampton Art College and had been invited to speak to us about artist's agents in the past, as Scarfe had done about cartoonists.

I knocked his door and he asked me to come in. After a brief exchange of pleasantries, he opened my portfolio, and whizzed through it at approaching 200 miles-per-hour. I couldn't have even focused my eyes on each new page that quickly, so heaven knows how he took it all in. He closed the folder and said, 'You're not good enough yet you will be one day goodbye.' There were no commas.

I staggered outside into the blinding heat and began to think to myself that this Art game was somewhat harder than I had realised. Dispirited, I caught the tube back to Notting Hill and flopped into the Chesterfield. The phone rang. It was my mother. She informed me that there was a job being advertised in our local paper, the Express & Star, for a junior Graphic Designer/Illustrator in Brierley Hill, which was two miles from our house. I applied for it. Why not?

Susan came to visit towards the end of the week and brought Kenny Stevens and his girlfriend, Margaret, with her. We did all the tourist things, saw the sights, drank too much, didn't watch the telly and spoke using semaphore so as not to risk any more confrontations with Jerry. On the last afternoon, just before we set off for Euston, I wandered up to the top floor to have a nose, as I'd not been up there before. I opened a door and found a small attic room with a made-up bed in it. A small note said, 'Tristram love (Geoffrey, sorry), here's your bed. Enjoy the stay and good luck! Tony.'
I'd been making myself at home in Tony and Helen's big brass bed all week.

Back in Quarry Bonk, I received the good news that I had been asked to go to Gavinbrook Design Consultants for an interview. It was a small office suite tucked into a hidden corner of Brierley Hill High Street, next to Marsh & Baxter's factory and offices. I was interviewed by a friendly, middle-aged Northern chap called Joe Oates, his Boris Johnson-like senior artist, Porridge (that's what everyone called him) and a younger partner, Tom, who wore a nice suit and did the non-artistic stuff, like seeing clients and finding work for us all to do. The final member of the team was a middle-aged secretary that I will call Jean who handled the phones and the clerical stuff.

I showed them my portfolio and they offered me the job, which was wonderful, as over 50 people had applied for it. Joe's main clients were food companies, crystal glass manufacturers, the odd restaurant, and Falstaff Silverware. They chose me because I was an illustrator, and many of the catalogues they designed had line drawings of silverware and cut-glass in them. I was never much of a designer, but luckily Porridge handled all that, which left me free to draw the pictures. I began straight away, and it was the perfect job to get me started. I had an office of my own, and all three of the directors were easy-going and friendly, as was their pet print rep, Rob O'Dell, who became a good friend. Some weeks I would be creating line-drawings of 50 or more cut-glass items or loads of silver-plated things ranging from kid's piggy banks to candelabras to illustrate catalogues, price lists or small press ads. The important thing for an illustrator is to have a range of styles. The more styles you have, the more money you can make. Fine artists paint what they fancy, but illustrators do what they're told. We have to be able to tackle any subject matter in a variety of styles. If I ever hear someone bleating on about only being able to draw flowers, or whatever, I turn my eyes heavenwards and sigh. Pictures are all made up of lines, tones and colours. That's all they comprise, so if you can paint anything, you can, *ipso facto*, paint everything!

In the course of my career I have had to tackle line-drawing, etching, woodcuts, cross-hatching, line-and-wash, loose drawing, tight drawing, Impressionism, Pointillism, Pre-Raphaelitism, silk-screen printing, surrealism, cartoons, magic-marker visualisation, caricatures, oils, acrylics, watercolours, pastels, hand-lettering, pencil drawing, nib-pens, scraperboard, posterization, abstraction, science fiction, murals…I could go on. I've had advertising agencies ask, 'Can you paint like David Hockney, Monet, Lowry, Leonardo, Rockwell, and each time I say 'yes, mate,' because if I don't say that, someone else gets the job instead. And once you say yes you have to back it up with a perfect result, or they'll never use you again. As I say to the students, this is a game for fanatics only. If you're just playing at it, pack it in now and work in a bank instead, because you won't last ten minutes. It takes hours, weeks, years of dedication before you can even make money at it. I will always be grateful for Gavinbrook for getting me started, but I knew I wouldn't be there for long. I was far too ambitious, and the last thing I wanted was to be stuck in some Brierley Hill backwater forever, drawing yet another Royal Brierley Crystal wine goblet.

Our location was a tad unfortunate. Marsh & Baxter, as you will be aware, made meat products. I was on the 1st floor, so as the occasional JCB tractor with its bucket hoisted high trundled past my window, I could see its contents, whereas the folks in the street could not. I can't count the number of times when I would glance outside just in time to see a huge bucket full of dead pigs pass by, inches from my drawing board. I was also a bit isolated and lonely, because often Joe would be out seeing clients with Tom, and Porridge, who worked at home in Kington, Herefordshire most of the time, only visited to deliver artwork and pick up his next assignment. That left me with Jean, who I was not overly keen on. The problem was, God, when creating her, had omitted to include Jean's Humour Gene. Some days, she'd wander in with a cup of tea for me (at least she did that) and sit on the edge of my table for a quick chat, again, so far so good. Watching me drawing, she asked one day, 'How good are you at art, do you think? How would you rate yourself on a scale of 1 to 10?'
I smiled at her and replied with a smirk, 'I am an artistic genius. Possibly one of the best in the whole of the UK.'

Instead of doing what, say, Tom, would have done, which is to whack me over the head with the Express & Star and add 'twat' for good measure, she stood up and spat, 'it's about time you got down from that high horse of yours, young man!' and stormed out. She didn't understand irony, or sarcasm, or banter. She took everything at face value. If you said it, you meant it literally.

Another day, after I had said something mildly sarcastic about someone, she informed me that 'sarcasm was the lowest form of wit', so, hearing that old cliché for the thousandth time and tiring of it, I asked her if she could name any higher forms of wit for me, off the top of her head. Flummoxed by this, she again stormed off into her office like I'd begged to see her tits or something.

Then it all came to a head one morning, when I'd dashed out of the house to catch the bus (I still didn't drive) and forgotten my office key. Consequently, I had to hang around outside until she arrived (late). I explained what I'd done, and instead of saying 'never mind', she rounded on me as if I'd stabbed a puppy to death. Apparently, it was time I grew up, time I acted more responsibly, time I did this that and the other, and then she barged past me, opened the door and stormed in, leaving me bewildered. She wasn't even a director, and technically, she was no higher up the food chain than I was. I quietly seethed and carried on working. As far as I knew, affable old Joe knew nothing about her tetchy way of talking to me when he'd gone out. Some days she was sweetness itself, and then, like Jekyll and Hyde, she would change without warning. The following week, I hopped off the bus and headed for the front door of the office. Jean was stood outside pacing the floor. I asked her what was up.

To my great delight, she had forgotten her office key and was waiting for me to arrive, so I could let her in. She was hoping the ground would swallow her up and I enjoyed every cringeworthy second of it. I opened the door and didn't say a word. Very dignified, I thought.

141

I stayed at Gavinbrook for a year, and then saw an advert for a designer/Illustrator at Dudley Borough Council, which I applied for. Again, thanks to my genial personality and genius with a paint brush (are you listening, Jean? That was what we on Planet Earth call a joke) I landed the job. I was based in Fisher Street at the Print Unit. There were just two of us, Paul Cobb and myself, and we were responsible for Dudley Borough's advertising posters, leaflets etc. This included the Library and Art Gallery publicity, and anything else the council needed.

Paul Cobb, in those days, looked like a clown without his make-up, and yes, I realise that I've used this description once already for Roger the coach driver, but it's the best way to describe Paul too, so I'm sticking with it. He was okay, and perfectly friendly, but he had this rather self-important way of answering the phone which always made me snigger. He barked, 'COBB' at it, as if he were the Chief of Police for the West Midlands. If I'd been on the receiving end, I would have been tempted to bark back, 'CHEESE' as if we were playing a word-association game.

My first ever job at Dudley was to get the balcony ready for the Queen and Prince Philip's visit to Dudley Town Hall. I thought every day would be that exciting, but sadly, it wasn't. I was handed various flags and coats of arms, and I had to dress the balcony. I remember that we were running late for some reason, and I'd only just finished my task when I saw, from the balcony, a posh Bentley sweep up to the front door, cheered by thousands of Dudley folk who were in and around the Coronation gardens. I dashed downstairs, but my progress was halted, thanks to Her Majesty and Prince Philip, who were progressing up the town hall steps. They entered the front doors, which is where I was standing with a ruler, a roll of masking tape and a scalpel in my hand. I was dreading Philip asking me what I intended to do with them, because that's the kind of thing he does. Knowing me, I would have come up with a spontaneous and totally unsuitable reply that

142

would have made the front pages. Thankfully, they just walked past, and I almost curtseyed.

I was still having to rely on public transport, but one big advantage with working for the council was that they insisted you learned to drive, which was the kick-start I needed. I booked a course of lessons with the BSM (curse these acronyms) and I was allowed to drive one of those old yellow council vans, as long as Paul sat beside me. His feet would be constantly operating imaginary brakes and clutches from the passenger seat, as if the van had dual controls, and I swear he never perspired that heavily when *he* was driving. It used to drive me mad, if you'll excuse the pun. My test date arrived, and true to form, I was half-dead with flu, but in a way, it helped, because I was feeling too ill to get nervous. All I wanted to do was get it over with so I could go home to bed. Miraculously, I passed first time.

I didn't waste time in purchasing my first car, a knackered beige Mini with shitty plastic imitation cosmic wheel-trims. Susan was working as a sewing machinist in a furniture factory at the time and had a knackered Ford Anglia, so we were now a 2-knackered-car family; we were moving up the social ladder! She had worked since she left school in the 5th form and had not only passed her test before me and bought her own car (if you could call it a car), but she also subsidised me to the tune of drinks, junk-food and the odd entrance fee to JB's club while I was a student. It was time I repaid those debts with interest.

Working for the council was not really the most inspiring job I could think of, but it wasn't unpleasant, and I was meeting lots of nice people. Charles Hadjamach (pronounced Hide-a-mac) was the curator of the art gallery at the time. I called him Charles Hydraulic and others, childishly, called him Charles Conceal-a-Coat. An affable Geordie boy, he was and still is a renowned glass expert, and not only lectures all over the world, but he has also been a BBC Antiques Roadshow expert. I never thought I'd ever know a BBC

143

Antiques Roadshow expert, but I now I know 2, the delightful and extremely amusing Will Farmer being the other one. How's that for a boast?

Basil Heatley was working over the road at Dudley library, and just as I'd had no idea about Tony Messengers' illustrious past, I didn't have a clue who Basil was either. It turned out that he was one of our best-ever marathon runners, the Mo Farrer of his day, and he famously beat the Japanese runner, Tsuburaya, into 3rd place in the 1964 Tokyo Olympics to come second, in front of the Emperor of Japan, no less. The Japanese runner, who felt great shame in being beaten, took his own life shortly afterwards, so I am told. These Japanese do take things seriously, don't they? It transpires that Dudley was a hotbed of talent, hiding in plain-sight. The town also boasted Duncan Edwards, whom his peers considered to be the best footballer in the world at that time, before the Munich air disaster decimated the Manchester United team.

I was still feeling a little upset about my beautiful, lost clarinet, and now that I had a regular income, I decided that it was high time I got myself another one. I kept thinking that all those years of private lessons (which had cost mom and dad 12/6d a time, a lot of money back then), were going to waste, and I had a skill that could no longer be demonstrated – a bit like being an Olympic cyclist who didn't own a bike. I popped into one of my favourite haunts, Modern Music in Dudley, and asked my old mate Bob if he had any decent second-hand clarinets for sale. He reached under the glass counter and produced a tatty brown clarinet case. 'This arrived half an hour ago,' he said. 'It would be perfect for you. It's a Boosey & Hawkes Emperor, B flat, ebony and nickel silver, so it's a very nice instrument, but it looks as if it hasn't been touched for ages and needs a good service.'

He handed it to me. I opened the box and assembled the clarinet. I held it and played around with the keys.

'This *is* mine,' I informed him dramatically, clutching my brow in shock. 'The one that was stolen when I was at school.' I was breathing rather heavily now and my heart was pounding against my ribcage.

'You can't be serious!' gasped Bob. He was a bit of a clarinettist himself, though he was mainly a drummer. He knew all about my stolen instrument because I'd mentioned it to him many times. 'How can you possibly tell?'

'This box once had my address here,' I began. 'See, there's a sticky patch where the blue address tape used to be.' (these tapes were produced by Label-Makers, which were very popular back in the day. They were small machines with the letters of the alphabet printed on a circular dial. You dialled the letter and clicked, and this embossed white letters onto blue, sticky-backed narrow tape. I hope you appreciate this full and detailed explanation.)

'These catches were originally gold metal,' I continued, sounding more and more like a young Sherlock Holmes, 'but someone has crudely tried to disguise them by hand-painting them silver. I know it's mine anyway, just from the feel of it. It's like being reunited with an old friend you haven't seen for years.'

Bob picked up the case, and we heard something sliding around under the vacuum-formed inner-section that held the individual clarinet parts in place. He removed it, and found a spare reed lurking there. It had TRIST 2A written on it in my handwriting. 2A was a class I had once been in at Tipton.

'Who brought this in?' I asked Bob. My nerves were jangling now.

'I vaguely know him,' said Bob. 'He's called Trevor I think, and he's been in a few local bands. He looks a bit like Robert Plant, very tall, long blonde hair…'

I experienced a Eureka moment. The only person who fitted that description was Trevor the caretaker's son at Tipton Grammar School. Suddenly, things were becoming clear. I paid for the clarinet and thanked Bob for his help, but I left the

145

instrument with him, as it needed a full service and new pads. I returned home, collected Susan and my dad, and we went for a drive to Tipton. I stayed in the car while Susan and Len rang his doorbell. Trevor opened the door and Susan asked him if he had a clarinet for sale. Suddenly, he looked a little panicky. He said he hadn't. They persisted and told him the police would be informed if he didn't cooperate. Imagine how this was going to look for a school caretaker, they suggested. He went back inside, reappeared shortly afterwards and began throwing money at my dad. He begged them not to tell the police, and foolishly, we didn't, though one clarinet and one upset pupil might well have been the tip of the iceberg. Dad demanded enough to buy the clarinet back from Bob, plus the cost of a service. That's all we asked for.

Just as the plywood sheep was returned half an hour after I asked for it, years later, so was the lost clarinet. It was a seriously spooky moment. Was there someone up there looking after me, a guardian angel or even the actual Angel of the Lord maybe; the one who kicks sheep into orchestra pits. It was a nice idea, but it was far more likely that I was just a Coincidence Magnet, and to prove it, here comes yet another one.

A few days later, I received an unexpected call from my old friends, City Boy, who were flying high with their hit single '5705' and already on their 3rd album. Steve Broughton, the front-man from Harborne, asked if I'd like to do two things for them. First, could I play clarinet on their new album? (I felt my knees buckle) and second, would I like to draw a picture of the lads to go on the inner sleeve? (I had to sit down quickly now.) Had he phoned a day or so earlier, I wouldn't have even owned a clarinet. I immediately said yes to both requests. They were recording at Rockfield Studios in Wales, which was owned by famous rocker, Dave Edmonds. The album was to be called 'Young Men Gone West', and I was to play clarinet on a track called 'Millionaire'.

Susan and I packed a bag and drove to Rockfield, which is a barn complex surrounded by open countryside. We were shown to our sleeping quarters (all very nice, thank you) and told that the chef was preparing dinner for all of us that evening. I had no idea these rock stars lived so well. Also recording that weekend were rock legends, Van der Graaf Generator, starring Peter Hamill, and Back Street Crawler, Paul Kossoff's next band after he left my heroes, Free. Only Paul had recently died of a heroin-induced heart attack while on a plane to New York, so they were soldiering on as best they could with a new guitarist. If not for this tragedy, I would have been meeting my guitar hero at dinner that evening, but in a way it was all for the best. There is nothing worse than finally meeting your hero and finding out that he was a drug-addled mess. I prefer to remember him at his magnificent best, a stocky little Jewish chap with a lion's mane of hair, making that old 1950's Les Paul scream and cry.

City Boy's producer was Robert 'Mutt' Lange, a South African who has produced not only five albums for City Boy, but also albums for AC/DC, Britney Spears, Def Leppard, The Boomtown Rats, Foreigner, Michael Bolton, The Cars, Billy Ocean, Bryan Adams, Lady Gaga, the Corrs, Maroon 5 and Nickelback. He was, around the time I met him, married to Shania Twain. His session clarinettist that weekend was Geoff Tristram, who'd never recorded a thing in his life, other than a demo record, and that was with a guitar. His clarinet highlights up to that point were, playing to the parents at Tipton Grammar School Prizegiving events, and erm... that's it really. But I wasn't nervous, that's the wrong word. Terrified shitless about sums it up.

Mutt was very pleasant. We went through the song a few times, as I'd never actually heard it until that day. He'd already recorded a brass band in the middle section of the song, and now he needed a clarinet to play along with them in the chorus and then add a fairly simple double-tracked solo in the middle. I improvised something on the spot that had a

New Orleans jazz feel, but he preferred something more fitting with the Northern brass band sound, and of course, he was right. He hummed the notes to me in my earphones from his mixing desk, and I replicated them on clarinet. We did a take. Jeez, those notes were mighty high, right at the top end of what a clarinet could achieve. Larry Homer had joined us that afternoon to experience it all. He is a cracking, rounded musician, far better than me, and has always enjoyed the recording aspects in particular. I'd introduced him to the lads a few years previously and they had become very friendly.

Mutt said what I'd played was fine, and then he got me to do it again. It's all about every note being perfect, taking breaths in the right places and so on. I did another. Then another. Then one more. Then another. I thought it would never end. By the halfway stage I couldn't remember what my name was. Another 16 versions and he was finally satisfied. 'He's a good musician,' he said to Larry as we finally wrapped it up. I wanted to get that cast in bronze with Mutt's name beneath it and screw it to the front of my house. I was so proud!

In a break between sessions, Van der Graaf Generator and City Boy played a football match in the field behind the studios. I always imagined that Peter Hamill, another one of my musical heroes, was far too ethereal to play football, but there he was, running around with the other lads. As weekends go, this was one of my better ones.

Back at Fisher Street, we were knocking out leaflets and posters like they were going out of fashion, and the print unit next door was constantly pestering us for our artwork, in order to meet their deadlines. One afternoon, a young printer named Evans whose Christian name irritatingly escapes me, was sat next to my A1 drawing board, impatiently waiting for me to cut and paste the final sentence of a council leaflet.

If I may briefly digress to explain the expression 'cut and paste', this refers to scalpels and cow-gum. Nowadays, everything is done on computer, so when we refer to 'airbrushing', for example, designers don't use a real airbrush any more (I still do, by the way), and the same goes for 'cut and paste'. Back in the 1970s, we'd cut up sections of text with a Swann-Morton surgical scalpel, spread cow gum on the baseboard artwork and position the text on the gummed page, removing surplus gum with that essential piece of 1970's artist's kit, 'The Cow Bogey'. This was a solidified ball of Cow Gum 'snot' that acted like a snowball, in that, the more gum you rolled it into, the bigger it got. Old hands in the graphics trade had cow bogeys the size of a human liver, and they were proud of them.

The young printer was nagging me to hurry up, so I glued down the final sentence, cut the surplus paper from it, cleaned up with my cow bogey and slammed my scalpel down on the drawing board theatrically.

'It's all yours,' I sighed. 'Finished!'

As we sat talking, neither of us noticed that my scalpel was quietly sliding down the drawing board and gathering pace as it did so. It reached the end of the board and then dropped through the air like an arrow, until it found Mr Evans's thigh, two feet below. Had it travelled handle-first, there wouldn't have been a problem, but, as Sod's Law dictates, it didn't, and the brand-new blade, which is what surgeons actually cut us open with, thudded into his thick, footballer's thigh doing around 30 miles-per-hour, and stood proudly erect and quivering.

Mr Evans interrupted his sentence to look down at his leg for the first time. His face, previously a healthy pink, turned white very quickly, and I thought he might faint. Curiously, his trousers showed that no blood had been shed, at least, for the first few seconds anyway. Then, an ever-widening red pool grew around the scalpel until it was eight inches in diameter. Evans gingerly grasped the handle, and wincing, drew it out with a sickening slurpy noise, whereupon the circle of blood quickly grew again.

By this time I was in hysterics. I laughed so much that I cried, and no matter how I tried, I couldn't control my emotions. There's something perverse about laughter, in that it will not cease even when it knows the occasion is not suitable for it. It seems to grow stronger and feeds on people's misfortunes, despite knowing full well that it is behaving reprehensively. I will never forget Mr Evans's freckled little face, as he gazed at me like a stricken rabbit, his lifeblood oozing out of him, and the more he implored me to help, the more I howled. Then he seemed to find strength from some hidden reserve and limped back to the print room in search of the first aid kit. Paul Cobb arrived at this point and asked what had happened, but I was too hysterical by then to explain it. I should add, if I haven't already, that I get this from my mother, Roob. She is a well-known giggler, and it's hard to stop her when she gets going. She initially laughs at the funny incident, but then she laughs at the sound of her own laugh, and from thereon-in it sort of spirals into madness.

It was around this time when I first met Tim Joplin, a local photographer, artist and raconteur. He would call round to Fisher Street and blag cups of tea in-between assignments for places such as the Black Country Museum, and if he wasn't with me, he'd be trying to blag tea from Charles Hadjamach over at the art gallery. We were to remain friends for many years, during which time we often laughed until it hurt so much that we literally begged each other to stop talking. I remember going to see Steve Martin's new film, 'Trains, Planes, and Automobiles' with him, and our laughter was embarrassing in a packed cinema. He used to laugh like a little pig that was being tickled, and make lots of silly snorty noises that cracked me up. Sadly, my close and much-loved friend, who contracted Parkinson's disease at 37, went on to become completely paralysed from an unspotted abscess on his spine. He battled on for far more years than anyone imagined he could, through sheer strength of character, and died in 2018, leaving his lovely wife, Dr Ruth Joplin, and his wonderful daughters, Bonnie and Ellie.

I cannot for the life of me remember how I got to know Grafreaks, a Smethwick-based design studio, but around this time they began to offer me some freelance work, which I did at home on weekends. I am not the most astute businessman in the world, but even I could work out that doing just two days' work for them paid as much as a whole week's wages from Dudley council. I had always dreamed of being a freelance artist, but it was a precarious lifestyle. Then, Godfrey Gilbert, the Brummie boss of Grafreaks and an Oliver Hardy-lookalike, promised me at least two days' work per week indefinitely, leaving me better off than working at Dudley, with three extra days to further increase my turnover. It was, as the Italians say, an offer I couldn't refuse. I handed in my notice and prepared myself for the next chapter in my hectic life.

I nearly didn't get another chapter thanks to the complete cretins I worked with thinking it would be a great idea to throw me into Dudley Leisure Centre's swimming baths on my last day, a ritual they performed on all leavers, unknown to me.

I have already touched on my time at Tipton, and my aversion to swimming baths. Put simply, if they'd succeeded, I would have either died of a coronary, or else of drowning.

They grabbed hold of me, and very quickly I realised what my fate was to be. I yelled to anyone that would listen that I could not swim and was terrified of the deep water for that reason (they were not only throwing me into the baths, they were throwing me into the deep end). My frantic pleas fell on deaf ears, and I was getting closer and closer to the edge. Panic then set in, and it was a case of fight or flight. As flight was difficult to organise, fight would have to do. I made it VERY plain what my problem was, and how I was going to break Paul Cobb's nose if we went a step further. There was

151

something in my demeanour, some piece of subtle body language maybe, that eventually convinced this bunch of idiots that I was not just protesting because I didn't want my hair to get wet. Thankfully, they let me go. I felt humiliated and silly, but at least I was alive. Knowing them, they'd have thrown me in and stood laughing as I sank to the bottom, thinking it was just me playing the fool again.

I was now heading for self-employment and I knew it was my destiny. I never worked for anyone again after that moment.

◀ *My mother, Ruby at 14 Thorns Avenue, Quarry Bank*

My father, Len (on the right) at the end of his National Service ▶

▲ Even as a toddler, I loved drawing.

The Freddy Field 'Hitler' hairdo. ▶

▼ Me and brother David, aged 4 and 6 months. What **is** he wearing?

◀ *Two Dickensian urchins, Anne Road, Quarry Bonk.*

David and me at the back of our house. Note the recorder and the Beatle hairdos, courtesy of Roob's pudding basin. ▶

Quarry Bonk Infants School. I'm the one on the back row with the women. The two cat masks were my earliest commission. ▼

▲ *The Darling Buds of May. Grandad Reuben, David, Len, Bertha and me at the caravan.*

▲ *One of Roob's legendary knitted jumpers.*

▲ *Granny Bertha sinks another Guinness.*

▼ *A carefree, loved-up Roob and Len in Tenbury.*

I always said my mother was a basket case. ▶

◀ *Granny Bertha in Tenbury Wells, peeling things on her Formica table.*

Me with dad's Austin Cambridge Shooting Brake. Reg No 5551 UK. ▶

▲ Me and Mally 'Lobes' Stevens outside 3 Anne Road.

▲ Reuben, David, Ruby and Bertha outside the New Inn, Knighton, near Tenbury Wells.

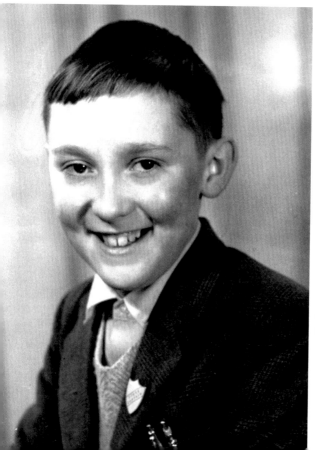

◀ Aged 11, a Yellow House Captain. Dig those biros.

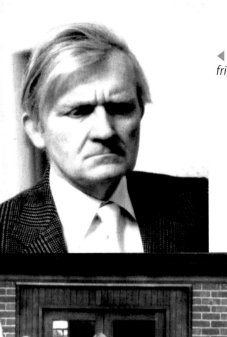

◀ *My art teacher and friend, Peter Trafford.*

▲ *Tipton grammar School circa 1967. I'm on the front row, fourth from the right.*

Me and Danny Sims in the Tipton Grammar School playground. ▶

◀ *Susan is the one on the right.*

Is it Paul Weller? No, it's me at 16. ▼

▲ *Who is that handsome Rock God? Aged 19, with my first Les Paul.*

Drawing Wilf's cut-price holiday home in Harlech. ▶

At Walsall Security printers with Miss World, Gina Swainson. ▼

◀ Jolliffe looking like a Latino drug mule.

▲ Tim and me at the Graduate Records opening. Ten minutes later he was unconscious.

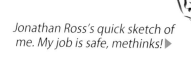

Jonathan Ross's quick sketch of me. My job is safe, methinks! ▶

Jamie and Laura at her Master's
degree ceremony in Lancashire.

▲ *The Limited Edition Martini Porsche, 103 Woods Lane, Amblecote.*

▼ *David and family, looking rather like 1950's Americans.*

David Tristram
wears the mask.

My friend Mike Timmins, a brilliant airbrush artist who died at 33.

Long-lost 'sheep' is rescued!

◀ The legendary Plywood Sheep.

◀ Guess who we went as!

*They call me Mellow Yellow.
Donovan poses with a living legend*

Chapter 14

Susan and I had saved enough to pay the deposit on a house in Woods Lane, Amblecote, opposite the Caledonia pub, as it was then known. I think it's called The Raven now. The house, a three bedroom 'link detached' (a slimy estate agent term meaning it wasn't detached at all; the equivalent of the furniture shop's 'faux' leather which means imitation leather, i.e. plastic) with a tiny garden that overlooked a field with a few cows in it, cost us £13,500. We got married on March 3rd, 1979, on a tight budget. Susan made her own wedding outfit, a 2-piece suit. She was handy with a sewing machine, as she spent her days making furniture for Walker & Homer in Colley Gate, and later, Pieff in Cradley Heath, the company that produced all that typical 70's white leather and chrome stuff. I wore an oatmeal-coloured suit with cream brogues and looked quite smart in a dated kind of way. At least it didn't look as bad as Steve Jolliffe's wedding suit, which had lapels that were 8-feet wide and would have taken off in a high wind. The wedding was at Dudley Registry Office, and the reception was initially at a Netherton pub called The Wheelwright's Arms and later, for our more intimate circle, at a local shopper's restaurant called The Loft, in the Churchill Precinct. The Ritz it wasn't. I was now 24 and Susan was 22. We were both born on the 19th April, so we never forget our birthdays, but it doesn't really matter that much as we never buy each other anything anyway.

I'd rented a small office above the Hearing Aid Centre, of all places, in Tower Street, Dudley, but I couldn't squeeze my large and extremely heavy Grant projector into the room, let alone get it up the narrow stairs, so Sue's mom and dad kindly allowed me to borrow their box-room. Consequently, every time I needed to make a print, which was very often, I had to drive two miles to their house. Tower Street was handy in one sense, because there was a small artist's materials shop literally next door, run by a kindly English gent by the name of Mr Harrison who could have been a character in a P.G. Wodehouse novel. Very old-school, very charming, bow-tie, excellent manners. The man who rented the office to me, on the other hand, was a surly, pompous git. Tell him hello from me, if anyone knows him.

I spent weeks in that room, spraying enough photo-mount to wither my lungs, as I prepared 100-page car parts manuals and the like for Grafreaks. Heaven knows what that did to my health, but when you're young and impatient, you don't think about it as much as you should. One week I lost my voice completely. I must have glued my larynx to my epiglottis. I went to Boot's to ask the pharmacist what I should do, but when I opened my mouth, no words came out. She smiled, handed me a medicine and said, 'Try that.'

Sometimes David would come and help with the paste-up jobs, once he'd completed his BA (Hons) in English and Music at Birmingham University. One day I gave him a sheet of Letraset (remember that?) to create a small dedication panel beneath a photograph that was to be framed and presented to man who'd done 25 years' service at a foundry. I picked the finished item up the framers and was just about to hand it to my client when I reread David's text.
It read:

To Jim, from all his frieds at the foundry.

Maybe a lifetime spent working in hot conditions had fried them all. Ever since that day, I have been aware of how important proofreaders are. There are basically four types of typographical or grammatical error. No.1, a slip of the finger that you spot and correct, No.2, the same, but you don't spot it and therefore don't correct it, and No.3, something you believe to be correct that actually isn't. That's why a fresh eye is required, and you can't proofread your own work. Oh yes,

154

and No.4, something that *was* correct till the proofreader altered it.

David's other classic was a picture frame caption that read 'Dudley Musuem', which was only spotted once it had been hanging in the museum for a year. Not that he was a terrible speller, by the way, the complete opposite, as you can imagine. It's just that Letrasetting causes temporary dyslexia. You get so involved with getting the letter exactly level and rubbing it down properly that you forget everything else. Thank God it's virtually obsolete nowadays.

After a short time working in Tower Street, I seemed to change my working address every ten minutes. It's been nearly 40 years since all this was happening, so the chronology of it is all a bit hazy, but I had a period where I worked at my new house in the 2nd bedroom and used the box room as my darkroom. Then I moved back to Dudley and worked in the newly opened Graduate Records offices, a very nice, spacious Georgian building in Wolverhampton Street. There were two more changes of address before I settled permanently at home in Wollaston in around 1990.

I also can't remember how I met David Virr, the boss of Graduate Records, but we got on instantly. He came from the Worcestershire country set, very well spoken, with a posh wife, Sue (yet another Sue and there are many more to come). In fact, he was everything I wasn't, but they say opposites attract, don't they? David had been running a second-hand records emporium in Dudley, not far from JB's at Top Church, and he owned a few shops elsewhere I believe, but he had his sights set on forming his own record label. He began with a few local acts, but his major breakthrough was the signing of UB40. From then on, his career rocketed. Soon came the swanky Georgian townhouse in Britannia Square, Worcester, and the aforementioned Georgian office in Dudley. David and Sue liked Georgian! I had designed a few sleeves for David, and he suggested a marriage of convenience. He would give me studio space for a low rent, and that meant he would have an artist on tap to manage his posters, leaflets and record sleeves. The offices had been specially refurbished, and David and Susan had an official opening, with a band playing on the roof, just as the Beatles had once done. Susan was great fun. She was tall and willowy and posh, with something of the Margo Leadbetter about her, albeit a trendier version. I don't usually like people like that but I made an exception for her. Tim Joplin and I were once passengers in her little VW Golf convertible (the car of choice for the posh Worcestershire woman about town), when she pulled alongside a car that was legally parked in a quiet Dudley street. The middle-aged man within it was eating his sandwiches and reading the paper. She rolled the window down, pointed at the road beneath his vehicle and said, 'Excuse me, I usually park there.' He hurriedly packed away his things, apologised, would you believe, and drove off. I don't know how she did it, I really don't.

Susan Virr had decorated the offices and filled them with flowers ready for the opening. Caterers were serving nibbles on silver trays and handing out the champagne. Jimmy the Con, the feared bouncer from JB's, was on the door to prevent gate-crashers. Tim had been invited because he often took photographs for the Virrs, and I remember Susan Virr once asking him to snap her, stark-naked, for her birthday treat. He produced some very arty black and white pictures of her draped over the furniture in her house, I recall. All very elegant. Nothing tacky. That afternoon I stood chatting to Tim by the fireplace in one of the large reception areas, and the waitress kept filling our glasses with bubbly. Tim came from a proper Black Country family, like me, but his was the type where three brothers and the old man would inhabit the pub all day Sunday and drink 16 pints before returning home for their huge Sunday lunch and a kip on the settee. He was sneering and dismissive of champagne as being a drink 'for poofs'. He nevertheless helped himself to a considerable amount. I walked away briefly to say hello to someone I knew, and when I got back, Tim was unconscious and snoring in the fireplace. Thank God the fire wasn't lit. Jimmy the Con was summoned to remove the remains. He slung the bulky, comatose photographer over his shoulder as if he were a sack of feathers and marched out with him to who-knows-where. One presumes the Georgian Resuscitation Room.

I also had to make my excuses and leave shortly afterwards, as I was in need of a dinner suit for a swanky birthday party I'd been invited to at David Virr's Brother-in-Law's house that weekend. There was a dress-hire place in Dudley town and I needed to pop over there and collect the suit before the shop closed. The walk across town in the crisp, cold air made me feel ten times as drunk as I actually was. I walked into the shop, and the manager handed me my suit in a plastic suit-bag. I wrote him a cheque and caught the bus home, and by then, I was in serious need of a lie down. The next day, the manager of the dress-hire place rang me and asked if I'd mind returning to the shop to write him another cheque. I asked why. Had I perhaps omitted to write the date, or sign it, or was the amount wrong? The man seemed a trifle embarrassed.

'Well,' he began nervously, obviously trying to find the '*mot juste*'. 'The truth is, none of us could make head or tail of it. It was just scribble.'

I rang Tim to see how his hangover was progressing. He was as near to a dead person as you can be, whilst still retaining a pulse. Jimmy had marched out of the building with Tim on his shoulder and dumped him in a nearby public gardens to sober up. Tim eventually woke up lying on a grave in a churchyard, covered in vomit. How he ended up there, no one knows. It is one of the great mysteries of the world, like how the pyramids were built.

I enjoyed my time at David Virr's place. We were like a pair of giggling schoolboys. I loved his daft, friendly face and his ever-optimistic outlook. He would greet me each day with 'Morning, Twit-Ears!' like he was a character in a Billy

157

Bunter novel. That said, the work ethic was unbelievable. Both of us were working ourselves into a stupor, he even more than me. I was incredibly busy though. I would typically have 13 jobs on my list, and every time I finished 3, another 12 would arrive. It was relentless. I was building up a good reputation as a skilled, punctual illustrator with a wide range of styles, and many of the big Birmingham advertising agencies were beginning to use me. Then there was David's in-house work, and I'd recently added another couple of clients to my ever-growing list. One was Swinford Motors, a Mercedes Benz and Porsche cars dealership in Lye, near Stourbridge, and the other was Embassy World Snooker, thanks to a speculative caricature of Ray Reardon that I drew one afternoon when I was at a rare loose end. I showed it to Ken Williams, The Power-Glide snooker cue manufacturer, whose elder brother was Rex Williams, a professional player and also the boss of World Snooker's governing body, the WPBSA. Rex showed my cartoon to the tournament director, Peter Dyke who worked for Embassy, the sponsors, and they commissioned a set of 21 cartoons of their top players, which you can still see all over the place in every snooker hall, and for sale second-hand on Amazon and eBay. This was the start of a 25-year association with the sport, and before you call me a hypocrite for being a committed non-smoker who, was in effect, working for a Tobacco company, let me first say that I broadly agree with you, but those who are without sin chuck the first cobble, as Jesus once said. Sometimes a once-in-a-lifetime opportunity arrives, as in, working for the BBC on one of their top sports programmes, and you'd be mental to say no. In my defence, it's very easy to get on your high horse about something, and have your principles printed on your T shirt for all to see, when there is nothing whatsoever for you to lose as a result of your piety. How many of us are as moralistic when it impacts directly on us financially? Imagine, if you will, that 100 people who claim to have high principles are quietly offered a million pounds each on the understanding that they forego their objection to whatever it is they objected to or disagreed with. Then, folks, we would know who the *real* principled people were, and I bet there wouldn't be more than a handful left out of the 100. If there's no great personal loss, it's easy to be a virtue-signalling goody-two-shoes. The plain fact is, I hated cigarettes, but obviously not enough to refuse a lucrative job with the BBC because of who their sponsor was. I notice that the sanctimonious BBC didn't object either. I also did some work for Peter Dyke when he wore his other hat, sponsorship director for the Formula 1 racing team John Player Lotus. After a successful season, Peter commissioned me to produce a cartoon of Ayrton Senna, from which 50 prints were made. I was asked to pop to an address in Surrey where the driver would sign the prints, so that Peter could frame them and present them to the team. I had no interest in Formula 1 at the time (I got to like it later when Damon Hill and Schumacher were tussling for the crown), so I sent a courier to get them signed instead. He returned with the prints, and Ayrton, who I'd never even heard of, signed one for me that said; 'Congratulation Mr Trist for the good job' in his broken English. A chap I only vaguely knew badgered me for it relentlessly so I gave it to him just to shut him up. He knew it was worth £1,000 and I didn't. You live and learn. Suddenly I was dealing with a few famous people, thanks entirely to my job. I got very friendly with most of the snooker people, and I have to report that they were down-to-earth, normal, friendly folks, with the exception of Alex Higgins who was a bloody nightmare.

David Virr had signed UB40, and everybody in the world seemed to be ringing him. I knew he had become friends with Richard Branson, and many other influential types, because we'd often chat about it over a cup of tea at his Dudley offices. The band were regularly on Top of the Pops, and of course, David had to seize the moment and milk it while he could. He must have put a million miles on the clock of his old Mercedes during that period, and he was knackered. Meanwhile, Susan Virr, bless her, always the party animal of the pair, was entertaining the great, the good, and the not so good at Britannia Square with lavish dinner parties. Sometimes, David would arrive home, exhausted, and discover loads of folks in his basement room that he didn't even know. It was even more galling when some Hurray Henry demanded to know who he was and what he was doing there.

I was asked to design UB40's first album sleeve, Signing Off, and I had no idea how it would take off at that point. It was just another sleeve. David and I went to meet the band and their producer, Bob Lamb, who used to be the drummer in the Steve Gibbons Band. As we all chatted about what kind of sleeve they fancied, band member, Astro, arrived carrying a two-piece snooker cue case. I had become very involved with Embassy World Snooker around that time, and I also played the game myself (not well) so I thought we had a mutual interest. I asked him where he played which caused the rest of the lads to fall about laughing. He opened the case, which contained a huge water-cooled turbo-charged hookah pipe for smoking marihuana. He hid it in there to avoid unwanted attention from the police. We spent another hour or so discussing business, in, shall we say, a very smoky, atmospheric haze. Then David drove us back to Dudley. I have never taken illegal drugs and never will, but that afternoon as we drove home, both of us felt completely stoned, and we giggled even more than usual.

The first album sleeve was a simple affair; just a giant copy of the Government's Unemployment Form 40. It cost them the grand sum of £110. A few years afterwards, once it had sold a squillion copies, the management of UB40 offered me a framed, platinum disc; something I've always wanted. Apparently, as sleeve designer, I was entitled to one, as were each of the band members and the producer, Bob Lamb. I said, 'Yes please!', whereupon they wanted to charge me

£150 plus VAT. I politely refused, as that was a lot of money in those days. Besides, when Tom Cruise won an Oscar, they didn't make him pay for it, did they? That said, I've regretted it ever since.

I went on to design their Singles Album and a few of their singles sleeves, but I didn't get awarded any framed platinum discs for those, which was just as well. I also designed album covers for Ossie Osbourne's keyboard player, Jezz Woodroffe, and later on, circa 1982, when City Boy had finally run its course and disbanded, for Lol Mason's new venture, the Maisonettes, who had a hit with the retro single 'Heartache Avenue'. The band sent me all the way to Paris so I could sketch a small, typical French café from life, as opposed to from a photograph. They wanted that life-drawing look; a bit unfinished at the edges, rather than a meticulous studio-drawn illustration. I traipsed around Paris on my own for the whole weekend, desperately trying to find such a café, but they were all huge Edwardian places, which the band didn't want. Eventually, on my final day, I found a perfect little café that fitted their wish-list, but the only vantage point was the middle of a madly busy 6-lane highway. Frustrated, I grabbed my Nikon camera, dashed into the traffic, nearly getting myself killed, and took a quick reference shot before leaping back onto the pavement. I then flew home. On the Monday morning after my Parisian weekend, I developed the film and sketched the sleeve's cover illustration from a photo; the exact thing that the band had expressly barred me from doing. I took the finished picture to a meeting in the boardroom at the Graduate offices and showed it to an expectant band. Lol smiled and said, 'Well done, Geoff. It was a worthwhile trip. You couldn't have done *that* from a photo, could you?'

The story of how the Graduate logo came about is quite amusing, as it happens. David had asked me to come up with a few alternatives, but he wasn't that keen on them. I drew a few more, but still he was dragging his feet. In fairness, the logo for a record company that's going places needs a fair bit of thought, so I could see why he was being fussier than usual. After the umpteenth rejection I tetchily folded my latest flop into a paper aeroplane and threw it out of the studio window in a fit of pique. As I watched it sail majestically through the window into the bright sunlight, I had a Eureka moment. I sketched out a circle and drew a paper plane within it. Then I added a few lines and a pyramid, just to fill the spaces. I showed it to David, and he said, 'That's the one. Perfect!' His second label's logo, 'Ready, Steady, Go!' took me about 5 minutes.

Meanwhile, David Virr was still haring around the country, going to meeting after meeting. Then one day, he fell asleep at the wheel through sheer exhaustion. His car careered off the road and entered a field, coming to rest once it hit a large tree. David was knocked unconscious and had suffered a huge gash across his brow. He lay there for ages before someone spotted him. For a while it was looking serious, but he recovered, albeit with a lovely scar across his head that had to covered by a strategically-placed blond fringe.

David eventually divorced Susan and promptly married yet another Susan, who I never really got to know. Then, Sue 2 left and he teamed up with the delightful Tina, a French lady, who was with him until he died tragically before his time, aged just 58, from an illness so rare that only a handful of people in the U.K. suffered from it. I was extremely upset by losing David, and even today, I regularly think about him.

The other David in my life had found himself a job at Beacon Radio, writing radio ads and jingles with another young graduate by the name of Paul Brighton. He was also doing a bit of work for one of the presenters, Dick Fisher, who had his own business. Another presenter was a gentleman by the name of Dale Winton. Yes, 'the' Dale Winton, no less.

Around the same time, I was beginning to accept jobs as a corporate events caricaturist, thanks to Glynn Edwards, a cartoonist who owned a magazine for the Graphic Design and Advertising industry called Adline. Glynn had been doing live caricature work for years, and he convinced me that it was a doddle and the money was good. You turned up in a lounge- or dinner-suit with a clipboard and a pile of specially-printed card featuring a company logo, and drew as many folks as you could in three hours if it was an evening, or 6 if it was a full day at an exhibition. You needed to have nerves of steel, a quick wit and a confident drawing style - no preliminary pencil outline; that was for sissies. It was straight to ink, and no dithering, no mistakes allowed and you had to finish your picture in five to seven minutes, max., usually with a big head, a small body doing something that typified the sitter, such as a sport or hobby. You also had to cope with awful conditions such as noisy, boisterous, dark rooms, idiots, people who spouted the same old hackneyed clichés at you (can you make me look handsome? Can you draw me playing golf/having sex? I can't even draw a straight line, don't make my nose too big, yawn yawn.) I worked as a caricaturist with Dale Winton as our host a few times at local car showroom launches and the like. David informs me that, whenever Beacon's presenters had to have their photographs taken, Dale would scurry off to the lavvie and apply his make-up. He was always good fun though, and I was sad to hear that he'd died, a few weeks before I began writing this. David went on to win two Sony awards for his radio ads, and Paul Brighton became a BBC Mastermind semi-finalist and a BBC politics presenter with a brain bigger than the Mekon from the Dan Dare comics. He could name Gladstone's cabinet ministers off by heart, but he also had a fantastic sense of humour. David informed me only last week that Paul suffered a massive stroke and is currently in a nursing home, struggling to communicate. Isn't life a huge pile of shit sometimes?

163

My corporate caricature work was not done *instead* of my 9-to-5 day-job. It was usually done *after* it, unless I had been employed to work at exhibitions for several days on end. Thanks to this extra-curricular activity, I made a good living and was able to travel all over the country and also abroad. I worked fairly regularly in Italy, Germany, America, Canada, and Holland, and generally, I had a great, if exhausting, time. Just for fun, I will now briefly digress from this chronological life-story to report on some of the worst caricature events I attended over the years.

I was asked to work at a Jaguar event in Castle Bromwich. There was a very brief, ten-minute reception, which only allowed me to draw one person, and then they called everyone in to dinner. To my horror, the dinner hall was pitch-black with laser lights whizzing about. The diners could not even see their dinners. It was disastrous! I asked a chap who seemed to be in charge how they expected me to draw in such conditions, and he replied, 'Oops! We never thought about that.' He told me to go home, but at least I got paid £300 for ten minutes' work.

I arrived in Milan for a 7-day exhibition and reported to my employer, who told me to put my equipment down and have a coffee before I got started. I thanked him and did just that. A sneak-thief ran past the stand and scooped all my equipment, including my brand-new spectacles, the A4 drawing cards, and my pens, into a bag and ran off. My employer sent someone into town to buy more card and pens, but I couldn't draw without my new glasses. He returned a short while later with some reading glasses that his secretary had lent him. Thankfully, they fitted my prescription, or as near as damn-it anyway, but unfortunately the donor must have been Dame Edna Everage. The specs had ornate pink and yellow floral designs on the outer corners and running down the side arms. Every time anyone looked at me, they began to laugh uncontrollably, and sadly, I was there for seven days. That's a lot of ridicule to soak up.

This tale did not directly affect me, but it certainly affected my good friend Chris Priest, who was the Close-up Magician of the Year in 2000. He approached a table of diners and told them who he was and that he was about to show them some magic. A drunken diner grabbed a party popper and exploded it directly into Chris's face. He was temporarily blinded and had to be taken to hospital before he'd even performed his first trick.

I was working at the Oil Baron's Ball at the Centennial Centre in Birmingham. I approached a table and was about to introduce myself when a man said, 'Fuck Off!' I know when I am not wanted, but maybe he should have been well-mannered enough to not presume that he was speaking for the whole table. It's important to remember that we are not rose-sellers trying to make a quick buck. Each entertainer was paid, on average, £300 to £350 for their 3-hour stint, plus accommodation if required, and more often than not £750 - £1,000 if it was Chris Priest. I strutted over to an adjacent table, where, by stark contrast, I was welcomed with open arms. Having drawn a few people there, I was about to move on when a gentleman from the obnoxious person's table asked for a caricature. I politely said no, I couldn't, and when he asked why, I suggested he ask the man who had taken it upon himself to speak for his table. A heated row then ensued between the two gentlemen, and I quietly got on with my business elsewhere.

I was at a hotel in Harrogate one evening, and I had already been drawing for way over my allotted time of three hours. I was shattered and it was time to head home. A man came over and began pestering me to draw just one more picture; the one request we cartoonists dread more than any other. I tried to

165

explain that I was exhausted and I had a four-hour drive ahead of me, but he was persistent, so I thought it would be easier to draw him than to argue. I finished his picture, he said thanks, and proceeded to fold it neatly into four quarters and put it in his top pocket.

One weekend, my mate, Geoffrey Bartlett, the corporate events caterer, asked me to work at a 'Generation Game' themed event for a large building firm. I had to draw a caricature of Frank Carson, the host, and then four staff members had a go. It was also my job to choose the winner. Frank arrived early, greeted us all and headed for the bar. Within 10 minutes, he was my best friend. He was drinking like a fish and offering to buy me shorts at 10am in the morning, but I politely declined and drank tea instead, as I had a job to do. Once the game show section had concluded, Frank headed back for the bar, and I was busy drawing caricatures around the dining tables. Out of the corner of my eye, I spotted staff members literally carrying Frank out of the room. It was rumoured that he had a plane to catch at the nearby Birmingham Airport, and he was legless. I thought no more of it, went home and had a rest. The next morning – and apologies for being a little base here – I was sat on the lavatory, mid motion, when the phone rang. I answered it, and it was Frank Carson, just saying hello. I chatted to this famous comedian and game-show host for some 15 minutes, even though I didn't know him from Adam, with my trousers around my ankles, and then he said, 'Lovely to meet you yesterday anyway!' and ended the call. It was one of the more surreal moments from a long and interesting career.

I was hired to work at a Christmas do for a large property company in Birmingham. One of the directors summoned me to his table and asked for a caricature. I need to keep people fairly still for five minutes in order to get a good likeness, but he was inebriated and not cooperating. I asked politely several

166

times but he didn't seem to be aware that I existed by then. I paused and asked one last time. His wife, who was similarly extremely drunk, took exception to my requests and slopped a huge, greasy chip from her dinner plate onto my half-finished drawing, thus ruining it. I was just about livid now, like a volcano about to erupt. I ripped the page off my clipboard and complained that I was not being treated with due respect and I was moving on to another customer. 'Oh dear!' she whined sarcastically, before emptying a sachet of conditioner from her handbag into my hair. I stood up, called over to the man who booked me and demanded my fee right there and then. I think there was something about my tone that convinced him to cough up without delving deeper into the matter. I went home two hours early, and around a year and a half later, I managed to calm down a bit.

One weekend I had to draw at an event at the Birmingham Botanical Gardens in Harborne. I asked a waiter where the accountants' Christmas dinner was and headed for the room. I'd drawn several people, when the boss came over and congratulated me on a good job, adding that it was a lovely surprise that the Botanical Gardens had laid this on for him. I explained that it wasn't the Botanical Gardens who'd arranged it, it was his own firm. He looked puzzled and didn't seem to know anything about it. This worried me, as he was the boss. I checked with him that there was only one accountants' Christmas dinner going on that evening, and the man confirmed it. 'The only thing is' he added, 'we're solicitors. The accountants are in the Garden Suite down the corridor.'

This is not about a caricature event that went wrong, but rather about the people who hired me to work at it, and how they wronged me. I was approached by a small husband and wife entertainments agency, based in Stourport, and asked to draw at a wedding at the Dormy House Hotel, in the Cotswolds. This I duly did, and the night was a big success.

The bride and bridegroom loved my work and everyone had a good time. The entertainments agency had agreed to pay a fee of £350, but for some reason, they didn't seem keen to hand it over to me when the time came. Once the usual fortnightly polite requests had failed to work, I rang the couple to ask when I could get my money. The husband was a nasty piece of work and got quite aggressive on the phone. I have said this before in this book, I realise, but isn't it interesting how people who are clearly in the wrong and without a leg to stand on, become aggressive, when maybe they should be contrite and begging forgiveness. I explained to this man that I had fulfilled the terms of his contract, driven miles and miles to the Cotswolds, worked for three hours, driven back, and wanted my fee, which was not unreasonable, and now, he was telling me to eff off, as he was getting effing sick of me 'pestering' them. He came up with the usual lie about it being in the post, but it never came. I ended up taking them to the small claims court. The judge found in my favour but told me she didn't think I had a cat's chance of getting my £350 because the couple had closed down the business I was suing and transferred everything to their other business where I couldn't touch it. The only person who profited by this complete waste of time was the rather snotty judge, who's lackeys in the small claims department took some money from me for bringing the case to court. So, if these entertainments people still exist and they want to book you to work at an event, tell them to sod off and say Geoff said *ciao*, and something in Italian about *un piatto che va mangiato freddo*.

And first prize goes to The Tia Maria Event in Troon, Scotland. A famous and rather eccentric PR lady, Lynne Franks (she was the inspiration for Edina, who was played by Jennifer Saunders in 'Absolutely Fabulous'), asked me to fly to Royal Troon Golf Club for the weekend and draw 25 American Tia Maria salesmen, who had presumably won the trip by selling bucketloads of the foul drink. Lynne booked the flights and a hire car, and I was to supply the 25 frames and the drawing card printed with the Tia Maria logo. I arrived at the club late on the Friday evening and asked the receptionist who the spokesman for the trip was. She pointed out a tall man in a Pringle cardigan who was getting hammered at the bar. I walked over, introduced myself, and explained why I was there. He replied, and I quote, pretty much verbatim:

'Look boy. We're 25 golf nuts from the States. Tomorrow, right after breakfast, we'll be on the course, and we'll get back late and then want to eat and drink. Ditto the following day. We don't have no room in our itinerary for no God-damned cartoonist. If I were you, boy (I loved that 'boy' bit), I'd get some shut-eye and then fuck off back to England in the morning.'

So I did, in spite of Lynne Franks' desperate protests. On the flight home, the stewardess asked if I'd like a drink from the trolley. I eyed the Tia Maria with delight and said to her, 'I don't want any of that shit for a start!' before laughing myself silly, much to the bewilderment of the poor lady. For many years I kept the 25 frames and the printed cards in my loft, to remind me what a crazy profession I had chosen. Just to add injury to insult, carrying the heavy bag of frames and card to and from Royal Troon gave me a painful hernia which required an operation.

***

As if my life wasn't hectic enough, with a new wife, new house and all the maintenance required for both, I had been doing a bit of teaching at Bilston College to further supplement the income. I was responsible for showing nursery nurses how to draw, as part of their BTEC diplomas. Incidentally, the Head and Deputy Head of Bilston Art College were Mr Artist and Mr Painter. Strange but true. Not long after that I landed a part-time place at Stourbridge Art College, which was situated in the old library building on the Hagley Road exit from the ring road, not far from the law courts.

Oh yes, and I bought myself a Porsche.

I'd been doing all the design and artwork for Swinford Motors since they became disillusioned with the previous chap, for whatever reason. John Edmonds, their Managing Director and Hank Marvin look-alike (I keep doing that lookalike thing; I must stop it) was an easy-going soul and a pleasure to work for, if a tad on the nervous, OCD side. He was constantly lining up the pens on his desk and he never left home without checking the front door eight times to make sure it was still locked. I came up with the jokes and illustrated their cartoon Christmas cards and later, from the mid-80s onwards, I painted a series of deluxe single-sheet limited edition, signed and numbered calendars that have quietly become collector's items. Customers would trim the calendar bit off when they'd finished with it and then frame the prints for their offices. John virtually gave me free rein to do whatever I wanted, and I don't think I ever let him down. Some of my slickest, most finished illustrations come from the 1980s period, when my technique had been more-or-less perfected and my eyes were still 20-20, like an eagle's. There were airbrushed sports cars, *trompe l'oeil* watercolours of Porsche and Mercedes Benz enthusiast's bookshelves, Norman Rockwell-style scenes with a car theme, and many cartoon greetings cards, not to mention hundreds of press ads. They spent a lot of money with me, and in return, I thought it only fair to buy the odd car from them. The one I chose was a 1-year-old Martini Porsche 924, a limited-edition model. It was white with flashy red, blue and black stripes, red and blue upholstery and a small plate by the gearstick stating that only 100 had been built. Not only that, there were only five of them in the Midlands. When I collected it from Swinford, I was terrified all the way home in case I scratched it. Proud doesn't even begin to sum up what I felt. At last, I could see tangible rewards for all that hard graft.

I was not so much burning the candle at both ends, as throwing it into the furnace and to hell with it. On the home front, I'd helped to land Susan a better job at Dunn's Photographic Laboratories, near to Cradley Heath railway station. She'd grown tired of making leather furniture and fancied a change. She has been there, on and off, ever since, with gaps for motherhood. The Stourbridge teaching job was not only to provide a steady weekly income (not that I needed it during that manic period) but also to give me a change of scenery that allowed me to socialise with other human beings, if you can call my old Stourbridge students human beings. Painting pictures is a very solitary, lonely existence, which is fine if you are that way inclined. For me, it was more a case of reluctantly putting up with it because it was necessary in order to do the job I loved. In truth, I missed having people to talk to, and the college provided that, once a week.

The Head of Graphics was David Craven, an extremely thirsty ex-advertising agency art director. I will always remember a wonderful tale about Dave farming out a design job to a freelance artist because he was too busy to do it himself. The freelancer then realised that he was also too busy, and duly farmed it out to a 3rd person, who then, realising that HE was too busy, farmed it out to…Dave Craven, who, out of sheer devilment, decided to do the job himself. Dave handed it back to the 2nd chap, who in turn handed it to the 1st chap, who presented it to Dave, who rejected the job and refused to pay for it because he said it was sub-standard crap.

The lecturer I saw a lot more of on a daily basis was John Elkes, a comical Welshman who had served his time at an art college in Liverpool. As was the norm, he didn't really have a clue about graphic design but he was a good college tutor nevertheless, with just the right mix of discipline and humour to hold the place together. John was fearless. If he saw someone drop littler in Stourbridge High Street, he would confront them, regardless of their size. Even at the end of his life, many years later, he was indomitable. Dying with cancer and nothing more than skin and bone, as my grandad Reuben had been, he insisted on climbing to the top of Clent Hills and shouting 'Fuck off, cancer!' for all to hear.

I used to draw a silly caricature of John at the time, with his little moustache, jutting chin and cropped, erect hairdo. This cartoon eventually morphed into Norman, of Norman & Brenda, my rather risqué greetings card range.

Another wonderful character from that esteemed seat of learning was Paul the technician. Originally, he had worked in the local art equipment shop, A.J. Mees, in Amblecote, but he later did the same kind of thing within the college, just as bandleader Ron Astle had done during my time at Wolverhampton College. I know this isn't really a subject for humour, but here goes anyway. Paul was afflicted by a very subtle form of Tourette's Syndrome or similar, but whereas the full-blown version involves swearwords, Paul just had a little, occasional vocal tic that sounded like the word 'cut'. He'd be talking away happily, and all of a sudden, his face would contort and out would come this word, apropos of nothing. My brother, David, once assured me that Paul was forced to take the lowly college job after being sacked as Hollywood's most disastrous film director. Just as the scene was going beautifully...well, you get the idea.

I was soon joined by friends of mine from Wolverhampton, namely Robin Greenwell, Denise Harrison (nee Serphentine) and the excellent airbrush artist, Mike Timmins. Mike would have been a bit like the younger brother I always wanted, were it not for the fact that I already had the younger brother I'd always wanted. This was, if my modesty will allow me to say so, a pretty formidable team...there, I said it. Not bad for a small art college that only offered a BTEC diploma rather than a degree. Mike was a brilliant artist who was signed to Artist Partners in London. You may remember Dominic Rodi whizzing through my portfolio in eight seconds and telling me I wasn't ready yet but I would be soon. In the interim, I had signed for Specs Art in Cheltenham instead, and with everything else going on all at once in this book, I nearly forgot to mention that. I was also getting more work than I could handle from them each month, just to keep life interesting. At least no one can accuse me of being lazy. Mike, meanwhile, was working for Dominic's outfit in Piccadilly, and not long afterwards, I began working for them too, as well as for Spec's. If you've been paying attention, you'll remember the cartoonist, Bill Kimpton, our exhibition technician at Wolverhampton. Well, he was also signed by Dominic, so it was all getting a bit incestuous. Mike's airbrush style was ideally suited to paperback covers, which was the bread and butter work for London agencies, just as our local Midlands design studios handled more mundane stuff, such as industrial brochures and leaflets. He painted covers for the likes of John le Carre, Agatha Christie, Jilly Cooper and many more authors that you've probably heard of. Then, just as he was getting into his stride, Mike became ill with Hepatitis C, which meant his work was disrupted by regular hospital visits.

Denise and Robin ran design studios with several staff members, so between us all we really knew how to nurture those students, something the students have never forgotten, bless them. We still keep in touch now and again, and they're all in their mid-50s now. One of them, Alan Birch, was also a talented actor, a member of a group called the Citizen's Theatre. My brother, then a professional copywriter and radio-ad creator with two Sony awards to brag about, was constantly asked by folks he met, on learning that he was a writer, why he had never written a book or a play. Bored with this repetitive enquiry, he decided to write a comedy play, just to shut them up. One day he handed me a manuscript entitled, 'Inspector Drake's Last Case', and asked me to read it. I did, and I laughed my head off all the way through it. Even on the cold page it was extremely funny, and it could only get better and funnier still when acted on stage. I told him I loved it, and he then asked if I knew any theatre groups that might stage it, just to get him started. As a matter of fact, I told him, I did, and one of the actors was at that precise moment sat in a life class next door trying to make a naked lady's breast look the same as the other one. I interrupted him to hand him my copy of the manuscript, and he promised not only to read it but to put it before his peers at the Citizen's Theatre, Pedmore Road, Quarry Bonk. This he duly did, and they loved it too, but didn't think they could stage it because, in their words; 'We only get 17 folks in for Shakespeare or Alan Ayckbourn, so we've got no chance with a chap nobody's ever bloody heard of.'

Despite this, somehow Alan persuaded them to give it a go. Theatre's are prone to giving Maureen a leading role because she didn't get a part last time, and letting old Graham have a go at directing because, even though he's hopeless, it's his turn. Predictably, this didn't wash with David. He told the Citizen's Theatre that not only was he going to direct it himself, he was also going to audition the cast to pick the best people, regardless of who hadn't had a go recently. This was far too much of a step for some of them, and a few swooned and had to be revived with a cold wet towel to the brow. Nevertheless, he wangled it, rehearsed them till they bled, and gave young Alan Birch the lead role, because he damn-well deserved it. He was, and still is, a great comedy actor, and now he even has an Equity card. The result was a total sell-out, with audiences falling off their seats laughing. The Citizen's, understandably, then asked for first refusal on the next play. Encouraged by this, David sent a copy to Samuel French, the famous theatrical publishers in London. He received a letter, which read:

'Dear David, we have read your play, and unfortunately....'
David tossed the screwed-up letter into the bin. His wife, Susan Tristram (yes, another bloody Susan) fished it out and read it.

'...and unfortunately, our M.D. is away in Japan at the moment, but we all think it is brilliant.' She gave him one of her looks. Some 25 plays later, David was announced as 'The Samuel French UK. Comedy Playwright of the Year 2015'.

The moral of this story is to read everything properly and take it in. And yes, dear reader, that applies to you too. If you're currently reading this in bed as a cure for insomnia, and one eye has already wilted, put it down now and start afresh in the morning.

One day, I needed to use Dudley Library to find some picture reference for a job I was doing. In those days, remember, Google didn't exist, so the library was our only resource. I parked the car just outside the Town Hall, where I'd once dressed the royal balcony, walked around the corner and strolled up the steps of the library. Half an hour later I returned to my car, and to my dismay, I realised it wasn't locked. I jumped inside and noticed that the ashtray was full of cigarettes. This was intriguing. Then there was a sharp rap on the window which made me jump out of my skin. A very aggressive man was swearing at me. I asked what the problem was, and he said I was in his car. I jumped out, and he seemed rather keen on punching my lights out until we both spotted another, identical Martini Porsche three cars away in the same street. There were only five in the whole of the Midlands, but two were within a few feet of each other. The following week I did a day of teaching at my old college in Wolverhampton. At 5pm I returned to my beloved car and reversed out of the underground car park, into a 2-foot-high concrete bollard that completely caved the back-end in.

Chapter 15

It was now the mid-1980s, and if you think my life was hectic before, wait till you hear what happened next. Everything seemed to come at once. Susan and I had sold our first house and were looking around for a new one. We'd put an offer in for one in the same street as Corbett's Hospital, but the owners pulled out of the deal at the last minute with no explanation offered. We were literally packed and ready to go when we found out. I rang the man to ask what had happened and he said that it was none of my business. We'd lost money on the survey and we were living out of a suitcase and ready to call the removal van, but apparently it was none of our business. Only in England can this happen. We looked elsewhere and found a potentially nice house in Eggington Road, Wollaston, so we offered the man the princely sum of £37,500 and he accepted. The particulars included a cooker and a garden bench, both of which he took with him, so when I arrived at my new house and spotted that there was a cooker-sized gap in the kitchen and a bench-sized empty space in the garden, I rang the man to ask where they had gone. He explained airily that they had mistakenly been taken to his new address in Belbroughton and were buried under loads of other stuff in a garage, and it was rather a pain for him to extricate them. I suggested that he should try, nevertheless, as he'd in effect stolen them. This seemed to upset him somewhat, and he informed me that I was being 'difficult'. I explained to him that that was nowhere near as difficult as I was about to get if he didn't return the cooker, at least. I could live without the bench. Is it me, or are more and more people becoming afflicted with acute moral-blindness nowadays? The guiltier they are, the more aggressive they get.

As if all this wasn't enough excitement for one year, we discovered that Susan was going to have a baby, which was due around January 1985.

Meanwhile, I was getting more and more work from Swinford Motors, and often I was struggling to cope on my own. My old friend Steve Jolliffe was a far better graphic designer than me, (most folks are, in fairness, but he's VERY much better) so I began to farm out the stuff I wasn't as good at, so that I could spend more time on illustration. This idea of ours grew, and soon we were having thoughts of creating a small design company, the way Robin Greenwell and Denise Serphentine (now Harrison), had done.

Dunn's, where Susan was now working, at least until the baby plopped out, was a labyrinth of rooms and corridors, with the main entrance in Chester Road and the old toy and model shop, once owned by Mr Dunn's brother, in Lower High Street around the corner. What people didn't realise was that the two were actually part of one massive building, and you could walk from one to the other without going outside. The old toy shop was on two floors. Mr Dunn rented us the entire shop, so we spent quite a few weekends and evenings decorating and having new carpet laid. We painted the frontage and added a sign, TRISTRAM & JOLLIFFE. It sounded better than JOLLIFFE & TRISTRAM, I thought.

Life at Dunn's was fairly mad. I finally had someone to talk to in the daytime, which helped, and also someone to bounce ideas off and get second opinions from. Also, my darling, ever-expanding wife was a few corridors away if I needed her or she needed me. My main sources of income at that time were Swinford Motors, Specs Art Agency in Cheltenham, a plethora of Birmingham-based advertising agencies, Thornton's Chocolates, Artists' Partners in London, Embassy World Snooker, Graduate Records, Oasis Art and Craft Products in Kidderminster (eventually taken over by French firm, Colart, which also owned Winsor & Newton, Pantone,

177

Letraset, Reeves and others), plus of course one-off clients, the teaching posts and the caricature events. Steve brought along his own regular clients, so we were snowed under most weeks. These were the glory years but we were too busy to realise it. We were relatively young and trying to make hay while the sun shone, but already I was finding it all a bit stressful. My nerves were jangling, and it's hard to paint well with a shaky hand and a brain that's too full. You need calm and solitude in order to paint, and my life was the polar opposite of that. After a year or so at full throttle, we decided that we needed an office junior, so we employed Amanda Bullas, a nice, friendly, pretty young lady with a good sense of humour, who had been one of my students at Stourbridge. Things didn't get off to a great start when she realised that we had a serious mouse infestation. I don't like killing things and neither does Steve, so we needed to come up with a humane way of catching the little buggers. We constructed a trap, which was basically a metal waste paper bin that had a ramp leading up to it, laced with scraps of food. We also placed tempting treats inside the bin, thinking that the mice would chomp their way through the starters as they climbed up the ramp and then leap into the bin to get to the main course. Once they were in, we were hoping that they wouldn't be able to climb out again. It worked. We went straight to the bin-traps first thing the following day, to find about 36 of the little devils in each one. We emptied the contents over the nearby park and filled two more bins with rodents the next day. If we'd been a tad more entrepreneurial, we could have opened a pet shop that specialised exclusively in mice. We'd have made a packet. We got used to hearing a scream coming from Mandy's office every ten minutes or so, as she spied yet another one whizzing around the skirting board. It can't have been pleasant for her. Women seem to be genetically programmed to be scared of mice, even though I think they are one of the cutest creatures on the planet. What was even more unpleasant for her was the Downstairs Floorboards

178

Incident. Apparently, we had a serious case of woodworm, so we had a carpenter in to tear up the affected floorboards and install new ones. The only thing was, we forgot to mention this to Mandy, so one day she arrived for work early, opened the front door and immediately disappeared into the abyss. It was only by sheer good fortune that she wasn't killed, as she shot in a downward direction like a bullet, into the dank underworld of the cellar, grazing both of her sides on the remaining floorboards as she fell. I am still grateful, to this day, that she was too nice a girl to sue us.

It's a corny thing to say, but it was only our sense of humour that held us together and stopped us going crazy. I would often return from a lavatory visit to find my sandwiches Sellotaped to a high light fitting. Jolliffe would then spend the rest of the day like a coiled spring, waiting for my revenge. You may have read earlier an Italian sentence that I frequently quote and wondered what it meant. *La vendetta e un piatto che va mangiato freddo.* Revenge is a dish best eaten cold. I left him in that state of nervy vigilance for days, before I struck. Then, once his guard was down, I got my own back. People pointed and stared as he drove home to Amblecote, and asked each other why anyone would want a personalised number plate with WANKER written on it.

Steve and I both worked for Oasis, a company owned by Chris Bagnall and his business partner, John Yeomans. They manufactured art and craft products, and their biggest seller was Paint-by-Numbers. I created hundreds of images for them in that typical chocolate-box style, and then converted my paintings into the lines and numbers that any of you who have ever tackled one will be familiar with. From an artist's perspective, it was fairly cheesy subject matter, but from the perspective of someone just trying to earn a living, it was very well-paid, and I was more than grateful for the work. We used to have this in-house joke about being a fly on the wall at an Oasis product development meeting. Chris would ask for subject matter ideas for their brand-new paint-by-numbers range, and John would suggest, a dolphin, an elephant, a pony, a tiger, a country cottage, a still life with fruit, an underwater scene, and a sailing ship, and Chris would agree and ring me to begin work on them. The following year, after much deliberation, they invariably decided on a dolphin, an elephant, a pony, a tiger, a country cottage, a still life with fruit, an underwater scene and a sailing ship, and Chris would agree and ring me to begin work on them. The following year, after much deliberation, they decided on...

Well, you get the point. It was always the same core images slightly re-jigged. Every now and again, however, I'd get a request for something a bit different, like, for example, Leonardo's 'The Last Supper', which was popular with the Roman Catholic countries. I painted it and it went down well, but then I had a call from Oasis, asking me to amend it slightly. In a playful moment, I had added a Mr Kipling Cherry Bakewell to Jesus's plate and they wanted it removed.

I eventually handed all my paint-by-numbers work to Fred Bradley, an illustrator who didn't have much work at that time, so I was, in effect, handing him many thousands of pounds that I could have kept for myself. Chris Bagnall, a good friend of mine to this day, was a little hurt that I no longer wanted to do them, but in truth I was not coping all that well with the demands being made on me, and I didn't want to use up my best years painting paint-by-numbers pictures, no matter how lucrative they were. I knew I'd hurt his feelings after he'd provided a huge chunk of my income, and I regret it to this day, but you have to do what you feel is right career-wise.

Fred was an advertising illustrator, as was I, but he looked more like a particularly dour funeral director, and had the same temperament as Eeyore, the depressed donkey from Winnie the Pooh. I always remember him delivering a large painting to a design studio in Birmingham one day, and the self-important junior art director, straight out of college, asked him to change a background colour. Fred objected, and argued that it was perfect as it was, but the art director insisted. Fred went away, reluctantly changed it (which is NOT easy, folks) and returned with it the following week, to be told by the young lad that he had changed his mind and Fred must now return it to its original colour. When Fred remonstrated with the youth, he replied rather snootily, that HE was the art director and Fred was a mere technician, who should shut up and do what he was told. Fred pondered this for a few seconds in silence and then tore the £2,000 illustration into shreds in the reception area of the design studio. 'Now shove that up your arse', he added, before marching out of the door. We artists can be a touch temperamental, it has to be said.

Many years later, Chris and John sold Oasis to Colart, who continued to use me on other projects, as and when I was needed. One year they asked me to quote for a new one-off range of paint-by-numbers designs, even though Fred was doing all of them by that time. I think they preferred my style for this particular project, hence the unexpected call. I decided to accept, as work had now become temporarily patchy for me too, and frankly, I needed the money. Fred found out and then rang me to casually ask what I'd quoted them for the work. I foolishly told him. He then rang Colart and informed them that I didn't really want to do paint-by-numbers any more, and I'd only quoted them to be polite, but he'd gladly do them if they wanted him to, and for less than I was charging them too, so they reluctantly accepted. With friends like that, who needs enemies, eh? What was that Italian phrase again?

I was still playing the guitar, but there had been quite a few changes which I need to belatedly bring you up to speed with, as I've been a bit preoccupied with all this art activity! Tobias had petered out some time back, but Kenny, my brother David, George and I had formed a new progressive rock outfit called Cleardays that clearly thought it was Yes. We played a few times and packed it in. David had also been playing with a chap from Walsall called Andy Leek, who then left to become a founder member of Dexy's Midnight Runners. Two years and a massive hit single, 'Gino' later, Andy left Dexy's (he wasn't keen on getting punched by the frontman, Kevin Rowland, apparently) and, incredibly, went back to David, this time joined by Kenny Stevens, to form The Andy Leek Band. After a brief spell there, Ken and David teamed up with Larry, Rob Lake, drummer Nick Parry and me to become the new-look Still, a progressive rock outfit that basically thought it was Genesis. We were pretty damned good actually, and were invited to play at JB's Club, Barbarella's in Birmingham, The Lafayette in Wolverhampton and several other venues locally. Meanwhile, Andy Leek made an album with George Martin, of The Beatles fame, and Martin went on record as saying that Andy was the most talented songwriter he'd worked with since Lennon and McCartney. In spite of all that, his debut album didn't make waves. Andy also wrote a song or two for Agnetha Faltscog – that's the blonde one in Abba to me and you, and he was married briefly to Andre Previn's daughter, as you do. Nowadays he lives in Bridgnorth and the last I heard, he was still fronting Andy Leek and the Blue Angels, a superb party band. Our band, Still, finally hung up their guitars around the end of 1978, a conclusion that was hastened by drummer Nick spending some time at Her Majesty's Pleasure for 'borrowing' a new vehicle from the Range Rover factory, where he worked. We often joked about him sneaking it out bit at a time in his lunchbox, the way Johnny Cash did in the song. I am delighted to report that, upon his release, the lad went straight and eventually joined Lol Mason's post-City Boy band, The Maisonettes. You can still find him on YouTube recordings of Top of the Pops playing 'Heartache Avenue'. He's the chap wearing the overall with the little arrows all over it, with a ball and chain attached to his ankle. Hey! I've just this second thought of a great nickname for him. You know how old-style gangsters were often called names such as Al 'Scarface'

Capone? Well how about Nick 'The Range-Rover' Parry? See what I did there? Nick as in steal....oh never mind!

Oh, and before we return to the Artist's Progress, here's one last music anecdote for you. I was with Lol and the other lads from City Boy in a Harborne pub, when Roy, their drummer, arrived and told the others he'd done some session drumming and singing with a manufactured band called Tight Fit. Roy was not only a great drummer but the main vocalist on City Boy's biggest hit, 5705 (Everyone was a singer in that band!). Apparently, the song was a remake of 'The Lion Sleeps Tonight', for which he had supplied the lead vocal, as the three people who constituted Tight Fit were nothing more than hired models who looked pretty but couldn't sing a note. Scandalous, is it not? He was fairly confident that we'd never hear of this single again, and he'd shamelessly taken the money and scarpered. The next thing we know is that this awful single was No1 in the UK charts for three weeks and spent the next 33 weeks in the top 40, thereby making old Roy a tidy packet in royalties.

Apparently, he and the lads were in this same pub some time later when the jukebox began to play the song, and Roy was stood next to it, singing along with it. A young lady in the vicinity remarked that he sounded awfully like the singer on the record, whereupon Roy explained that it was actually him. The girl considered this for a brief moment and then replied, 'Fuck off, you lying wanker.' Roy never did find out which Swiss finishing school she once attended.

During our tenancy at the Dunn's building there were a couple of incidents that were truly memorable; even more so than Mandy falling through the floor. One day I had pulled my car halfway onto the pavement outside our offices to avoid causing traffic congestion in Lower High Street. I need to explain here that the pavement was extremely wide at that point, and the fact that two of my wheels were on it did not impede pedestrians, not even those who were pushing a pram.

183

In fact, you could have been pushing a skip on wheels and you'd still have sailed by with ease. I had parked there because I had to load up my car with exhibition panels, and I was about half done when an old bloke walked past and started mumbling under his breath about blocking the pavement. When it began to grate, I asked, 'Excuse me, what's the problem?'

He started banging on about motorists 'thinking they could take over the pavements' and so on, and in normal circumstances, on narrow pavements, in domestic situations, I totally agree, only this wasn't like that. For a start, if I'd parked on the road, there'd have been a line of traffic stretching back to Dudley within three minutes. I explained, as politely as I could, that he was still able to get by with no difficulty whatsoever. I also added that he could have been one of a line of can-can dancers and they'd still get by without touching the sides. But no, he kept banging on and on until I began to see red.

'How wide is the gap you have left to get through, you stupid twat?' I asked. 'I am loading a car. I will be gone in a few seconds, but you can't help but get involved, can you, even though it has not caused you a moment's difficulty.'

Still he kept on, and on, and on. Again I tried to explain that the pavement he had available was wide enough to land a Lancaster Bomber without scuffing its wings on the office wall. And still this idiot would not shut up. Suddenly, above my head, I heard the office window open, and I saw my pregnant wife's head peer out. Then, at approaching the same decibel level as a Jumbo jet revving up, she screamed:

'YOU. YES YOU, YOU MORON. GO AWAY NOW, OR I WILL COME DOWN THERE AND...'

There was no need to complete the sentence. He shot up the high street like a whippet.

My favourite story of all is the Holiday Romance Paperback saga. In those days I used to illustrate quite a few paperback book covers for Dominic Rodi's Artist Partners Agency in London, as did my mate Mike Timmins. One cold, rainy November I was given the cover of a Messenger Books (no relation to Tony) 'romance' paperback to paint. These were similar to Mills & Boone's output, if you are familiar with those. The plot, if we can call it a plot, was that a girl is on holiday in Majorca, and decides to go for a swim, but the sea gets a bit too choppy and she's not exactly Rebecca Addlington, so she fetches up on a bit of rock and she's stuck there, gasping for air and frightened. Suddenly, a millionaire passes by on his yacht and spots the damsel in distress, so he strips down to his undies, dives in, saves her life, and they fall in love. The scene they wanted to show on the cover was the man swimming towards the girl, with his boat in the background. The only trouble was and still is, I can't just make this stuff up. None of us can. We need good reference material to work from. The view from my studio window was a derelict Victorian factory. There was no beautiful girl on tap, no hunky bloke, no turquoise sea, no yacht, nothing. I was staring at a piece of white watercolour board and thinking, 'bloody hell, I have to finish this by Friday'. On occasions such as these, you have to think on your feet. 'Who do I know who's beautiful? I asked myself. Why, Susan of course, but she was busy printing photographs next door. Then I thought of Marcia. She was a model from Cradley Heath, and the handsome hunky millionaire in the story could be played by Dave Grainger, her boyfriend (a man that I had nicknamed Grave Danger). He fitted the bill perfectly.

Excellent. That was the figure reference sorted. I could make up the rest of the scene from a Thompson's holiday catalogue. I rang Marcia and Dave and asked if they'd pose for me for £50. Half an hour later, they came up the stairs (we had floorboards again and no mice) and popped into my room. I told Marcia she'd have to strip down to her bra and pants, so they'd resemble a bikini, and drape herself over a small glass coffee table, which would play the part of the rock. I then asked Dave to strip down to his 'Y' Fronts and lie on my Hostess trolley. I wheeled him behind Marcia and asked him to pretend he was doing the front crawl. Then I asked Marcia to pretend she was half-drowned and gasping for air. She said, rather predictably, 'I can't, I feel stupid', and I didn't blame her.

Seeing his 50 quid potentially in jeopardy, Dave chipped in. 'Come on Marce, pretend your gasping for air, do some panting.'
Marcia did her best. It sounded as if she were having a painful orgasm. I began clicking away with my trusty little Nikon camera, and then I turned my attention to Dave, stretched out on my trolley, smiling at me as he did the crawl. I told him not to look at me and grin, but instead to look at Marcia with a concerned expression. I took a few more pictures of him. Meanwhile, Marcia was still gasping and panting and squealing like she was in a porn film. I needed one or two more pictures of Dave and that would have to do. It was getting surreal. I aimed the camera, and again, he was looking at me instead of her. I was about to tell him off when I realised he was actually looking past me this time. I turned around. The milkman had just walked in.

I am the kind of person who gets embarrassed very easily. I went bright red. If you want the precise colour, it was Pantone 205. The milkman just stood there and took it all in. he was staring at a scantily-clad Marcia, who was still in the final throes of orgasm – the dying embers, shall we say, which quickly ceased when she spotted the milkman ogling her. I daresay Dave also felt vulnerable, his arms set in a front crawl position and only a pair of skimpy pants shielding his manhood. I just wanted to die, there and then. Eventually the milkman snapped out of his reverie and said, 'That's £3.86 then, please Geoff.'

I ushered him out of the room into the corridor. Thank God Steve had gone to Swinford Motors and Mandy was delivering a job. I'd never have heard the last of it. I dug deep in my pocket and gave him the cash.

'Any pasteurised for the weekend, mate?' he asked, smirking.

I mumbled, 'No thanks,' a beaten man. Then he uttered a sentence that truly made me squirm.

'Look Geoff, we're all adults, mate. What you do in your own time is your business.'

It is fair to say that I still get flashbacks about this one.

Changing the subject seamlessly, one thing I learnt about running a business was that I had to be a bit more astute with money. I've never been tight-fisted, and I have a tendency to give things away on a whim. Take Ayrton Senna's signature, for example. A well-known advertising agency in Birmingham asked me to paint a picture for a large billboard ad, showing a man in a sou'wester rowing down a flooded street with his faithful dog, in order to get to his local pub. We had been experiencing extensive flooding in England at the time, and Worthington's Brewery wanted to feature this in the ad. The caption at the bottom read, 'If it's Worthington, it's worth it!'

I asked for £1,000 at the time, but the agency beat me down to £750, which I reluctantly accepted. One of my old Stourbridge students worked at this particular agency, and he gave me a ring. The agency, he assured me, had charged the client £10,000 for the painting. I am not naïve. I know they mark-up the work we produce, and that doesn't bother me. What does bother me is making me take a pay-cut, when their margin was already astronomical. Artists, from time immemorial, have been ripped off. We seem to be considered fair game.

It was the early-80s now, and I had begun to work for Walsall Security Printers, which printed postage stamps for the government, as well as fancy labels for spirits' bottles such as Famous Grouse.

I had always wanted to design postage stamps, children's books, book covers and record sleeves, because these were the kind of fantasy projects we were given at art college, which wasn't the real world. The reality for most artists and designers who weren't based in London was boring industrial brochures and press ads, but I was incredibly lucky, and often in the right place just at the right time. I ended up doing all the fancy stuff!

I designed several sets of stamps in the early 1980s. My first was for Miss World, Bermuda. There were four stamps featuring Miss Gina Swainson, who I was lucky enough to meet at the printers. We had out photographs taken together, and interestingly, my brother is on those photographs with us, though I can't think for the life of me why.

I designed a ten-stamp set for the Lake Placid Winter Olympics that featured the medal winners in each category. I had to contact a picture library to hire press photographs of the ten gold-medal winners to work from, which Walsall Security Printers were paying for. The only problem was, none of us knew who the winners were. There was no such thing as Google then, no Olympics magazines in the shops, so my research was leading nowhere and my deadline was fast approaching. In desperation I rang the Olympic Association in Lake Placid and asked them, and this deep-voiced Yank on the other end of the line said, 'Sorry, Geoff. We *should* know who they are, but we kind-of don't!'

At that time, Susan and I had a tiny Cavalier King Charles puppy called Lucy, the 1st of 3, and she was left in our kitchen whenever we were busy or had to go out, as she was not yet house-trained. We had to leave newspapers all over the floor and collect them all up when they were covered in dog-poo and wee. It's a delightful pastime and one I'd recommend to everyone. I'd elected to work from home for a short while so I could look after the dog, as it was easier for me than

Susan, who had a proper job. I opened the kitchen door and was met by... well, you can imagine. I was on my hands and knees cleaning up this awful mess and thinking to myself that I had better, more pressing things to do. I grabbed the pungent cover of the Express & Star and tried to drop it into a black bin-bag. Meanwhile, a vile, runny, Cavalier turd was slowly sliding down the page *en route* for my kitchen floor. As it slid, snail-like - and I swear this is true, - it revealed in its wake the names of the 10 gold-medal winners listed in the sports column. I swear I saw a shaft of heavenly light suddenly appear through the kitchen window, accompanied by a choir of angels.

I was also asked to design Spain's World Cup Football stamps, again, a set of 10, and finally, fanfare of trumpets please, my proudest stamp-related moment, the Royal Wedding Stamps for Charles and Diana.

Another highlight from that era was the cover of Trivial Pursuit. Mine was the CD ROM version as opposed to the familiar boxed game we all know and love. I'd been given the job by Spec's Art, and told to liaise directly with Hasbro, the manufacturers. The idea was to illustrate subject matter that cropped up on the question cards, so my painting was to be a montage of Madonna, Michael Jackson, the Leaning Tower of Pisa, a Bakelite radio, a dolphin and so on. I was preparing my master tracing in the darkroom when Hasbro rang me. They asked, could I make sure that I made Michael Jackson larger than Madonna, as 'Michael's people' insisted on it. I went back into the darkroom and began to alter my tracing. 10 minutes later, Hasbro rang again. Apparently, 'Madonna's people' were now demanding that she should be at least as big as Michael Jackson. I grunted and returned to my sweltering hot darkroom. I may even have sworn under my breath. Then, blow me down, if they didn't ring again, having heard from 'Michael's people' once more. In fairness, the Hasbro chap was just as exasperated as I was. I calmly explained that I was just a humble artist who wanted to get on with things and to meet their deadline, which was looking ever-more unlikely if I kept getting interruptions.

'Look', said the frustrated Hasbro designer, 'we've made a decision. Ditch Jackson. They're being a right pain in the arse.'

'Great,' I replied, 'but what do I stick in that big gap where he used to be?'

'Good point!' he said. 'What do you fancy?'

'Me?' I asked, shocked that he'd asked me. 'Well, I'd stick Shakespeare in there. He's ten times more famous than either of them and he's local too.'

'It's a deal,' he laughed. 'Get on with it.'

And that is why Shakespeare is on the cover of Trivial Pursuit's CD ROM version. I'm rather proud of that, as it happens. And as befits a world-renowned Coincidence-Magnet, Shakespeare would once more enter my life in spectacular fashion in 2016.

I had appeared on television a few times, thanks to the World Snooker Tournament. They were advertising my caricature prints on the programme, and Susan and I were invited to the Crucible in Sheffield each April to watch a few games, have some dinner at the restaurant and doss about in the players' lounge. We got to know Dennis Taylor, Steve Davis, Eddie Charlton, John Parrott, John Spencer and presenter David Vine, amongst others, and I have to report that they were all nice people. As the years progressed I would also get to know the next generation, and even the one after that. The finals always coincided with our joint birthday, and one year, Susan and I were invited into the commentary box to watch the semi-final. I remember Steve Davis being one of the players but I've forgotten who his opponent was. I have a terrible memory as you've probably gathered. The commentators that night were the legendary 'Whispering' Ted Lowe and the man who invented the upside-down snooker spectacles for Dennis Taylor, namely, Jack Karnehm. Ted was focussed on the game and speaking into his microphone.

'It looks as if Steve is going to try for that plant in the corner pocket and then screw back up the table for the pink.'

And then suddenly he added, 'Commentate on this next shot, would you, Sue?'

He thrust the mic into Susan's face, and I saw her drain of colour. There were only eight million folks listening in, so there was no real pressure, I would have thought, but then again, she isn't a show-off like me. She gurgled a bit and was just about to take a stab at it when Ted started sniggering and told her he'd turned the mic off and it was a joke. If push came to shove, she could probably have done it, after a fashion. We've watched so much snooker over the years that she knew her way around a snooker table.

Having got to know a couple of the show's producers, I was asked to create a framed cartoon of Peter West, the sports commentator, which was to be a retirement present from the BBC. I was told to visit the mobile film-editing van which was parked at Worcester Cricket Club during a test match and lie to the occupants that I was a lackey from the BBC. Peter would be there, and also Richie Benaud, the famous Australian commentator. The idea was to create a montage of amusing incidents from Peter's career, so I had to casually probe him for stories all afternoon without letting on that I was a cartoonist. Talk about under-cover work! I'd also been asked by my mate, Tim Joplin, to collect as many autographs as I could for him, as he was a real cricket nut.

The afternoon went well, and I had amassed a good few anecdotes for my secret mission, hopefully without arousing Peter's suspicions. I decided to ask Richie Benaud for an autograph for my friend Tim, and he took the autograph book from me with what can only be described as an expressionless face. I gave him my fountain pen, but instead of taking it, he just stared at it. Things were getting a tad uncomfortable, as I couldn't fathom his intentions at all. His face was more inscrutable than Fu Manchu's.

'Erm, what's the matter?' I asked.

'Take the bloody top off it,' he barked in his surly Australian accent.

'I'm not really sure that my friend Tim would want the autograph of someone who can't manage to take the top off a pen,' I countered, instantly regretting the day, earlier on in my life, when I elected to have the filter between my brain and my mouth surgically removed. He stared at me some more, removed the top and scribbled on the autograph book. I decided it was time to beat a hasty retreat, having harvested enough material to begin the Peter West cartoon.

Later that same week, Glynn Edwards, the cartoonist and boss of Adline, had sponsored a glitzy event for the advertising industry in Birmingham City centre, and sent Susan and me two tickets for it. We didn't particularly want to go but we had nothing much on and the entertainment was free, so we set out in the swanky Martini Porsche. Susan had a posh frock on and I was wearing my new dinner suit, because it was that kind of event. We got as far as Mucklow Hill island, Halesowen, when my tyre decided to deflate rapidly. I realised that our evening was over before it had begun, because the spare had a dangerous bubble in it that I was meaning to get replaced when I found a second, which I never did. I pulled up, grabbed the tyre jack from the boot, and tried to undo one of the wheel nuts. It was stuck solid. They all were. I sighed a trademark heavy sigh. At precisely this moment, an AA van appeared, and kindly pulled up to see what the problem was. I explained the situation to the chap, who looked and spoke just like Lenny Henry.

'Leave it to me!' he smiled, winking at Susan. He applied the jack and grunted a lot. 'I can't shift it,' he begrudgingly admitted, suddenly looking as deflated as my tyre. 'I'll have to go back to base and get one of those electric doodahs, like they use in the Formula 1 pits.'

I thanked him brokenly. I was getting cold and extremely fed-up. Then he coughed a little, polite cough and asked if I was a member. I had foolishly let my membership lapse, so I had to write him a cheque for 30 quid. ten minutes later he returned and made short work of the nuts, just like my hamster used to do. He grabbed the spare from the back of the car, and his face changed again. 'It's got a huge bubble in it,' he said. 'You'll have to crawl home and get this sorted tomorrow.'

I told him I already knew about the bubble. He swapped the flattened wheel for the bubbled one and asked if he could do anything else for us. We thanked him and said no, we'd be okay. He duly left and I returned to the driving seat. I turned the key, and the car responded with a sickly 'groan, groan, groan, phut' noise. The hazard warning lights, which had been on for ages now, had flattened the battery. We sat there fuming. Then Lenny Henry drove past again and pulled up to see why we hadn't moved yet. He applied the jump leads and got the car running again. He gave it a good old charge for a considerable amount of time, to make sure it would start next time. We removed the key, replaced it, repeated the procedure and it worked perfectly now. Lenny bade us goodnight and left. It was now around 10 o'clock, and we'd set out at 7pm. The sky was pitch black, but thankfully there was a full moon. I grabbed the huge bunch of keys and held them up to the moon to help identify the ignition key. And here you will have to take my word for it, with regard to what happened next. It sounds far-fetched, but I swear I am not exaggerating.

The ignition key, silhouetted against the moon, seemed to rock a little from side to side. Then it fell in half.

I looked at Susan, and she looked at me. Neither of us could get our words out. Metal fatigue had claimed my key at the precise moment I showed it to the moon. It could only happen to me. I rang my dad, and he came to fetch Susan and take her home, so she could get the spare car keys. He dropped her off at Mucklow Hill what seemed like hours later, and then we crawled home at 20 mph thanks to the enormous bubble in the spare. We got home at midnight, exhausted and frustrated in equal measure. The next day, Glynn rang to say we'd missed a great event.

Not long after that I began working for Dr Dorian Dugmore, who used to be a professional footballer, but had since completed his PhD in Cardiac Rehabilitation. He founded Action Heart, the Dudley-based charity, and then left to work in Toronto for the large rehab centre there, before eventually returning to England to work for Adidas in Stockport. One day I was asked to visit their offices and draw caricatures of the Adidas staff, which I duly did. When I'd finished, Dorian asked me to drive my car over to the nearby warehouse, as they had 'a nice surprise' for me. I popped my head around the door of the warehouse, and saw two large cardboard boxes, sat side by side. One was labelled 'David and Victoria Beckham', and the other was labelled 'Geoff and Sue Tristram'. The warehouse-man explained that David Beckham was in a meeting in the room next to where I'd been drawing and he was coming over later to get his box. He dropped mine into the boot of my car for me and told me what was in it. It was £2,000 worth of Adidas sports gear, he said. I was stunned by this. I got home and within seconds, the human locusts had stripped the box bare, leaving me with one pair of socks.

Chapter 16

One relatively warm and sunny afternoon in January, Susan and I were outside our new house, painting the rendering white. She shouldn't have been painting a house as she was, on paper at least, only a few weeks shy of giving birth to our first child, but you know what these hardened Black Country women are like. In the olden days, some of them used to give birth standing up while they continued to make chain, so slapping a bit of paint on a house was nothing. We eventually packed it in around 7pm and retired, exhausted, to the kitchen to fix some food, as the Americans say, when they actually mean prepare. I know I'm being pedantic (who, me?) but your cheese sandwich would have to be broken in some way if you needed to fix it. Maybe the crust might have fallen off, for example, and you had to Sellotape it back on. The Americans also believe that the past tense of sneak is snuck, so they're beyond help, grammar-wise. So anyway, we flopped down onto the settee with plates on our laps and decided to watch Dallas. It was the episode when we all found out who shot J.R. Just after she had finished eating, Susan glanced down at the old leather Chesterfield and realised that it was wet. Water seemed to be gushing from her legs. She gave me a look of panic that said it all. Her waters had broken, and I had to drive up to the Rosemary Ednam Maternity Unit, near Dudley, in a bit of a hurry. We gathered her over-night things as quickly as we could and dashed – well, I dashed, she waddled, leaving puddles in her wake – out to the Martini Porsche, which I'd just had valeted at great expense. She plonked herself down onto the passenger seat and instantly drenched it. They say having a baby is expensive, and the little devil had already begun to cost me money. I drove to the Maternity Unit, a bag of nerves, and they took Susan from me. I paced the corridor in time-honoured fashion and was called into the room just in time to see Miss Laura Anne Tristram emerging. There was no screaming from Susan, no calling me a son-of-a-bitch for causing all this pain, no hysteria. The Black Country wench just got on with it, even though it must have come a bit sharp, like a paper-cut or something maybe, and once little Laura was cleaned up and introduced to her mommy and daddy, Susan announced to the room that she could murder a pint of lager. And they say romance is dead. You don't get that sort of thing in Jane Austen novels.

We never found out who shot J.R. Ewing, and to this day, I still don't have a clue. I *can* tell you that, had we known the trouble, worry and heartache that children cause, we'd have got ourselves a pair of guinea pigs instead.

After a spot of much-needed paternity leave, I had to report back to work, so that we could keep young Laura in the Farley's rusks to which she had become accustomed. Sue had to pack in her job at Dunn's until Laura was old enough to go to school, so that meant I was in sole charge of paying the bills and the significantly increased mortgage on our new house.

We were the first of our group of friends to have a baby, if I remember correctly, but not long afterwards, several of the others followed suit. As Laura changed from baby to toddler to infant, I remember lots of get-togethers at each-other's houses with Robin and Elaine Greenwell, Denise and Phil Harrison, and Mike and Susan Timmins, and, like all people of a certain age, the conversations inevitably centred around houses, mortgages, jobs and kids. Looking back on those times, and I mean no offence to anyone here, we all played the new-parent game, each of us agreeing to be enthralled by a friend's child for the simple reason that we wanted our friends to reciprocate and be enthralled by ours. It was a marriage of convenience. Later, the predictable dinner-party conversation with all people of our age would be about which schools we sent them to, and then of course it was universities, eventually followed many years later by conversations about illnesses, the medicines we now needed to take and who was seriously ill or had died. It was, and still is, rather depressingly reminiscent of reading Shakespeare's Seven Ages of Man.

When not entertaining at home we all used to frequent a wine bar in Harborne called The Rock Candy Mountain, if we could find a babysitter, but now, the sixth-form obsession with Guinness had matured into a liking for Liebfraumilch, Blue Nun, Soave, Lambrusco and Riesling. Well, it *was* a long time ago, and we were at the beginning of our wine-drinking odyssey.

Back at the ranch, I'd had a call from an Advertising Agency based in Shrewsbury about producing an advertisement for Eco-Bale, which was foodstuff for cattle packaged in what looked like an unappetising black binbag. They wanted me to paint a picture of a couple of cows in the depths of winter watching as a helicopter dropped the black hay bags into their field. I needed visual reference as usual, which meant a short drive to my nearest farm. I spotted a rustic sat on a tractor, so I explained what I was up to and he gave me the go-ahead. I was busy photographing the cows when a Range Rover arrived and screeched to a halt right beside me, covering me in dust. A man with a florid face, a checked shirt and a flat cap wound the window down and began ranting at me and asking what the effing hell I was doing. This threw me, as I was led to believe the rustic on the tractor was the farmer, but it transpired that he was just an idiot on a tractor. I tried to reason with the driver, but every time I opened my mouth this overly-aggressive individual began ranting again.

'What do you think you're effing doing?' he bellowed, but when I tried to explain he interrupted me and screamed, 'Get orf moi land!

197

Exasperated by his bolshie attitude, I asked him, 'Do you want me to tell you what I'm doing or get orf your land? I can't do both at the same bloody time.'

This retort only seemed to make him worse. I decided that the best form of advance was to retreat, or whatever the saying is. I drove to the next-nearest farm, where I encountered another rustic on a tractor, almost identical to the first one. I made sure that he was the boss this time, insisting that he sign forms to that effect in triplicate, and then, once I was convinced, asked permission to snap his Friesians, which isn't a strange sexual euphemism, by the way. He said (and I've attempted to write it as he said it, so read it to yourself using an accent similar to Long John Silver's, from Treasure Island, as portrayed by Robert Newton):

'No prarblem moi friend, but I can see you's gart your best suit arn, so step carefully. There's a really narrow strip o' grarse, the width of a carpet toil, and then the fence an' the cows. You needs to be careful, 'cause if you falls backerds there's a 3-foot drarp into a huge pool of liquid slurry an' it stinks to hoy heaven.'

I thanked him for the advice and strolled over to the field with my trusty Nikon. When I got there, it was as he had described it. In front of me was a nice cow that was doing exactly what I wanted it to do, which was to quietly chew on some grass and mind its own business. Worryingly, however, to the right of her was a very aggressive young bull, with his head down low, scuffing the grass with his front leg and snorting hot air through his flared nostrils, like he was about to do battle with a Matador. He had taken an instant dislike to me, for whatever reason. Maybe it just saved time. I had one eye on the cow, one eye on the young bull, and yet another eye on the pool of liquid cow-shit behind me. I decided to get cracking so I could get out of there as soon as possible. I raised the camera to my eye, and all of a sudden, I felt a terrific blow to my testicles, followed seconds later by an unbearable, searing pain. I crashed backwards down the muddy slope and ended up prostrate in the slurry, which quickly engulfed my best Yves Saint Laurent double-breasted suit, the one I went to interviews in. I thought to myself, 'That bad-tempered bullock's head-butted me in the bollocks'. My groin was still throbbing wildly and I think my eyes must have disappeared into the back of my head. It was then that I heard a plaintive, faraway voice on a tractor.

'Oi fergot to warn you 'bout the 'lectric fence. That one's a bugger an' all. It's wired up to the mains!'

It took me around three weeks before I could see the funny side, thought both Susan and Jolliffe seemed to find it hilarious right away. It was not all bad news, however. I would now not need Viagra ever again, and if I turned the one way, given the right weather conditions, I could sometimes pick up Radio Shropshire on my dick.

A couple of years later, my brother came to see us and suggested a merger with his own company, Contact Creative Communication. He and Dick Fisher, who you'll remember was a presenter at Beacon Radio, had formed a company and were doing extremely well. They made radio and TV ads, and corporate videos, and also staged conferences with a partner by the name of Trevor who supplied them with staging and lighting equipment. David reckoned that adding a graphic design arm to the business would be a great idea, especially if we were 'all under one roof', as the cliché goes. We gave it a lot of thought, and eventually joined them back in Dudley, not far from Graduate Records, in Wolverhampton Street. It was another large Georgian 3-story building, and once more we all chipped in and redecorated the place from top to bottom, ably hampered by our new junior artist, the wonderful Stephanie 'Swampy' Marsh, an amusing Sedgley wench who also kindly baby-sat for us.

I really don't know how we had the energy for all this enterprise; especially me, with a young girl to look after. It would kill me nowadays.

Work continued to be hectic and at times overwhelming, and then Susan discovered that she was pregnant again, which would have meant Laura would have a brother or sister a couple of years younger than she was. This was exactly as we'd hoped, but I didn't figure on the amount of work that I was having to cope with at Contact. It's important to remember that my job is not like a lot of other jobs. To function properly and concentrate, I need inner-peace and solitude. That's not some woolly hippy ideal, or an example of extreme prima-donna behaviour, but a fact. I had to concentrate to such a degree that even someone opening a door too loudly could potentially ruin a painting. A phone call at the wrong time would snap my concentration in two. I always liken it to performing brain surgery, but without the blood. A millimetre either way and the patient dies. Thankfully, death was never an issue, but starting again on a picture that had already taken three weeks certainly was. Those who have never had to focus to that extent will think I am laying this on a bit thick. In my defence, I often had to suspend my breathing momentarily as I painted a line so accurate and fine that any interruption would have resulted in a spoilt picture. Take a look up-close at my 'serious' pictures from that time and you'll understand what I mean by mega-concentration and mind-numbing detail. Ideally, I needed to be a monk in a cell, and my hairstyle was heading in that direction, but instead I was in a busy building with phones going off all the time, and people constantly in and out of my room. Add to that a head so full of stuff that I couldn't sleep very well, and it becomes extremely difficult to function. The already fragile nerves begin to fray. Then, when I couldn't take any more stress, God opened my studio door and threw in a live hand grenade.

Not long into her pregnancy, Susan discovered that her waters were leaking. When all else failed, she was eventually admitted into hospital for the foreseeable future and told she must have absolute bedrest in order to try and save the unborn baby. The trouble was, we had a daughter at home who needed her mother. My own mother stepped in and helped look after Laura each day while I tried to work, and after work I'd visit the hospital and take Laura with me. Sue's parents also helped as much as they could in what was a very tense time for all concerned. Susan was not coping too well in hospital. She thought her child was forgetting about her, causing her to get very weepy and emotional, which was unlike her. One day the doctor would be concerned that the baby had contracted a serious infection, and the next, they assured her it hadn't. We were on the world's worst roller-coaster ride. It was vital that they kept Susan wrapped in cotton wool until the baby was viable, and that was some time off. I was turning up for work as soon as I could, because I was the only person who could do my job, but I was so fragile that one afternoon I just sat at my drawing board and cried my eyes out. Then one day the doctors decided that the baby should be born by Caesarean section. One of them asked if Susan had eaten any food that day, as they were concerned about the anaesthetic. She replied, 'Only the hospital dinner, which can't be described as food.' Unfortunately, in spite of its taste, it was technically classed as such by the anaesthetist, so the operation had to be delayed until the inedible crap had passed through her system. They eventually wheeled her down to the operating theatre, and were about to administer the anaesthetic, when she decided to go into labour. She gave birth on the trolley as she waited for her operation, to a baby boy that we'd decided to call David, after my brother. The doctor sat down with us and said, 'Congratulations. After all that stress, you gave birth to a healthy little boy.'

The next day, things began to go wrong. You can always tell that there's a real problem when the vicar arrives and wants to christen the baby early, just in case. David died on the 20th of May, 1988, aged just one day. The nurse brought him to us in a private room and we were allowed to hold him for quite some time before they took him away again. Susan was absolutely distraught, as was I. I had never seen her cry that way before, and I never have since. In hindsight, I feel that it did us both good in the long term. We got it out of our systems there and then, rather than harboured it for ever afterwards the way some couples do. That evening I had to go home and put Laura to bed. The hardest thing I have ever done was having to explain to her that the little brother she had been expecting home soon had died. With alarming naïveté, I never realised we would have to have a funeral. I thought they just took the baby away and that was that, when they were only a day or so old.

The undertakers supplied a tiny white coffin, no more than two feet long. When Susan saw it, she fell apart all over again. I would even say that she temporarily lost her mind with grief, at one point asking me to go to the funeral home and get her baby back. Jeez, it was tough to see. The funeral was every bit as grim as you can imagine, as they carried this tiny coffin to its resting place. The only consolation for us was that we were crying about an awful experience, and not for the loss of a child we had grown to love. In truth, we had never known him. He was a day old. Imagine how we would have felt had he reached the age of, say three or four, and then died.

We healed well, considering what we'd been through, and were able to move on, and I am convinced that our initial outpouring of grief helped this to happen. We didn't bottle anything up. You sometimes hear people say things such as, 'There's not a day goes by that I don't think about the baby that died.' From my own experience - and I know this will upset some readers - this is a glib statement; a maudlin cliché that we allow people to say without questioning the accuracy of it. The truth is, after an initial period of grieving intensely, you begin to think about such tragedies less often, maybe when you're a bit down, maybe on an anniversary, but every day... I don't think so. That is just a hackneyed figure of speech.

I went back to work as soon as it was wise to do so, and I encouraged Susan to pop in a lot too, so that she wasn't on her own. I never liked being in those offices, for whatever reason, in spite of having my brother and his wife Susan around (she was the company secretary). I think I was quietly tiring of being in an organisation, in the same way that I tired of being in a band. My work demanded that I was a free spirit – it was what being an artist was all about. I needed to follow my instincts and go where my heart took me, without having to answer to anyone. I have always been the same. I also hate being told what to do or being told off, but in my defence, I am so self-critical that I really don't need others joining in. I give myself a far-worse time than others could.

After three years in Wolverhampton Street, I decided that I wanted to be on my own again. Steve and I split up amicably, and we both headed home. We still work together to this day, but as freelance artists, not as a company. My only real problem was *where* I would work. I couldn't bear to find yet another small office to rent, so one weekend I walked into my recently renovated garage and stood there, staring at the room for what must have been hours, until Susan had to come in and ask what was up.

'I've decided,' I said, 'that I am going to turn this place into a home studio.' She probably gave me one of her looks but I didn't notice. I was too busy trying to imagine where the desk, the drawing board and my Grant projector would go.

The following week, Len Hale and Daryl Jenkins, our pet carpenters who had just replaced all of our windows with nice new mahogany ones and renovated my garage, were invited back to ruin their handiwork and convert my garage into a studio with a darkroom. They thought I'd gone mad, wasting all that money, but I've been here ever since, and after 28 years, I am not going anywhere else until they build me my own mahogany box with brass handles.

Working at home, I discovered, had many advantages and a few disadvantages. On the plus side, I found myself laughing out loud in a slightly unhinged way as I listened to local BBC radio traffic reports of huge jams on the M5. I also saved on rent and petrol, and I was putting in longer hours, thanks to my four-second commute to and from the office. On the down-side, I would get visited by all and sundry for a quick coffee and a chat, and it was awfully difficult having to explain to them that it might have been *their* day off, but it wasn't mine. Often, I would have crippling deadlines to meet and, being the obsessive type, I tended to put in long, uninterrupted hours as a rule. Some days, after one of these visits that could last one or two hours, I fantasised about showing up at *their* office, or bank, or school, and chatting with them for hours at their desks, just to see how *they* liked it.

I registered for V.A.T. when I was forced to, thanks to my earning a decent amount of money in those days, and one morning I had to endure the customary visit from the V.A.T. man. I opened the door to a pony-tailed lad in a suit, who couldn't have been more than 19. I invited him in and offered him tea and biscuits while he began examining my bookwork in forensic detail for hours. Being the informal, friendly type, I asked him to call me Geoff, rather than Mr Tristram, but even at that tender age, the corporate broomstick had been inserted so far up his arse that he refused, adding that he preferred to keep things formal in case the results of his scrutiny proved problematic. I left him to it and carried on painting. Susan, who had delivered his refreshments, and was famous for her catchy nick-naming skills, popped into the studio to announce that she had christened him 'Vat-Boy'. Hours later, he tapped on my studio door and told me that he had concluded his investigations and I owed the V.A.T. office the princely sum of £3.97. He delivered this news as if I were

Ronnie Biggs. Then, just as he was about to leave, he asked about the caricatures I drew. Apparently, he couldn't think of anything to get his parents for Christmas, which was fast approaching. Slightly surprised by this, I told him I'd need two decent photographs and a few suggestions for their favourite pastimes. 'And as to cost,' I added, 'A full colour, framed caricature is £250...plus VAT.' I added the final part of my quote with a flourish, and I intended it to sting. He said he'd be in touch.

A few days later he knocked on my door again, but this time he'd let his hair down, both metaphorically and literally. He now wore jeans and a leather jacket and someone had surgically removed the broomstick from his back passage. I told him to come for the cartoons on the day before Christmas Eve. He arrived, collected the pictures, which he was delighted with, and then came the awkward bit. He took £500 in cash from his wallet and handed it to me. No V.A.T. had been included. He explained that he did discos in his spare time, and he'd just been paid for a weekend's work at a club, so I could have the cash. I wasn't quite sure what to do. Should I make a fuss, remind him of the V.A.T., or just take the money? Was this a clever sting operation by the V.A.T. office, I wondered? Surely not. It was far too elaborate for that. I bit my lip and took the cash, and off he went, into the night. I mentioned this to my accountant right away and he advised me to take out the V.A.T. content of £500 and declare it, just to be safe, meaning that the pony-tailed little git had just, in effect, lost me around £85, plus the standard tax on top. I just loved the hypocrisy of it all. The V.A.T. man makes sure that we pay up, but he's not so keen to do so himself.

David's business partner, Dick Fisher, was married to a woman named Cynthia, who worked for a company called Altecnic, near Stafford, that were distributors for a large Italian firm called Caleffi. Altecnic had heard about my caricaturing skills via Dick, and offered me a job at the

205

Interbuild show at Birmingham's NEC. I spent several days drawing their customers, and one day, a group of smartly turned-out Italians arrived on the stand and stood watching me drawing. One of them, a young man called Luca Bonini, asked if I was willing to draw for them in Milan. I told him that 'willing' wasn't a big enough word for it. I was thrilled at the prospect. Little did I know that I would become almost one of the family and work there for over ten years. Luca and I are still friends, and I still go on holiday to his town and con him into buying us dinner while we're there, being as he is considerably better off than we are.

Caleffi's huge factory was situated near to Lake Maggiore, an idyllic spot in the Italian lake district. Nearby are Como, where George Clooney lives, Orta, a small jewel of a lake favoured by the locals, and Garda. It is pretty much Paradise on earth. Silvino Berlusconi has a large villa on Maggiore, the dirty old devil, and Madonna was thinking about buying a magnificent place that I drove past regularly whenever I was there, the last I heard. That's just to give you an idea how heavenly this part of Italy is, if you discount the fact that you'd have to share it with the aforementioned celebs. The lakes are surrounded by the Alps, and just a few miles away is Switzerland, where everything is three times more expensive. We may have had to work hard at the Milan Exhibition Centre, which was like the NEC with spaghetti (as opposed to Spaghetti Junction), but each night we travelled back in our own deluxe tour bus to the magnificent towns of Stresa or Arona, and our gorgeous hotels. The first time I saw the place, I knew I was in love.

Each day I had to set up my stall on the stand, and once I'd had a coffee and had my equipment stolen by pick-pockets, draw the Caleffi customers non-stop until around 5.30pm. On average, that meant at least 40 people per day. It was exhausting, and I'd be a gibbering wreck with drool dripping from my mouth by the end of a session. As with any exhibition event, there were all kinds of people there. One day

I was merrily drawing away when Luca popped over and explained that the next chap to sit for me had a scar on his face and was a bit sensitive about it, so could I leave it off, per favore? I assured him that this was not a problem. Almost as an afterthought, he added that the man had done time for murder but was now a plumber. Caleffi, I must explain, made central heating valves and equipment for the plumbing industry (comically, many Italians often pronounce the 'B' in plumber and plumbing). The entire area is famous for bathroom furnishings, taps and so on, in the same way that Stourbridge is, or at least was, famous for glass.

A man the size of a small Alp sat down opposite me and just grunted. I gestured for him to sit facing a certain way, and then noticed that this 'small scar' was in fact dissecting his ugly face from hairline to neck and was around an inch deep. He looked like Popeye's nemesis, Bluto, would have looked if he'd got his head stuck in a bandsaw and couldn't find the off switch. It was impossible to leave the scar out; it was his main feature. I fudged it as best I could and handed it to him, holding my breath in anticipation. He grunted and walked away, but at least he didn't murder me, and that's always a plus in my book. Quite soon afterwards a good-looking slim chap in leathers sat down, and as I began to draw him, Luca's dad walked behind my sitter and gestured in a very Italian way with his hands. First, he made a praying gesture by clasping his hands together and, raising the fingertips to his lips, he kissed them. Then he did that thing where you pretend you've tying a ribbon into a bow and you're now pulling it tight. He smiled and walked away. After I'd handed my drawing to the man in leathers, I copied the gesture to Luca and asked what his dad had meant by it.

'Can't you speak Italian yet? You've been here a whole day,' he enquired with mock severity. 'It means, of course, please Geoff, make this picture perfect!'
The sitter was apparently the current Italian Moto-GP champion, hence the 'request'.

Luca was fluent in just about every language I'd heard of. It wouldn't surprise me if he could talk about central heating radiators in Swahili. He'd chat away in his native Italian and switch effortlessly to perfect English when talking to me, albeit with a strong Italian accent. Then a German customer would drag him away to have a very technical and complex discussion about valves and boilers, in perfect German, mind, and when a Spanish and Portuguese pair arrived, he'd translate everything the German had said to him in both languages so they could understand it. I don't know how he does it. If I learn German, and I did for a while, it goes into one ear and all my 'O' level French disappears out of the other one. I often mix two languages up and get something unintelligible. I did, however, manage to teach Luca some Black Country dialect, and he is very proud of being able to now say 'How beenaya, me wench,' whenever he meets Susan.

One evening he invited me to his parents' beautiful apartment on the lake for supper. (They also own an ancient, magnificent house in a nearby village where they live in summer) Luca's brother, Maurizio, who is also fluent in English, was there too. Their parents did not speak a word of English, but we got by with Luca or his brother translating for me. That day at the exhibition, I'd asked him to teach me a few sentences so I could personally thank them for supper. I also wanted to send them some of my cat-art prints (of which more later) as a present, because they loved cats. I practised the words endlessly in my head, and I felt I was now ready to have a go. I tapped a glass with my spoon, the way people do when they want the audience to be silent, and I launched into it. Seconds later, Luca's mom and dad were staring at me with incredulity, and Luca and his brother were in hysterics. It took Luca around ten minutes to control himself. He had removed his specs and was wiping his eyes, and every time he tried to explain my mistake, it set him off again. I was horrified.

It transpired that I'd mixed up my German words with the Italian ones and created a very unfortunate hybrid.

What I actually said was, 'Thank you for dinner, and when I get home I will send you some photographs of my penis.'

His folks presumably thought that this must be a strange old Black Country custom.

In the past I have also asked for a rabbit-full of tea in a German café and told a promotion girl on our stand that I wanted her, carnally. I was actually just telling her that it was quite hot in the exhibition hall that day. A friend of mine, at the equivalent exhibition in Frankfurt, thought he'd told the hotel manager that he needed some more soap, and when he got back from the exhibition there was a tub of Colman's mustard waiting for him in his room.

While we're on this topic, my friend, Geoff Bartlett, owned a swanky French restaurant that had real French staff, imported from Paris. One night the chef complained that the duck still had bollocks in it. He meant bullets, or 'shot' as we would have said.

Every evening our posh tour bus would collect us and drive back to the lake. We'd get an hour to freshen up and then it arrived again to take us to dinner. The English distributors were there, as were others from Portugal, Spain, Germany and the U.S.A., and Caleffi treated us to fabulous dinners at a different restaurant each night. I tended to hang around with the two Americans, Bob Webber and Ed Clarke, who were from Dallas. Bob was a very funny, droll individual, and Ed was an ex-American footballer who was built like a brick lavatory and tended to shoot anything that moved and wasn't human. He was also a recovering alcoholic, so Bob was always checking that the waiter had brought alcohol-free beer for his business partner rather than the real thing. I asked him one evening what would happen if he accidentally drank proper beer. Bob gave me a look, winced a little and said,

'He'd almost certainly end up fighting and smashing the joint up.'

At the first restaurant we ever went to on the lake, the waiters served a tiny little plate of spaghetti for the first course. I wolfed it down and asked if I could have some more, as I was still starving. The waiter brought over another plateful and that disappeared too, so he kindly fetched more. Then Luca slipped over to say hello, and discreetly mentioned that it was a ten-course meal, so maybe it wasn't the best idea to have four portions of the first course. I felt such a fool, but that was nothing unusual for me, it has to be said.

Each spring we alternated between the Milan and the Frankfurt Exhibition Centres. One evening, when we were in Germany, we went to a huge bierkeller-cum-restaurant where we were served steins of beer by ladies in traditional dress. The house speciality was a frying pan with a huge sausage in it that was presented as a spiral, like a Catherine wheel, so that it filled the pan. It looked quite formidable when it was curled up, and if you unwound it, it was as long as a garden hose and took around three weeks to eat. We all sat on huge trestle tables, eating our mile-long sausages and drinking lager from stone vessels that held at least a gallon. On a distant table, a crowd of Germans began singing typical German drinking songs, so the English folks, being defiant by nature, began to sing too, which encouraged the Italians to do likewise. I don't know if you've ever seen Casablanca, but for a moment I thought World War 3 was about to kick off. Bob and Ed, the Americans, had been to see clients and arrived late, which is somehow fitting.

After dinner, we all went for a walk to the river, and we watched with interest as a group of German fishermen were winding in a giant net. It was extremely slow progress and the nets seemed full, so we all hung around for the best part of an hour, keen to see what they'd caught. Well, there was nothing on TV. As spectator sports go, it was bloody boring, but none of us wanted to miss seeing the catch. Then one of the

German fishermen wandered over to us and asked why we were so fascinated in seeing some old fishing nets being washed and stored for the evening.

Ed, always one with a load of anecdotes up his sleeve, told us about his new speedboat, moored on the lake where he owned a log cabin, just outside of Dallas. The boat had cost him around $100,000, and he'd fitted a shrimp net to it. His friend assured him that if he whizzed around the lake for an hour or two, he'd catch a huge netful of shrimps and crayfish, which they could then barbecue that evening. This he did, and meanwhile the family were cooling the beers, preparing the salad and lighting the barbecue. The mighty speedboat pulled up to its mooring point, right outside the cabin, as the partygoers looked on with anticipation. Ed lifted the net out of the water and saw his first ever haul of shrimps. Actually, the use of the plural there was misleading. He had wasted two hours and gallons of fuel to catch one, solitary, scared little shrimp. Ed felt so sorry for it that he threw it back into the water and they ordered pizzas instead.

Ed had a friend by the name of Ron Gard, whose hobby was collecting rare decoy ducks. These, for the uninitiated, are carved wooden ducks which are used to lure real ducks onto the lakes, so that Ed and his friends can shoot the crap out of them. Ron had a $9,000,000 collection of these things. Yes, you did count the noughts correctly; nine million dollars' worth of carved wooden ducks. Ed wanted to commission me to travel to Dallas, photograph some of the rarest ducks in Americana settings and then produce four highly-finished watercolours which would then be made into limited edition prints. The Americans were, apparently, mad for these ducks, which were regarded as important folk art, and if one was carved by Elmer Fuddbucket in 1888 it could fetch a quarter of a million dollars at Sotheby's, New York. Ed reckoned the prints would do well, if he advertised them in huntin', shootin' and fishin' magazines all across America, and he'd make a

211

tidy packet. He was already a millionaire, but apparently, he wanted a bit more. I duly packed my bags and headed for Dallas, as you do. I may have missed the 'Who Shot J.R.?' episode when Susan's waters broke, but I was making up for it big-time now!

I had a terrific time there, it has to be said. I stayed at the log cabin in a large bunk-house in the grounds, where Ed put his mates when they came to use his clay-pigeon shoot in the woods that he also owns. I must say, at this point, that I am SO anti-hunting that I had to bite my lip sometimes when they talked about killing deer, bears, ducks and anything else that they could think of, but in spite of Ed being my polar opposite in virtually every department, we somehow got on really well, though I was far more like Bob Webber, his business partner, in nature. I got the Dallas guided tour, of course. We drove to the precise spot where Kennedy was assassinated, and I saw the grassy knoll and everything. We also drove past Southfork, but Ed couldn't remember who'd shot J.R. so he wasn't much use. I purchased proper Woody and Buzz 'Toy Story' figures for Laura, and, while I was staying at the lake, I had my very own quadbike to get around on. We visited Ron Gard and photographed his beloved ducks, and I had to wear white gloves before I was allowed to touch them. His house was FULL of ducks. It was bizarre. Back at Ed's holiday cabin I arranged some of Ed's own humble $3,000,000 collection of decoy ducks in folksy settings and took loads of reference pictures. One composition called for an old chunk of wood to sit a duck on, so I went down to the lakeside to collect a few logs I'd seen strewn around there. I lifted one promising-looking log and a huge rattlesnake reared up and hissed at me. I found that this worked wonderfully well as a laxative. I beat a hasty retreat and Ed decided to treat me to a clay pigeon shooting lesson to take my mind off nearly being killed by a serpent. I'm not boasting, but you can call me Annie Oakley from now on, and I don't mean because I am transitioning and now want to identify as female. Then we went out for a pizza in the evening and the waitress asked me what I wanted to drink. I asked for a lager, and she seemed shocked. The entire area was in the bible belt and was also a no-alcohol zone. Can you imagine that in England? I was climbing the walls by 9pm like a drug addict going cold turkey. I never realised that I was that kind of artist. The problem seemed to be that I could easily do without a drink until someone told me I couldn't have one.

One of Ed's young friends arrived and was really curious to see what a real-life Englishman was like.

'I hear you don't have guns in England,' he said, with an incredulous tone to his voice. I confirmed that this was largely true. He shook his head and said, 'Well I'll be darned. What on earth do y'all do with yourselves?'

I returned to England and began work on the paintings. Three months later, the prints were made and signed, and I shipped them to Dallas. They were lovely, I have to say. We designed a nice press ad, and Ed placed it in just about every relevant magazine in America. I daresay some of you will sense another 'solitary shrimp' moment coming up here. We sold the grand total of 12 prints. It turned out that, whilst your average American is mad about decoy ducks, this doesn't extend to liking paintings of them. That's a different kettle of shrimps altogether. You live and learn.

I went on to draw caricatures for Bob and Ed's company at the exhibition centre in Atlanta, and I would continue to visit Lake Maggiore as a caricaturist for ten more years. I also painted portraits of Mr Caleffi's grandchildren during that time (which you can see in the picture section of this book), and even attended Luca's wedding to Elizabetta. I still visit the area fairly regularly, but now, just as a tourist. It is my second home, and nowadays Susan comes with me, and she loves it too.

I was enjoying working in my new little studio, and now that Laura was at school, Susan was finally able to go back to

Dunn's. She'd put the baby disaster behind her and was moving on, but she did make an appointment to see a consultant about the possibility of having another child. He squirted some blue fluid into 'her tubes', whatever they are, and then he examined the scans. Apparently, the tubes were blocked and the chances of having another baby were extremely slim without a lot of 'poking and scraping', as he put it. I explained that I was perfectly willing to do lots of poking, but I don't think that's what he meant. Susan seemed satisfied with this answer and discontinued that line of enquiry. She had one healthy child, she said, and that would have to do.

Then something quite remarkable happened. The blue fluid that the consultant had used must have been Toilet Duck, because it unblocked her tubes. We weren't using contraception because she wasn't able to conceive anyway, only now, she was, but we didn't know. She became pregnant again, and nine months later, Jamie Finn Tristram arrived, all 9Ibs 1oz of him, the big bugger. When we compared his first photograph with the one we took of our baby David, they were identical in every way, and even though it's utterly silly, I like to think that our little David came back and had another go – a reincarnation if you like, only with a name-change. The names Jamie and Laura were my idea. I wanted simple, Celtic names that wouldn't embarrass them when they grew up, and would go well with our unusual, ancient Celtic surname. The Finn bit was Susan's idea. At the time she was madly in love with Neil Finn from Split Enz, and later, Crowded House. She actually wanted to call our new baby Neil, but I wasn't having any of that nonsense. As a final footnote to all this, baby David would have been 30 this year.

We were halfway through the 1990s now and things were going in the right direction. Laura had a little brother to fuss over, work was still plentiful and I wasn't paying rent for offices any more. I'd sold my lovely Martini Porsche to Glynn

Edwards and bought a blue one, which was followed by a shiny red one. Jeez, I realise how shallow this makes me sound now. Glynn and I did an awful lot of caricature events together over the years, but on one occasion, he asked me to work in London with him and I couldn't make it. He did the job by himself, and on the Monday morning, he rang me to tell me how the evening had gone. Apparently, it was a very swishy affair at a Mayfair Art Gallery, and many of the guests were very camp indeed. A couple of men, who had already been drawn by Glynn, suggested he now drew David, whoever David was. They led him into another room, and there, sat chatting to friends, was David Hockney. Glynn sat down next to him and drew his caricature, and Hockney reciprocated with a quick doodle of Glynn. As soon as Glynn got home, he decided to get a valuation from a posh auction house on this five-minute sketch. It was, conservatively, they said, worth £12,500.

In the background, my radio was playing 'It Should Have Been Me' by Yvonne Fair. I snatched it off the shelf and whacked it against the studio wall.

I was still working for Swinford Motors, who were now sponsoring Worcester Cricket Club. Jack Edmonds, John's father and the chairman of the company, was friendly with Ian Botham, and they had supplied him with a Mercedes Benz as part of the sponsorship. Steve and myself were asked to organise a photographic session at Peter Moss Photography, Halesowen. A Minerva blue convertible Porsche 911 was driven into the studio, and Ian was photographed in his cricket gear alongside the dream car by my lifelong friend, Nigel Reed, a loveable village idiot from Bristol. His accent is quite similar to that of the rustic farmer on his tractor whom I mentioned when recalling the 'Legendary Electrocuted Testicles Incident'.

This concluded, I asked Ian (a lovely chap, regardless of what you might have heard, by the way) if we could pop

215

outside so that I could take another photograph of him for a caricature illustration that Swinford needed. We strode out into the sunshine, and almost immediately, we stopped the traffic, or rather, he did. People instantly recognised him and shouted 'Beefy! We love you!' A double decker bus, loaded with passengers, ground to a halt, and passers-by waved and yelled.

It couldn't have been much more dramatic had it been Paul McCartney.

Chapter 17

Just when things were beginning to settle down, we were beset by a series of awful tragedies. My friend Mike Timmins became seriously ill with hepatitis C, an illness that had dogged him for a few years. He'd often had to spend weekends in hospital due to this evil disease, but I didn't realise what a state he was in. One weekend, he was rushed to the Queen Elizabeth Hospital, Birmingham. He was placed on a ventilator, surrounded by his family, and he never regained consciousness. His beautiful, gentle-natured, funny young Liverpudlian wife, Susan, and the twin girls, Jennifer and Elizabeth, were devastated by Mike's death, aged just 33. To make things even worse, Susan was expecting a third child – one that Mike would never see. He was one of the best airbrush artists in the country, in my not-so-humble opinion, and destined for great things. This was unbearably cruel in so many ways. I'd experienced the death of grandparents, and that was awful but sort-of expected, whereas this was a total shock, the first of my young age-group to die. I attended the funeral in Sedgley and I was so distraught, I could hardly speak to John Brierley, the kindly Foundation tutor who'd come to pay his respects, because every time I tried to, my lips began quivering and the tears started again. I was in such a state. I had lost my best mate in the Art world, and the world had lost a brilliant artist and a truly gentle, likeable soul who was loved by all that knew him.

Then my grandmother, Bertha, died at a care home in Wollaston, just a street away from our house, on the 13th March 1998. She was 90 years old and had dementia. We knew something was wrong several years before, when she refused to undress for bed in front of her TV because she thought the people in the telly were watching her. At the care home she would spend hours 'polishing work surfaces', because as a young lady she was in service to a wealthy chain-making family – all very Upstairs-Downstairs – and now she was reliving her past. My poor mother had been walking up the gruelling hill that was Quarry Bonk High Street every morning to look after Bertha, walking back home, doing her own housework and shopping, and then repeating the trip each evening to make sure her mother was okay, before returning, exhausted, for an hour in front of the TV before bed. This continued until she was so wiped out that the care home became her belated, albeit reluctant solution. My dad, meanwhile, had been doing exactly the same thing for his mother, Elizabeth, until she shuffled off her mortal coil a decade before in 1987. I never once saw that lady smile or have fun. Her death certificate listed, amongst other things, 'Chronic Depression'.

Shakespeare once wrote, 'When sorrows come, they come not single spies but in battalions.' Lesser mortals often say that trouble comes in threes.

My dad had already suffered a ruptured aneurysm which forced him to retire early. Thankfully, he survived it by the skin of his teeth, after a doctor at Russell's Hall Hospital finally, at the 11th hour, realised what it was. Oddly, I watched an episode of E.R. around that time, and when the emergency patient was examined by George Clooney, Noah Wyle or whoever it was, and was made aware of the exact same symptoms that my dad had described to *his* doctor, the TV doctor shouted immediately, 'Get this man to surgery, his aorta is about to burst!'

The Russell's Hall doctor, however, didn't have the foggiest idea, and initially told my dad to take a couple of paracetamol tablets. After the last-minute emergency operation that saved my dad's life, the surgeon showed him a Y-shaped mesh tube that he'd fitted within the aorta so that the artery could grow around it and repair itself. He also told my dad how much they cost, which was a hell of a lot, apparently. Len told the surgeon that he could probably have got them cheaper from B&Q, or failing that, he could have made one for himself at work. Maybe Len should have been running the NHS. He'd have certainly put a stop to all that waste that we keep hearing about.

Dad was never quite the same after that operation, and a few years later he was diagnosed with emphysema, which has to be one of the cruellest of the diseases in our benevolent God's repertoire. He ended up hooked to oxygen cannisters which helped his failing lungs to breathe. The hospital visits became more frequent, and he died during one of them, in distress and alone, just after my mother had left at the end of visiting time. I was a regular visitor, as you can imagine, but I couldn't go that particular evening due to a work commitment. Imagine how that has haunted me ever since.

I cannot adequately describe the effect his death had on me, or on my brother for that matter. The funeral was awful. I have just tried to type that part, and I've had to erase it. I know it's supposed to be cathartic to get it out of my head and on to paper, but it took me so long to get over our beloved dad's death that I really don't want to open that wound again. Once more I find myself dabbing moist eyes as I sit at the keyboard, some 19 years later, and I really can't drag myself through that again. Besides, I wanted to make you all laugh with this memoir, not depress the pants off you. Let's just say that he was one of the finest people I ever met...shit, here I am again with the waterworks. Move on.

I did warn you that I knew 'Hamlet' inside out, didn't I? Well, he was criticised by his wicked uncle, Claudius, the new King, for grieving too long for his father, which was a damned cheek, considering that it was he who murdered him. Claudius deemed it to be 'not natural'. Well, I struggled to get over it too, though I consider it to be perfectly natural. My counter argument was always that people who grieved less than me simply didn't love their dad as much as I did. This was a completely different scenario to losing a 1-day old child that I didn't know. I had 60-odd years of wonderful memories haunting me and it broke my heart. I sank into a depression, and suddenly I knew what Granny Elizabeth felt like. It wasn't an all-consuming depression like hers, however, but more like a dull, aching, empty void that wouldn't go away. I got up, shaved, worked, joked with colleagues, and ate, but there was no joy in my life. I'd be given some prestige job or other; an album sleeve for a famous band, a set of commonwealth postage stamps maybe, and once-upon-a-time, I would have been thrilled, but during that dark period I greeted it all with the same enthusiasm that I felt when designing a deadly-dull double-glazing leaflet. There were no peaks and no troughs in my life. Everything was monotonous and flat. It was like moving from the Highlands of Scotland to live in Holland. Hamlet once told his friend, Horatio, that while most people saw a magnificent sky full of beautiful clouds when they looked heavenwards, he just saw a foul pestilence of vapours. Well, that sums it up exactly. I would pack in working as soon as I deemed it acceptable, often at around 3.30pm, go to bed and sleep just to numb the pain, waking up at 8pm for my bottle of Shiraz and dinner. I found the time between work and Shiraz-o'clock was a kind of No Man's Land, so I simply slept through it in order to make it pass more quickly.

As soon as dinner and the bottle were finished, I wanted to sleep again and put an end to another awful day. I must have been great company for Susan.

I had been to see my friend and G.P., Dr John Firth, about a minor ailment, the name of which eludes me, and he recommended that I took Omega 3 fish oils. He added that, if I were lacking that particular vitamin, the effects on my under-performing brain might be beneficial too. I think he was aware that I wasn't my usual, jovial self.

I took those capsules for around three weeks, and then something quite remarkable happened (and no, this book is not sponsored by Boot's). It was as if a cork in my head had suddenly popped, and a great eruption of creativity was bursting forth like champagne on a Formula 1 podium. I instantly felt better and was putting in a full day at work again. Out of the blue, apropos of nothing, I had the urge to write a comedy novel... in short, I'd got my mojo back, whatever one of those is. Instead of slinking off to bed, I sat down at the old keyboard and began writing a story called 'A Nasty Bump on the Head', which was a fictional effort based on my experiences at junior school. Incidentally, for my seven readers out there, I chose that title because I'd heard that Roald Dahl had never written a thing until he received a nasty bump on the head, which somehow turned his dormant brain on, bigtime, and the rest is history, as they say. My book was about a character who likewise received a hefty blow to the cranium, but the title had a double-meaning. It also referred to my new-found verve and creativity.

I spent most of my spare time writing that book, and to say it was cathartic is a huge understatement. I sat laughing my head off as I wrote it, to the extent that Susan often feared for my sanity. Suddenly, she was longing for the days when I'd just fall asleep upstairs and give her some peace. I never bothered to try and find a publisher, because part of the fun was to learn how to set up my own, mini publishing house, which I called The Drawing Room Press. This was so-named because I wrote my books in my art studio, which was also the room where I drew pictures. I love puns and wordplay, me!

I painted my own book cover, naturally, and got Steve Jolliffe to do the graphic design. I asked my brother's advice about specialist book printers, as he'd had to get several of his playbooks printed in the past. I also researched how bookshops were able to order books via the ISBN number, and how registering my book with Nielsen Book Data would make my publication official, meaning that the National Library would request a copy for posterity. Registration also guaranteed free ads on Amazon. It was all a very steep learning curve, but I needed a new hobby to keep me awake between the hours of 5 and 8pm, and this was it. Like most things that I enthuse about, I tend to throw body and soul into it and become obsessed, a bit like Mr Toad from Toad Hall only marginally better looking.

The first book went down extremely well, and there is no thrill to compare with discovering that lots of total strangers have ordered a book that you have written. I decided that my next attempt should feature the same protagonist, David Day (named after my brother, and the surname was short for daydreamer). They say 'write about what you know', so next, I came up with 'Monet Trouble', which echoed my time at Tipton Grammar and Wolverhampton College of Art. The basic premise of the story is that my imaginary baddie, Lord Hickman, has commissioned David to forge a Monet, which is then substituted for the real one which hangs in the Lord's stately home. Hickman is planning to leave his wife - who holds the purse strings - for another woman, and he wants the money from the Monet, which actually belongs to his wife, in order to finance his new lifestyle. Unbeknown to Hickman, his wife has also asked an artist to forge the Monet, as she suspects, quite rightly, that her husband has similar plans. And then it gets even more complicated.

My comedy hero was and is Pelham Grenville Wodehouse, whose beautifully elaborate, farcical plots with their hilarious set-pieces have always been my inspiration. I remember, in my first book, deciding to have Mrs Kettle lying dead beneath her open till with a huge bump on her head, and wondering what might happen next. I asked myself, what Wodehouse would have done, and my answer was that, every time David entered the shop, throughout the entire book, he would constantly find the same woman dead beneath the till, even after her funeral had taken place. Then all I had to do was work out how that could feasibly happen. Seemples, as those pesky meerkats are always saying.

My next book was 'Vincent Gough's Van', surely the best title for a comedy novel ever, and that was David at art college again, solving a murder mystery. The entire plot was a joke version of Hamlet set in Wolverhampton, circa 1972, and I don't think it dawned on anyone that it was a reworking of the Shakespeare play, which shows how well-read my readers are.

Actually, that brings up a very interesting point. I have a nice bunch of readers (isn't BUNCH a funny word, by the way?) who collect the books that I write, which is extremely gratifying, and many of them tell me that they'd never read a book in their lives until someone foisted one of mine onto them and nagged them into reading it. These people then went on to collect every book of mine, bless 'em. I think a lot of folks are frightened by books. They fear they are too intellectual, in the same way that they fear the opera, the ballet, or Shakespeare. (Actually, I'm with them on Opera and ballet!) They were usually handed one of my comedies by a friend, and promised that the areas and landmarks mentioned in the story are places they will know well, and this, I'm sure, is the bait that lures them in. Then they begin read to a chapter of something that's more akin to 'Trains, Planes and Automobiles' than 'War and Peace', and they find themselves laughing out loud at set-pieces – an embarrassing moment, a piece of slapstick, a bizarre sequence of events maybe - something they see in their mind's-eye, like a clip from a comedy film. Then they relax a little and wonder what their fear of reading was about. Books ARE for them after all, and they want more of the same.

In other words, my books appeal to folks who don't read.

I think there is a huge gap in the market there, and I've even come up with the catchphrase, 'Geoff Tristram, the man who writes books for people who don't like reading books.'

The trouble is, book publishers are always looking for the subtle, exquisitely-written masterpiece of gloom, angst and depression, and they fail to realise that there's a massive untapped market out there for the lightweight, daft Ealing Comedies like the ones that I write; laugh-out-loud situations with maybe the odd poignant or reflective moment. Film makers get the idea, but the book people are lagging someway behind. A lot of best-selling novels are about undiluted misery. Don't get me wrong. I adored the Khaled Hosseini's 'Kite Runner' and 'A 1,000 Splendid Suns', tragic as they are, but where's the literary equivalent of 'Father Ted' or 'Fawlty Towers?'

All this has probably given you the erroneous impression that I'd packed in painting. Far from it. Writing was my hobby, painting was my job. I was still caricaturing my way round the world (good idea for a future retirement project there!) and working for my usual clients, plus a few new ones. A Birmingham company by the name of The Gift Business, headed by my old friend Trevor Jones, who used to work for Birmingham Art Gallery, asked me to paint them a cute cat sleeping on a bookshelf, which they intended to use on multiple products such as diaries, jigsaws, prints, collector's plates and so on. I painted the picture, my first ever of a cat, and everyone seemed to like it. It certainly made the Gift Business a lot of money, but naïvely, I had sold them the original and the copyright for £1,000, which meant that my involvement in it was over, regardless of how much money it made. The success of that image was duly noted by companies such as Spink, Wedgewood and Royal Doulton, and soon they were asking me to create cat images for their collector's plates. I was also busy painting more of the same for The Gift

Business. Before I knew it, I was 'An International Cat Artist', even though I didn't even own a cat.

Adverts for my plates were being featured in the Sunday colour supplements, along with the typically gushing prose that accompanied the image.

'This exquisitely detailed painting of Marmaduke, an adorable cat who's taking a catnap on his master's bookshelf, was created by one of the World's premier cat artists... handcrafted with a 24-carat gold border to beautify and enhance your home... pay no money now, but we'll eventually fleece you for £200 over a 3-month period.'

You'll have seen this tosh before, I'm sure, but it's all rather weird when it's you they're talking about. The good news is that I learnt my lesson from the Marmaduke painting. I was now telling the ceramic companies that I wanted to retain the original artwork and the copyright, so that I could create other uses for the 25 or so cat paintings I had amassed, once the initial useage, i.e. the collector's plate, had run its course. For those of you who are not *au fait* with the rules of illustration - and why would you be? - the illustrator's fee is for the right to *use* a painting, not to own it, unless of course this is agreed beforehand. Once the picture has been scanned and used on the product in question, the original must be returned in good condition to the artist, who can then sell it as wall decoration only, thus giving him or her another bite of the cherry. The new owner of the original cannot make money out of the image in any way except by selling it on as more wall decoration of course, unless they don't mind risking an expensive law-suit. Conversely, the artist cannot simultaneously license his image to a rival company that produces similar goods, but, subject to the type of contract that is signed, the image can sometimes be used on other types of goods, which again, increases the income for the artist.

225

That's more than you needed to know about copyright, but an inexperienced artist reading this book might be helped by that brief and simplified excursion into copyright law. Different rules apply to fine art and private commissions. For example, if you commissioned a portrait of your beloved granny and I charged you £5,000 for the privilege, I couldn't then demand the original back from your living room wall!

Trevor Jones was a very nice chap, and we got on really well, to the extent that we regularly went out as a foursome for dinner. In fact, can I take this opportunity to blame him for my red wine habit? I drank white before he nagged me to try it, and I've been trying it regularly ever since. Trevor was borderline posh and rather dry, but always amusing. As the business got bigger, he was forced to delegate, and I was informed that I would be briefed on jobs by another chap in future. This all went terribly wrong, so for once I will be diplomatic and refer to this new fellow as 'M', a bit like they do in James Bond movies.

'M' was one of those people who spoke with such convoluted sentence structures that the unfortunate listener would be either insane or asleep within minutes. Possibly both. He would blather on, adding so many commas, colons, semi-colons, sub-clauses, N-dashes, M-dashes, hyphens, bracketed sections and then more brackets within brackets within brackets, that after the first part of the sentence you literally couldn't fathom where you were, and death by cyanide pill seemed like the best alternative. The trouble was, he had to meet clients and talk to them about my work, and half the time they just gave up after five minutes and went somewhere else instead. I remember a couple of incidents where he took the client to the edge of reason. The TV programme, 'They Think It's All Over' had seen my snooker caricatures and wanted me to draw some spoof cigarette-card caricatures for their Christmas annual, featuring famous sportsmen and women. Nick Hancock, the presenter of the TV show, was to write the deeply sarcastic text on the back of each cigarette card. The whole annual was a wonderful spoof of the old schoolboy's annuals of the 50s, with excellent copies of Beano and Dandy favourites such as Lord Snooty and Chums, Desperate Dan and so on. I was so looking forward to it, I can't tell you. The company wanted to brief me directly, but 'M' wouldn't allow it. Instead, he drove them mental with rules and regulations, clauses and sub-clauses, indecipherable gobbledegook and 30-mile-long sentences, that they gave up and decided to try elsewhere. I rang them, begging for the job, and asked them not to think any of that was my doing. They reluctantly agreed to proceed but insisted that they dealt with me exclusively. 'If we never, ever have to talk to that clown again', they added, 'it will still be far too soon for us'.

'M' eventually branched out on his own as a picture licensing agent. He immediately probed me for new contacts, as he didn't seem to have many. I helped him out, and one of the many, many contacts I gave him was Embassy World Snooker. It transpired that he had informed Embassy that he was my sole agent from that point on, so any work had to be channelled through him. Embassy did as they were told, not realising that this was a complete, utter, despicable lie. So full marks for guessing which was the very first job they passed to 'M' instead of handing the client my own phone number, as they previously always did. Yes, you're right. The TV programme, 'They Think It's All Over' who liked my Embassy cigarette cards and wanted spoof ones done for their Christmas Annual.

'M' would often visit our house and get me to submit rough ideas for one of his potential customers. He would do the same with four or five other artists, and we'd all create ideas for a pitch, free of charge. Usually, one of the group would get the work, but the others got nothing. It didn't matter to 'M' however, as no one ever got paid for the speculative work anyway. In all my time with 'M', I never landed one single job from that approach, so I gave up. Another genius idea of his was to call at my house and then ask if he could do a bit of work in our front room. He would be provided with tea, coffee, biscuits and so on, plus, in the winter, a fire. A typical visit could last all afternoon or even longer. Are you forming the opinion that I was an idiot yet?

One such day, after I'd been at the receiving end of one of his interminable sentences, I suddenly excused myself, steamed through the house passing Susan on the way, *en route* for the studio, which is situated in the garden. I went in, slammed the door behind me and screamed a ten-minute long, primal scream, which everyone in Eggington Road must have heard. I then calmly walked back into the house, past a shell-shocked Susan, and into the front room. Both 'M' and Susan heard it. You couldn't NOT hear it, but 'M' said absolutely nothing and carried on where he'd left off. Rhinos had thinner skin than that man. He was a Picture-Licensing Pachyderm.

'M's best ever ruse involved a transatlantic collaboration. He had his portfolio of English artists that he 'represented' - I use the word sarcastically. He met an American licensing agent by the name of Lance Klass at an NEC trade fair, and persuaded him that by joining together their portfolios, Lance would have access to his English painters and 'M' would likewise have access to Lance's American people. If Lance found a job in the U.S.A. for an English artist, he and 'M' would share the cash, and vice-versa. On paper, this sounded excellent, but sadly and somewhat predictably, it was Lance who was getting all the work. 'M' would inform me that my artwork was going to used on a calendar, or a jigsaw, or what-have-you in the U.S.A., but strangely, nothing came to fruition. Each time I enquired, 'M' said the job had fallen through.

Then, one day I saw Lance's email address online, so I sent him a note to ask why none of the jobs had materialised. Within seconds, the man was on the phone to me. I reeled off around 6 projects that 'M' had said were not going ahead, and guess what? They had not only happened, but 'M' had been paid handsomely for every one of them. Lance and I suddenly smelled a rat; we were astute that way. By my reckoning, 'M' had been sitting on £5,000 of my cash for a year. He was doing so badly that he was in no position to pay me my share, so instead, he pretended the jobs had been shelved. I rang my solicitor, who popped to see 'M' right away. He explained all about fiduciary care, and other such solicitor-type terms, and how 'M' was facing jail unless he coughed up. The man must have been desperate. I knew him to be a lot of things, such as boring, indecipherable, hopeless, and a man who used three crook-locks on his car - yes, really - but I didn't see him as dishonest, and I don't think, deep down, he was. He'd just got himself into deep waters and was desperate. And there we leave the saga of 'M'. I'd say that we live and learn, but maybe I don't.

From that day onwards, I linked up with Lance Klass, so now I had a licensing agent in America, which sounds very grand indeed, I'm sure you'll agree. Ever since that time he has made it his job to get my cat images onto as many products as possible all across the world, and he even pays me, unlike 'M'. When I travelled to New Zealand for a dream holiday, the first thing I saw in their equivalent of WH Smith, was a shelf full of my cat jigsaws that Lance had negotiated, and right next to them, one of Bill Kimpton's which he hadn't. I can't tell you how thrilled I was. Susan just sighed and said she was going to look at the shoes.

It wouldn't be me if I didn't have a few disasters while I was Down Under. One evening we pulled onto a camp site in our hired motorhome and were allocated a space. It was a beautiful, balmy evening and all around us were campers of all nationalities in open-fronted tents, caravans and motorhomes, enjoying barbecues and fish and chip suppers. I walked round to the back of our van to empty the chemical lavatory and immediately trod on something lying in the grass.

229

At first, I thought it might be a snake, but then I remembered that New Zealand didn't have any. The next second, all hell broke loose. The hosepipe, which the last camper had not replaced onto its stand, reared up some 12 feet in the air like an angry serpent and started spraying a high-pressure jet of water over everything in its wake. The hosepipe was going absolutely crazy. Most hoses are turned off at the tap, which is fixed at the top of a wooden stake, but this one was situated at the business-end and I'd inadvertently turned it on when I trod on it. Campers were getting absolutely drenched, and their suppers were ruined. The jet blasted through an open caravan window to my left and soaked a pair of Germans who were watching TV. A Dutch family was strafed by it as they sat outside their tent cooking sausages. It was carnage. I eventually managed to grab hold of the pipe, yank it back to earth and turn the tap off, but not before everyone with a 20-metre radius was wringing wet and wanted me dead. The next morning, we woke early and decided to sneak off before we were assassinated. Later that day, *en route* to a new site, Jamie needed the toilet and couldn't wait until we got there. He popped into the miniscule motorhome lavatory while I continued driving, and did what he had to do, before flushing it. Then we heard a scream, and Susan dashed to see if he was alright. He'd pulled the wrong lever and turned the shower on. He was completely drenched, as was our large collection of bog-rolls. Maybe this was the previous campsite's retribution for the hosepipe attack, but my own theory is that Jay inherited the chaos gene from his dad.

If you fancy another 240 pages of New Zealand mayhem, treat yourself to 'Mr Maori Goes Home.' That's as shameless a plug as you will ever get. In my defence, I sent a copy of the book, my personal favourite if I really had to choose, to Margaret Thompson, the Managing Director of Penguin Books, New Zealand. I heard nothing for several weeks and forgot I'd sent it. Then I had a lovely email from her saying that it was one of the funniest books she'd ever read. I rest my case.

As you can imagine, I was very keen to get my own back on 'M', but not by means of a drive-by shooting or by burning his house down. No, what I did was to create a cartoon character called Malcolm - oops! Did I just accidentally reveal 'M's name there? Anyway, no harm done. Not to me anyway. I came up with a pair of dimwits called 'Malcolm and Glenda', and then I roughed out some 350 greetings card jokes featuring them. The scenarios were a mixture of surreal and seaside postcard double-entendre. At that time, I had been writing loads of captions for 'Emotional Rescue', the greetings card company that specialise in those 1950's black and white retro photograph cards with the irreverent funny captions. Virtually every card company does that now, but they were the ones that invented that genre. I showed my new 'Malcolm and Glenda' ideas to Dave, the managing director, and it is fair to say that I have never experienced such an overwhelmingly positive response. Even his battle-hardened script editors, who'd seen it all, done it all, and were not easily impressed, laughed their socks off at my outlandish jokes, which of course thrilled me no end. He promised me that this would be the 'next big thing', and trialled 20 of my cards in two flagship stores for a month. Disappointingly, they only sold averagely well when compared to his other big hits, 'Norbert and Val', and 'The Odd Squad'. After a lacklustre trial period, Dave reluctantly gave up on our new project, but I was not convinced that I had been given a fair trial. A new idea, be it a comedy series or a cartoon character, takes time to seep into the public consciousness. Take 'Father Ted', for example. The first time I saw that show on TV it completely washed over me. Then, by around episode four, I was convinced that it was the funniest thing since 'Fawlty Towers'.

231

Dispirited, I took my designs back and tried them out on Jim Driscoll's company, Galleon, and guess what? Exactly the same reaction. Everyone in the boardroom was in stitches, and each cartoon seemed make them laugh more than the previous one. Jim reckoned that we should forget greetings cards and concentrate on film, as he had made a fortune with his children's show, 'The Shoe People' (incidentally, he offered me the job of illustrating that, and I turned it down because I was too busy at the time, and I couldn't quite see the attraction of it. I think I was born stupid). So now, Galleon wanted to own it, and the first thing they did was make a pilot cartoon episode of 'Malcolm and Glenda' and try it out at the Cannes Film Festival. The only problem was, the short film was absolute shit. Just awful! And guess what? Everyone else agreed with me. Then, just after Jim had bought the rights, I had a phone call from Dave at Emotional Rescue. He said he was phoning with his tail between his legs (sounds tricky unless you do yoga). In the interim period, my 20 cards had now all become top sellers, and he wanted to proceed after all. Only he couldn't, because Jim now owned 'Malcolm and Glenda'. A year or so passed, and Galleon had no intention of persevering with it, so it sat on a shelf unloved and neglected, gathering dust. Sadly, I couldn't do anything with it either because I no longer owned it. Eventually, some years later, I went back to the drawing board and came up with 'Norman and Brenda', which was sort of similar but different, if you follow me. It was my solicitor's idea to do that, because this crazy *impasse* was restricting my trade. Malcolm, a.k.a. Norman, has now had more homes than George Clooney, though in Malcolm/Norman's case, none seemed to be suitable. He did a short stint with Paper Rose in Nottingham, and Saffron cards in London. Now he's back with me, awaiting his next outing. Maybe this is the curse of 'M'. Whatever he touches, turns to shit. However, I continue to be optimistic that he'll actually make me some money one day.

Back in the real world, not only did work continue to engulf me, I was also totally besotted with writing. I wrote a new book every year, like clockwork, and occasionally, two. Most were based on my experiences and tweaked accordingly for comic effect. The characters in my books were almost all based on people I knew, which occasionally caused me a few embarrassing moments when they subsequently found out. It didn't help that I would often use a pseudonym that was almost identical to their real names, and in Larry Homer's case, I couldn't even be bothered to change it. For example, Dylan Weldon was in fact my mate Dylan Waldron (oh surely not, really?) and Katie Black was based on Kate White, my buddy from the Foundation Course with the brassiere allergy. Tony Messenger was the inspiration for Claude, the evil Head of Graphics in Vincent Gough's Van, though for once I had the good grace to change the name completely to match Hamlet's wicked uncle's.

I have now written 15 comedies and a rather swanky, illustrated coffee table book about the history of JB's Club, and despite the protestation that each book is definitely my last, in truth I can't see me packing it in any time soon.

I continued to draw caricatures at events, but I was getting a tad weary with it all, if the truth me told. It had paid well and given me the chance to meet lots of nice people, and some of them were famous too, but sometimes, when I studied my events diary and saw all those dates scattered around in there; Saturday, Harrogate, next Wednesday, the NEC, Friday week, London, the following Saturday, Rotterdam, and so on, I would quite literally (and I use the word 'literally' literally here) feel my stomach churning. I had two children now, one around 15 and the other 6, and I wanted a touch of normality. I was living a charmed life in many ways and it seemed churlish to moan, but I was getting washed out.

I'd got to know loads of famous snooker players and folks from the BBC, and suddenly, people from the tennis world

233

too, thanks to Geoff Bartlett getting me a yearly gig at the Dow Classic in Edgbaston. This following section is all very name-droppy I'm afraid, but I was just a chap from Quarry Bonk and I couldn't help but get a little star-struck.

I drew everyone who kept still for too long at the Dow Classic. Kitty Godfrey, the 1920s Wimbledon winner sat for me, as did Teddy Tinling, the famous tennis clothing designer. I drew Pam Shriver at Geoff's posh French restaurant one evening during the event, and I am ashamed to admit, I didn't know who she was. I used to draw caricatures with little action bodies back then, so I asked the lady how I should portray her. She suggested I draw her as a tennis player, which prompted me to ask, 'Do you play yourself then?'
She replied, 'Just a little'. She was actually the world No. 3 and was married to James Bond actor, George Lazenby. She was nice, and I always remember what huge feet she had.

I worked at football events too. I drew the entire Red Arrows Squad and their wives at Aston Villa one Saturday, and they invited Susan and me to Scampton aerodrome to watch them practising their manoeuvres. I always remember Gordon, or 'Red Leader', as he was known, being fascinated by my drawing skills.

'I wish I could do that,' he told me. 'I'd give anything to be able to draw.'
I was flabbergasted. His comment sounded totally genuine, and not just a touch of harmless sycophancy.

'But you are the leader of the Red Arrows,' I reminded him. It just shows that the other man's grass is always greener. We stayed friendly for a while and I drew some cartoon entries in their official Red Arrows scrapbook. Sadly, for me at least, the team changes personnel regularly, so when the new chaps took over, I lost that contact.

I met Gary Lineker at a golf event, and drew him and his lovely ex-wife, Michelle, who also asked me to draw a cartoon portrait of the family, which I did. I was, surprisingly, slightly less enamoured of Gary. By the time he sat for me, I was exhausted after eight hours of sketching, non-stop. I made the mistake of telling him I was tired, expecting an iota of sympathy, and he curtly replied, 'Then you should have chosen another profession then, shouldn't you?' I bit my lip and made his ears even bigger.

I drew Ian Hislop at The Centennial Centre in Brum and he asked me what the dessert was that had just arrived at his table. I told him it was bread and butter pudding and it was a favourite of mine. He pushed it towards me in disgust. 'You have it then,' he said, so I did. When he shook my hand as he left, it was the wettest, limpest, most effeminate handshake I'd ever encountered, which was a great surprise.

Bob Monkhouse was also there to share the after-dinner speaking with Hislop, and he stood watching me drawing the top table for some time. I asked for his autograph on my menu, and he wrote, 'To Geoff, you're the best!'. He probably said that to everybody. Bob was a superb cartoonist before he became a comedian, and worked for D.C. Thompson's who published the Beano and the Dandy, amongst others. I have treasured that menu ever since, even though, if I'm honest, I found him a bit smarmy on T.V. Much nicer in real-life.

I was working at a show in Earl's Court, London, one week when I realised that Jonathan Ross was next door, working for a mobile phone company on their stand. One of the reps asked me to pop round and sketch their guest, so I did, quaking with fear and nerves at the prospect, for some reason. I wasn't usually that bad. Jonathan was lovely, I have to say, and he could see I was a bit twitchy because a film crew had arrived to record the incident. He spontaneously grabbed my clipboard and drew me. He, like Monkhouse, was a keen comic fan but, unlike Monkhouse, just an enthusiastic amateur artist. His drawing of me was, shall we say, hardly a Michelangelo, but I still have it in a drawer in my studio. He handed the picture to me and said, 'Now draw me, Geoff. You surely can't do worse than that!' It was a kind, clever way of diffusing the situation. He then asked if I'd do a 'proper' full-colour studio caricature of him and ring him when it was done and framed. I did so, and he suggested Susan and I come to see his TV show in London and hand the picture over there, rather than trusting it to the Royal Mail, who have a habit of jumping up and down on their parcels in the back of the van before they deliver them, just to soften them up a bit. I handed it in at reception, and we took our seats for 'The Last Resort', as his show was called in those days. I looked on, astounded, as he came onto the set to much applause, clutching my cartoon of him. He proceeded to show it to the cameras, and made me stand up to take a bow. Two spotlights were trained on me as he cracked a few jokes at my expense before I was allowed to sit down again. I had previously mentioned to him a charity evening I'd organised in memory of Mike Timmins, and before we parted company, he handed me signed pictures for the auction. I thought all of this was above and beyond the call of duty. I know Jonathan took a public hammering over the 'Manuel Affair', so hopefully this will redress the balance a little. I can't stand Russell Brand, mind you!

Our paths were to cross again several years later when Penguin Books, who I work for occasionally as an illustrator, was pursuing him for the rights to his autobiography. Rob Williams, their then Creative Director, was actually a close friend of mine from the Black Country area – the Halesowen/Quinton border to be exact. He asked me to create the artwork for a comic featuring Jonathan as a superhero character, which was subsequently printed and sent to his house. Can you imagine an avid comic fan opening the mail to discover a very limited-edition comic (one copy only) that was all about him? Surely that would clinch the deal, I would have thought. Sadly, it didn't, because Jonathan didn't want a ghost-writer (good man). He, being a supreme wit and a decent journalist, wanted to write it himself or not at all, and he simply didn't have the time. Rob Williams, incidentally, is worthy of a mention himself. He began as an art student in Halesowen, but quickly realised he preferred writing. He

236

found himself a job as a copywriter for publishers Hodder & Stoughton, and was eventually head-hunted by Penguin, where he rose through the ranks to become Creative Director, handling books by the likes of Jamie Oliver and many, many more. He once commissioned the most expensive cartoon I've ever painted, a large billboard ad illustration for a Jeremy Clarkson book. Then Rob left Penguin, much to the dismay of his loyal staff, to join the BBC Writer's Team. He began writing 'EastEnders', 'Holby City', 'Doctors' and other soaps, and moved on to write 'D.C.I. Banks'. Then he was given his own peak time 9pm slot for a 3-part drama called 'Chasing Shadows'. The last I heard, he was writing something for Spielberg. Jeez! And to think when I first knew him he was a junior goalkeeper at the Wolves and an art student. I love it when one of our lot does well, don't you? And he's one of the nicest chaps you'll ever meet too, which is even better.

I'll finish this name-dropping chapter with a great tale about Steve Bull, the Wolves and England footballer who I got to know because of my work. I'd painted a couple of pictures of him; one showing the moment he scored his 306th and final goal for Wolves. Having seen the earlier of my two paintings of Bull, Blackburn Rovers wanted me to paint a picture of Alan Shearer. I was thrilled of course, but I asked if I could take my own reference shots rather than use another photographers work. Alan's manager mentioned that Alan would be in Birmingham over the weekend, so we met up and I took the shots I needed. At the end of this session, the charming and friendly Shearer asked if I'd like the boots he'd been wearing as a souvenir. I accepted, naturally, but after he'd left, I realised that he hadn't signed them, so now they were just a pair of Umbro boots that could have been anyone's. I seized my opportunity to rectify this when Alan moved to Newcastle. The team were playing at the Molineux, so I asked Bully, via a mutual friend, if he could get my boots signed. He said he would sort it out for me, so I gave his friend the boots. After the match, on Monday morning,

Bully's friend dropped the boots off at my house in a cardboard shoebox. I opened it and saw, in beautiful, neat silver writing: '*To Geoff, best wishes, Steve Bull*'.

▲ My pencil portrait of Grandad Reuben, aged 11 (I was 11, not my grandad).

▲ David and I play Subbuteo in front of the gas-fire where my hamster came alive again, like Jesus.

- Shop - window posters
- Hand drawn to your own specifications
- Very low prices

Apply :—

Geoffrey Tristram

3 ANNE ROAD
QUARRY BANK
S. STAFFS

▲ An entrepreneur at 15. My first business card.

▲ One of my many forged banknotes, drawn with my 13-colour biro in 1965.

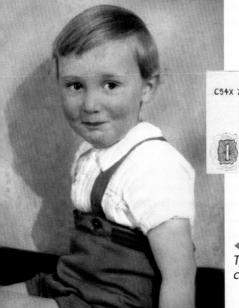

◀ A clothing model for a Tyrolean cross-dressing catalogue.

▲ Susan and I tie the knot at Dudley Registry office.

Ray Reardon

Embassy Snooker Celebrities

▲ The cartoon of Ray Reardon that led to my 25-year association with the BBC and Embassy World Snooker.

▲ Steve Jolliffe supplied the poses for my snooker caricature bodies.

◀ Tim Joplin and Laura.

▲ My beloved Boosey & Hawkes
Bb 'homing' clarinet.

▲ Me looking intelligent
and thoughtful in our
Dudley offices.

Susan, looking like a Pre-Raphaelite
artist's model, in Tony Messenger's
London house. ▶

Larry and Anne
Homer, my friends
since… well, forever!

My old caricature leaflet, featuring Ian Hislop, Gary Lineker, Jonathan Ross, Dennis Taylor, Alan Shearer and Ian Botham.

▲ Steve Jolliffe, Tess Belt, Ian Botham, Nigel Reed and myself posing in front of a Swinford Motors Porsche 911 Turbo.

▲ Jolliffe and Botham in Halesowen.

Susan in Malta, circa 1976. ▼

Len invests in 'Robert Plant's Patent Miracle Hair Restorer' ▼

▲ Luca and Elizabetta Bonini, my friends from Lago Maggiore.

▲ Susan is fascinated by the Red Arrows' pilot's cockpit.

▲ Me with the late John Elkes and Mike Timmins at a Stourbridge art college event.

Margaret Thatcher and a realistic waxwork of Caricaturist Glynn Edwards. ▼

No Other Desire
Frances Ramsay
MESSENGER BOOKS
•Holiday Romance•
RESORT GUIDE INSIDE

◀ A pair of posers, 'Orgasmic' Marcia and 'Grave Danger'.

▲ I discover my artwork in a department store in New Zealand.

◀ Me looking particularly noble in front of my painting of the Caleffi children.

Susan, David Virr and his partner, Tina. ▼

▲ David and Susan at the Edinburgh Festival to see one of his plays, darling!

▲ My lovely nieces Emma, and Lois, who currently lives in Australia. Something we said, perhaps?

◀ Laura and Jamie show off their immaculate, filling-free teeth.

▲ Susan and I pose for a Tim Joplin portrait.

◀ Sue's mom, Nancy, and Roob at the Four Stones Restaurant in Clent.

Chapter 18

Around the beginning of the new millennium onwards, I was being asked to give talks to art societies. They'd spot little articles about me in the local papers and ask if I could do a painting demonstration at their weekly meeting. I was never a fan of demonstrations. They'd all sit around in hushed reverence, watching me twiddling my little paintbrush back and forth as I explained all about tonal values, how to mix colours and so on, and it was all a bit intense. I like to paint in solitude, not with 40 folks watching me, even though I'd had to get used to that as a caricaturist. To break the ice, I'd entertain them with stories about my profession, exactly as I've been doing with you, dear reader, and bit by bit I was turning it into a comedy show. I'd also bring original paintings to show them, but the expensive frames were getting bashed in transit, and slithering all over the place in the back of my car. As if this wasn't bad enough, I had to load and unload the car each evening and put everything back on the walls at home before I crawled off to bed. I explained all this to my brother and he suggested that I create a PowerPoint presentation on computer instead. He showed me how to do it – he's a really technical whizz-kid, whereas I am the village idiot when it comes to computers. He's used to staging plays and company conferences, remember, so he knew all about stage-lighting, sound-equipment, computers, mixing-desks, microphones and so on. I compiled a talk based on what I'd been doing at the various Midlands' art societies, and called it 'Confessions of an Artist'. Once I'd worked out how to turn my new laptop and projector on, I was away!

I've been performing this talk now for around 15 years, and when I eventually decided to pack in travelling the globe as a caricaturist, it took over as my new extra-curricular, sociable

239

and hugely enjoyable way of making a few extra quid, even though the rates of pay didn't compare, with caricature events paying three times as much, on average. Recently I changed the name of the talk to '40 Years Spent Watching Paint Dry', which was skilfully adapted to create the title of this book.

I have delivered this talk locally, to just about every Art Society, W.I., Rotary Club, Probus, Round Table, University of the 3rd Age (sounds like a mysterious hippy cult but it isn't), History Society and Parents-Teachers Association that exists, and some of the societies even ask me back the following year to hear it again, thanks to the fact that most of the ageing members can't remember what happened yesterday, let alone a year ago. For those with better memories, I now have another offering entitled 'A Mixed Bag of Clangers', which focusses on cock-ups and errors of taste in the Art, Advertising and Publishing Industries, plus some hilariously awful Chinese-to-English translations.

As with all aspects of my life, some of my talks have been memorable, often for all the wrong reasons.

I did a talk one evening at a tiny Church Hall in Broome, not far from Stourbridge, to around 30 W.I. ladies, around ten years ago. I began with a rather unkind joke about Rolf Harris (and this was before the big news about his seedy sexual preferences got out), followed immediately by a totally unrelated silly anecdote about Clive Everton, the snooker commentator. Just so as you won't die wondering what they were, I'll quickly tell you. My opening spiel used to be:

'Good evening! I'm a great believer in the old expression, 'You get what you pay for', so don't expect this talk to be much good. I am a fine artist *and* a cartoonist, which is unusual. You're usually one or the other but not both, with the possible exception of Rolf Harris, who is neither'.

The Clive Everton story was about when he was commentating with Dennis Taylor at the Crucible. Having made two schoolboy errors with his calculation of how many

240

reds and blacks Steve Davis needed to win the frame, and having subsequently been corrected twice by Dennis, Clive rocked back on his chair and whacked his own head with his palm in a gesture of self-loathing. Having reached the point of no return, the chair continued to fall backwards, and Clive, who was a big man - some might say fat - reached out in desperation for something to cling on to, to prevent him from potentially falling through the tiny commentary box and down a flight of stairs. The only lifeline he could reach was Dennis's tie, which was now tightening around his neck like a noose. Sensing that he was about to throttle his partner, Clive selflessly, if a little reluctantly, let go and landed with a huge bang, narrowly avoiding a potentially fatal trip down the stairs Meanwhile, all the TV viewers heard was this:

'He'll need two reds and two blacks to win, Dennis.'
'That's actually three reds and three blacks, Clive.'
(Utter silence for 30 seconds)
'Arrghh, splutter, choke, gasp!'
'BANG!'

I looked at the audience. 28 ladies were laughing. Two of them were glaring at me.

'Have I upset you two ladies in some way?' I asked, puzzled.

'No, not really,' said one of them, lightening a little, 'It's just that, this lady here is Rolf Harris's niece...'

I gulped audibly.

'... and I, believe it or not, am Clive Everton's wife.'

I was about to perform my talk in a large church hall in Tamworth, but my satnav was playing up and it kept sending me in and out of a housing estate, which had made me extremely late. Frustrated and stressed – I am a punctuality fetishist – I parked outside a hairdresser's shop and tapped the window. A lady came to the door to greet me. I'd left the car running so I didn't have time to go inside. I asked if she knew how to get to the church hall. *She* didn't know, she said, but the chap having his hair cut did. I shot into the salon and he told me the instructions. 'Out of here, left, first right'. I thanked him and returned to where my car had been, right outside the shop. Only now it wasn't there. In the time it took me to hear one sentence from a man with a short back and sides, some git had stolen it. It contained a brand new, never used before, virgin laptop, my projector, a screen, 50 comedy novels, a pile of limited-edition prints, 100 greetings cards from my Norman and Brenda cartoon range, 100 of my cards featuring the cat images, my Crowded House CDs, my electric toothbrush and my sandwiches (cheese and ham with lettuce), a carrot, and a bag of Hula Hoops. I had 100 people waiting to be amused and educated in the church hall. I was at least 50 miles from home. Possibly more. It wasn't ideal.

Once the police had finished with me, two lovely, quite elderly ladies from the church hall took me all the way home to Stourbridge, bless them. When I explained what had befallen me, Susan gave me one of her looks. The insurance people wouldn't pay up because I'd 'abandoned' the car and left the engine running. The police eventually found the car but the other stuff had disappeared. I'm hoping the scumbags cleaned their teeth after they helped themselves to my sandwiches.

My talk for the Mayor of Walsall was also quite memorable. We were in a small church hall, next to a beautiful 12th century church, St. Michael's, in Rushall. I'd had some technical difficulties with the equipment which had made me a bit nervy, but thanks to my friends Kathy and John who stayed calm and kicked the projector till it worked, I was able to begin on time. Antonio, an affable Italian and father of the mayor, introduced me and I stood up to talk. Just as I did that, a man in the audience who I didn't know from Adam, rose to his feet and started banging on about the forthcoming Town

Cryer's competition. He must have prattled on for 10 minutes, as I stood there with a puzzled and frustrated expression. Eventually, Antonio got him to sit down, and once more I was about to say good evening, when the almightiest din began. The St. Michael's bell ringers had begun their practise session, and thanks to it being a humid, sweaty summer's evening, all of our doors and windows had been opened. I imagine this was how Quasimodo must have felt, up in that bell tower in Notre Dame.

'The bells, the bells, they made me deaf, you know!' I mouthed to myself. People in the audience were smirking now. Someone dashed out to silence the bell ringers, and once that had been accomplished, I once more set about entertaining those present. Just as I opened my mouth, a lady sprang from the kitchen and asked, 'Who wants cake and who wants sandwiches?'

I slumped to the floor and buried my head in my coat, sobbing theatrically.

I was asked to speak at a very snooty event in Stoke-on-Trent. NADFAS is an organisation that provides speakers from the world of the Arts. It's all very highbrow, and the audience members tend to be retired professors, teachers and intellectuals, with a scattering of National Trust types. It was a large event by my standards, 350 folks in a nice theatre, with plush red, ramped seating. There were giant screens on stage, like the Tory party conference, and here was I, a buffoon from the Black Country, about to deliver a talk that was more akin to 'Carry on Camping' than Kenneth Clark's 'Civilisation'.

A posh lady who was in charge told me that my talk MUST NOT last longer than an hour, as the members always put just enough money in the parking meters and liked to be away promptly. I laughed and promised to mention this in my talk, and she blanched beneath her tan. 'On no account must you do that,' she insisted. 'They will not find that remotely funny.'

I don't know what this says about me, but whenever someone talks to me in that way, it gets my back up, and some devil sat on my shoulder whispers in my ear, 'Do it! Don't let that old bag tell you what to do.'

I was introduced and I walked onto the stage, and over to my lectern. I began.

'Ladies and gentlemen. I will keep this brief. I am reliably informed that you lot are so tight-fisted that you can't bear to feed the parking meters an extra penny, even when a genius like me is entertaining you. What I intend to do it stop speaking mid-anecdote, even if it's side-splittingly funny, so you can all scramble off to your car park and bugger off home. I actually disagree with the lady down there, who said you were tight, as it happens. I think it's because all your previous speakers were so bloody boring you couldn't wait to leave.'

This could have gone one of two ways. Thankfully, it went mine, and they all laughed their heads off, and continued to do so throughout my one-hour stint, which finished, (on purpose) with half an anecdote. I looked theatrically at my watch and shut down, like someone had removed the batteries from a Duracell Bunny. The audience begged me to finish it, so I did. I glanced down at the lady, who appeared to be in shock. I gave her a look that was meant to leave her nursing a mass of contusions, at the very least, and an additional look that said, 'Don't tell me what to say and do in future.' I am such an arrogant git sometimes, but I do think I am right about that. Some people can cramp your style, just before you go on stage, a bit like the chap from a local Art Society, many years ago. Just before I went on, he said, 'I want you to keep this clean. No swearing, no smutty stuff please. We had a woman sculptor here not long ago who said, 'bloody' on two occasions and it did not go down well.'

Talk about throwing cold water over me at the wrong moment. I ask you! I waltzed up to the front and said, 'Ladies and gentlemen, that chap over there has warned me that you dislike risqué stories or smutty humour. My talk is called 'Confessions of an Artist', and most of it is like that, so I'm afraid I can't really continue.' I sat down again.

There was uproar. 'That man doesn't speak for us,' said one artist, glaring daggers at the committee member in question.
'We LOVE smutty stories,' shouted another lady. It turned out that the gentleman was trying to stamp his own, rather fuddy-duddy morality on the proceedings, just as the man who told me to 'Fuck off' at the centennial centre had done, but in a different way. In his case, he presumed he was speaking for his entire table in not wanting the services of a caricaturist, which is always a dangerous thing to do.
Nowadays, if anyone makes a beeline for me and tries to tell me what to say, I nod politely in all the right places and then do exactly as I wish.

The largest talk I ever gave was at the Spring Conference of the Women's Institute at the County Showground in Staffordshire. A lady had seen me doing my thing at a small Walsall event and asked me if I wanted to speak at an event for her. I said yes, of course (I say yes to virtually anything, me) and then she explained that it would be in front of 750 women. There was a small team of techie people to set up the stage, which had three giant screens. At the back of the hall they had a proper mixing desk, like Led Zeppelin used at the O2 arena. I don't usually suffer from nerves when I speak, but I admit to a certain frisson of something or other on that day, especially when the lady told me that my warm-up act was the Chief of Police for Staffordshire, and the person who did my spot the previous year was Michael bloody Portillo.

Thankfully, they were a fantastic audience. The sound of 750 folks laughing is truly wonderful, but can you imagine what 750 folks not laughing is like? I know that might happen one day but I try not to dwell on it.

I'll wrap up this W.I. sequence with a very funny incident that happened when I did a talk to around 40 W.I. ladies from

245

Langley, in the Black Country. At the end of my talk, the treasurer called me over to the old upright piano in the corner of the church hall that she leant on to write her cheques, and asked how much she owed me. Me being a complete idiot, I replied, 'Just £14,000 please'. She said something along the lines of, 'Geoffrey, you *are* a fool! Now how much is it really?' I then told her the proper amount, which was only around £80, and she signed the cheque and handed it over. I grabbed it, said thank you, strolled over to my car and drove in the direction of home. I was halfway down Mucklow Hill, Halesowen (the place where my old Porsche had a flat tyre and Lenny Henry saved me) when I glanced down at her cheque. It said, 'Pay Geoff Tristram, the sum of £14,000'. I looked at it several times, the way Stan Laurel looked at something he couldn't take in properly. I scratched the top of my head, drove to the roundabout and shot back up Mucklow Hill to Langley, where I found the ladies still tidying up and putting away their unsold jars of jam and stacking the chairs. I showed it to the treasurer, and she was horrified. I had, in effect, accidentally used the old magician's trick of misdirection on her as she wrote it. She quickly wrote me another one and destroyed the expensive one.

'It's not that I *wouldn't* have robbed you,' I explained, 'but having sat through the endless minutes of your last meeting before my talk began, I know for a fact you've only got £108.57p in your account.'

Chapter 19

You may be wondering what my children were up to while all this was going on. Then again, you may not, but permit me to tell you anyway. Laura turned 16 as the new millennium arrived, and Jamie was just 7. After spending her junior years at St. James's in Wollaston, Laura moved on to Edgecliff High School in Kinver, excelling in Art, as her dad had done. She then went to King Edward's in Stourbridge to do her 'A' levels, and onwards to Birmingham University to do a B.A. (Hons) in The History of Art. Personally, I'd rather do it than talk about it, but each to their own. Let me quote a small paragraph from one of her course-work books about Post Modernism, and see if you can make head or tail of it.

Following a prescription of Albrecht Weimar, Habermas considers that the remedy for this splintering of culture and its separation from life can only come from changing the status of aesthetic experience when it is no longer primarily expressed in judgments of taste, but when it is used to explore a living historical situation. That is, when it is put in relation with problems of existence. For this experience then becomes part of a language game which is no longer that of aesthetic criticism.

Ah, right, well that's clearer now isn't it? Somehow, she managed to get a very respectable 2:1 degree in this gobbledegook and then she moved to Lancaster University to do a Master's degree in Publishing. So far so excellent, you may say, but even before the Birmingham degree was completed, cracks were starting to appear. I have thought long and hard about this next part of my story, and how best to explain it, but I am struggling. Let me just say that, in spite of

247

being a rather beautiful girl who was also a superb proofreader, with the ability to plough through dirge like the stuff I just showed you and actually almost understand it, she was becoming a deeply troubled individual. She had a wonderful, idyllic childhood with parents and grandparents that loved her, but by her late teenage years things began to go wrong. I have my own theories, as does Susan, but this is not the kind of book to delve into all that. I want to keep it as light as I can. Suffice it to say that she fell apart in spectacular fashion, causing us, and her, untold grief and stress. Anyone who assures me that they have the perfect family, and that their daughter or son would never go that way, can I just add a word or two of caution? Do not shout too loudly, because life has a nasty habit of punishing sanctimonious people who are too confident about things like that. Laura has been struggling for many years. She went through a horrendous period when we really thought we would lose her, but by sheer determination she somehow managed to gain two degrees, both to high standards, whilst in the grip of something truly destructive and awful. These days, she seems to have crawled through that long, dreadful tunnel, and she can maybe see the light at the other end now, though she is still some way off getting out of that tunnel altogether. She variously lived and worked in the Warrington and Manchester areas, Lancaster, Bristol, and the lovely Portishead, and each time she had to come home because of her many problems. There were numerous addictions, alcohol-related incidents, anxiety, depression, physical illness; the whole gamut, all of which aged Susan and me by around ten years and took its toll on poor Laura. If you ever wondered where my hair went, now you know. We all hope she will get things together and begin living, because her life has been on hold for so long now. And to the people who helped to get her into this state, well, you know who you are, and I hope you can live with it, whatever part you played. I daresay you are cosy, middle-class office workers, musicians, teachers, scientists, receptionists, and bank clerks nowadays and that was just a phase you went through, but spare a thought for this pair of exhausted parents who don't cope quite as well as they might. You are free of it now, but you left behind the damaged goods for us to try and repair and moved on. Not everyone can live like Keith Richard or Amy Winehouse for a longish period and get away with it. I'm glad you all took whatever you took and survived, but look what you left us with. She was a young, naïve teenager when the damage was done, and at 34, I fear it may not be completely reparable. My best year ever would not be about being asked to paint the Queen's portrait (though that would be nice) or to be given the O.B.E. for services to Art (I can dream) but instead, it would be to see our beloved daughter get herself straight, spread her wings and fly. 34-year-olds with a Master's degree do not belong in the tiny spare room, living a semi-reclusive life without a job. I fear that one day, she will wake up and think, 'What the hell have I done?' but by then, it may be too late to make amends.

I didn't ask Laura to edit this book, because it might have been a bit too emotional for her, but she is quite simply the best, most eagle-eyed, forensic proofreader around, and I know that, when she gets to this section, it will make her cry, but I couldn't leave it out. I just couldn't. I hope she understands the difficult decision I had to make. I also hope she'll forgive me for the hundreds of typos I've probably left uncorrected. She can edit the reprint.

Jamie, meanwhile, grew into a strongish-looking, handsome lad (he didn't get either of those qualities from me) who took up cricket at the age of 9. He played for Edgecliff, his senior school, and Enville Cricket Club, and became a nifty leg-spinner who still holds the record, as far as I am aware, for the most wickets taken in one season. Sadly, for Susan and me at least, because we loved watching him play cricket, he decided to 'retire' from the game before he even reached 20. He just got fed up with having to spend entire weekends playing it, rather than the 90 minutes that footballers set aside. Maybe he'll return to it one day. A lot of them tend to, once they've got the pubs, clubs, parties and loose women out of their system. He did his 'A' levels at Halesowen College and decided he didn't want to go to University and get into debt in order to gain a meaningless degree, so he eventually became the Deputy Manager of an internet sales warehouse instead. If you ever need a glow-in-the-dark Elvis dog-collar or a set of Michael Jackson coffee mugs, you know who to ask, but hurry! He will shortly be leaving his job to work for Will Farmer at Fielding's Auctioneers, and he is quietly thrilled about it. There'll be more about Jamie in due course. I have two delightfully silly anecdotes about him to amuse you with. In case I forget, just remind me to tell you about 'the wrong bus' and 'the dead fly in the bath'.

As the new century progressed, I began losing clients through no fault of my own, but also acquiring a few new ones. Suddenly, I realised how fragile working relationships can be. I had worked for Tarmac for quite a time, thanks to Chris Reynolds, (or Cristiano Reynaldo as I often called him) their financial director. He gave me lots of cartoon work to do, which he mainly used to illustrate slides for his business talks. Chris was a nice man, and he would occasionally invite Susan, Jamie and myself to the Tarmac box at the Molineux to watch Wolves games and have dinner. One evening he invited me to a Tarmac dinner there which was to be followed by a 'humorous guest speaker'. When I arrived, Chris whisked me up to a private lounge to meet this speaker before the dinner began. His guest had his back to us and was ordering himself a drink as we arrived, so we strode over to say hello to him. Chris politely tapped the man on the shoulder and said, 'Excuse me, Steve, can I introduce...'

Steve Davis, six-times World Snooker Champion, spun round and said, 'Bloody hell, Geoff! what are you doing here, mate?'

250

I have never seen Chris look so deflated. It was his big, show-off moment and we blew it for him. It was extremely funny though, and I, in stark contrast, felt totally inflated for ages afterwards, and it really made my night. Steve Davis, I have to say, was a brilliantly droll after-dinner speaker, who reminded me of Nicholas Lyndhurst. A new career beckons, methinks!

Sadly, Chris left Tarmac, and with him went my connection. I never worked for them again. I had worked for Art giants, Winsor & Newton for years, and then a new bunch of young managers arrived and wanted to try new suppliers and new ideas – the New Broom Syndrome. Steve Jolliffe and I went to meet some of them in London, hoping against hope that this new regime would continue to use us, and we were introduced to a gorgeous young Brazilian lady who was to be in charge of briefing freelance artists from then on. We couldn't believe our luck, and we had to wipe the drool off our train seats all the way home, as we fantasised about her sexy looks, friendly nature and husky South-American accent. Sadly, all this was just skin deep, and what lurked beneath was the most vile, ambitious, nasty piece of work I have ever encountered. She made the bunny-boiler woman from Fatal Attraction seem like Mother Theresa. I am a strongish character, and can look after myself, at least verbally, if not physically, but her antics actually made me quite ill, until one day I couldn't stand the drip-drip-drip of mental torture any longer, and I screamed down the phone, 'DON'T YOU DARE SPEAK TO ME LIKE THAT AGAIN, YOU EVIL BITCH!'

Call me deeply intuitive, but I reckon that was the precise time when things began to unravel for me at Winsor & Newton. Not that I am using this book to settle old scores, you understand. I wouldn't dream of it. She was eventually sacked I think (I hope), and a far nicer chap took over, but it was still the beginning of the end for me.

So that was two companies lost, both of whom gave me thousands of pounds-worth of work every year. Next came Carillion, and I suppose I can count myself lucky that they didn't owe me a fortune when they eventually went under some years later. Incredibly, my demise at Carillion was a mirror-image of the Tarmac scenario, in that my friend John Thorpe, the Art Director, retired, and once more, my only contact there suddenly vanished like last year's snow. Now things were getting a tad desperate for the first time in my career.

Thankfully, a brand-new client arrived by the name of Ravensburger, a big, well-known German company that specialised in making high-quality jigsaws, amongst other things. I had created jigsaws for a company called Past Times several years previously, thanks to a very good idea that popped into my head one day as I was painting yet another cat image. My simple reasoning was that a lot of people loved puzzles and a lot of people loved cats, so why not combine the two? I came up with 'The Cat Conundrum', which was a picture of two cats in a curiosity shop, surrounded by all manner of strange objects. I'd purloined the basic look of the piece from Kit Williams, the famous illustrator and author. If you remember, he had very strange eyes that seemed to operate independently of each other. In hindsight, it was a miracle that he could paint at all with eyes like that, let alone be brilliant at it. His first book, Masquerade, was a beautifully illustrated piece that was laden with hidden clues, both in the text and in the accompanying pictures. A talented woodworker and a gold and silversmith too, Kit had fashioned a hare from solid gold, inlaid with precious stones, and with the help of Bamber Gascoyne, the original host of University Challenge, he buried it in a secret location in the British Isles. The book was a glorified treasure map, and before long, thanks to some excellent publicity, half of the people in Britain were out digging up Britain's beauty spots and looking for the golden hare every weekend. Each double-page spread of the book contained a page of riddles, an intriguing illustration full of clues, and a typographical border that was actually a coded sentence. It was this concept that I

252

'borrowed' – I prefer borrowed to stole – for my Cat Conundrum images. My painting of the curiosity shop contained 49 items that began with the letters CAT (and lots of items that didn't, of course) and it was framed by a cryptic border of letters, as Kit's had been. To win the prize, which was a one-off, signed and framed giclee print of my painting – well, I couldn't afford solid gold on my income – you had to decipher all 50 clues. Past Times had a chain of shops in the UK at the time, and they sold good quality art objects such as frames, jewellery, ceramics, jigsaws, books and so on, so the fit was perfect, as the advertising people say. I had been introduced to Past Times by a local charity that had occasional dealings with them. At the subsequent meeting, one of their representatives and I met one of the buyers at Past Times, and it was pretty obvious from the word go that they were pretty keen to proceed with my concept of a cat puzzle competition within a jigsaw puzzle, and a prize for the winner. The charity was angling to get a mention on the cover of the box and a small percentage per sale. I presume Past Times thought that helping out a charity as well was a decent thing to do. The Past Times buyer explained that there was £1.80 per puzzle on offer, to be split between the artist who had invented the concept and painted the artwork, and the charity, who shall remain nameless for reasons that will soon become clear. How we split the available money was up to us. The charity person began by suggesting that they would need at least £1.70 per puzzle to consider having their name on the box. Nice opening gambit! I am not a mathematical genius, but I could see right away that this was somewhat biased in their favour.

'So let me get this straight,' I said. 'You want £1.70 for an introduction, and I get the remaining ten pence for coming up with the concept and doing all the complex artwork?'

'Yes,' said the Charity Lady, 'but remember, this will be in all the shops, and your name will be on it, and it could make you very well-known.'

'Skipping over the bit about me *already* being well-known for a second, will it pay my mortgage this month?' I asked. I saw the Past Times lady look at me with a look that clearly said, 'I'm as gob-smacked as you are, mate!'

'Would it not be fairer,' I continued, to reverse those sums in my favour, or better still, for you at least, split the £1.80 down the middle even, bearing in mind I invented the concept, and each painting for the mooted series of four puzzles takes weeks to work out and costs around £3,500 to paint, whereas you are getting money for, in effect, doing nothing much.'

The Charity Lady's hackles seemed to rise rapidly at that point, which gave her the look of a disgruntled porcupine.

'We would not consider having our name on the box for less than that,' she said firmly. I could see her point. They had a nice, swanky new office block and a fleet of new company cars to pay for. Some weeks there'd even be a small amount of money left for the good cause they represented, so it was important to cling onto every penny.

I looked askance at The Past Times lady, who seemed to have made a decision.

'Then we won't have your name on the box!' she smiled. It was all so simple, I wish I'd thought of it. To say the last part of the meeting was a tad frosty was an understatement. That day, I saw another side to charity that I didn't care for. It was quite sad actually, that they were so greedy, because they could have done okay out of the deal, and now they would get nothing. There was another lady from the charity that I liked a lot, and she seemed genuine and had a true interest in the charity's work. I'm sure she would have compromised and come away with something still worth having, unlike the lady in the meeting who was intransigent and far too business-like for my liking. The charity lady that I *did* get on with left soon afterwards, because she had been diagnosed with breast cancer. Past Times proceeded with my Cat Conundrums, which became one of their top ten best-selling products for the next four years. A few years after the first puzzle hit the

254

shops, I received an email from the lady that left. She'd seen the jigsaws in the shops and said they looked good. I asked how her health was, and added that it was not the same after she left and the nasty cow from the meeting took over. I received a reply later that day. It was rather curt. It said:
'I AM the nasty cow from the meeting.'

Ooops! So where was I? Oh yes, well after Past Times collapsed, I asked Ravensburger if they were interested in carrying on with the Conundrums. They tried two new ones, which did okay, but they seemed to be far more interested in my cartoon work. My contact there was Sarah Stevens, who I like immensely, and we are nowadays a formidable team. We've also been through remarkably similar tough times in the past, which helped forge our close friendship. She asked me to illustrate a cartoon puzzle collection called 'The Best of British', which featured typical scenes from UK life. Sarah would hand me a snappy title, such as 'The Beach', 'The Department Store', or 'The Canal Boat Holiday', and I had to create a large, complex full-colour image, usually 30 by 20 inches in size, and packed full of verbal and physical jokes. Each painting usually took at least two weeks of solid work to create, and jigsaw fans seemed to love them. Later on, I also invented another type of puzzle for Sarah, entitled 'What If?' Bafflingly, the box lid shows a completely different picture to the one on the actual jigsaw puzzle, and this is because history is changed by a simple 'what if?' statement that is printed on the box. For example, one puzzle shows Leonardo da Vinci in the town square of Florence, painting a ridiculous cross-eyed woman stuffing her fat face with a hotdog. Next in the queue for a portrait is La Gioconda herself, or The Mona Lisa, as she is better known. Leonardo is turning to her and says, 'It's no good moaning, missus. This is my last one for today.' So, in my version of history, the Mona Lisa was never painted. The image on the actual jigsaw turns out to be a modern-day art gallery, and guests at a private view are looking at a collection

255

of works by Leonardo. Centre stage is a hideous painting of a lady with crossed eyes, sucking on a hotdog, which the visitors to the exhibition comment on with hushed reverence. The Mona Lisa is of course not part of the show.

I have now painted 70 or more of these jigsaw images which are sold world-wide. Ravensburger is by far my favourite client nowadays (no offence intended to the others of course), and whilst the jigsaws are extremely labour-intensive and often quite gruelling, they are great fun too.

In 2007, Embassy World Snooker and the BBC got in touch again. I had produced a set of snooker caricatures many years before for them, but now the players I'd drawn were no longer in the Top 20, with a few notable exceptions such as Steve Davis and Jimmy White. A few years after my first set, Embassy asked for an updated Top 16 set, featuring the new crop of players, but now this too was largely out of date. For my new collection, the producer explained, they wanted me to draw the players live on TV. I reached for the kitchen table to steady myself, and the terrified gulping noise I made could be heard from the end of our street.

'Oh, and one other thing,' he added nonchalantly, so as to get it under the wire without too much resistance, 'we also want you to interview the players while you're drawing them.'

It is fair to say that this caused me some consternation, to put it mildly. I could draw, yes, and I could talk for the national side, but to do both simultaneously? It was the artistic equivalent of patting your head and rubbing your stomach in a circular motion at the same time, or whatever that thing is that's difficult to do. Me, being me, I couldn't possibly turn it down, but it exercised my brain fairly solidly from that point onwards and prevented me from getting my eight hours each night.

Nevertheless, I turned up at the venue and took a load of artistic props with me in the car, with which they created a

256

'set'. They had two settees facing each other, one for the star player and one for me, with a coffee table in the middle. Behind me were my easel and oil paintings to give it the artist's studio look. I was, in effect, being given my very own chat-show, to be aired four times a day, in between snooker sessions for the duration of the tournament. Thankfully, it wasn't live, as I'd feared it was going to be. Instead, each day for four tough days, just before the tournament began, I was handed an itinerary. 10.30am, Steve Davis, 12.30pm, Jimmy White, 1.30pm, lunch, 3.30pm, Stephen Hendry, and so on, until I'd drawn and interviewed all of the top 16 players in the world. I was given a few stock questions to fire at them, and I could add whatever I wanted beside those, within reason. Luckily, I was not a newcomer to snooker, and I knew how to play it, albeit badly. I knew the terms used and how it all worked, so I wouldn't make a fool of myself there, hopefully. Also, most of the players knew me to at least say hello to, and felt comfortable, because I'd been attending the Crucible for many years. The big problem for me was drawing and talking at the same time. I was desperate to avoid dribbling and/or going all quiet because I was trying to concentrate. There was also that big black BBC camera with the cameraman in headphones behind it, and that ominous huge lens that kept zooming in and out to get the close-ups. All of this filled me with a nameless fear.

I got started, and even though it was nerve-shredding at first, I quickly settled in. I was hardly Jonathan Ross, but I kept the conversation moving as I drew, and we had a few laughs along the way. I think most of the players seemed as nervous about sitting for me as I was about drawing them, which helped in a strange way. Usually, I draw caricatures in one go, straight out of the brush pen, but because of the extra pressure of TV, I decided to do preliminary, very light pencil sketches in advance. My usual, devil-may-care relaxed pen technique was a tad twitchier than it should have been, but generally

257

speaking, all was well. Then they reminded me that Ronnie O'Sullivan was next, and I began to fret again. I'd been told, wrongly or rightly, that he was 'a bit of a moody bugger'. If he was not in the right frame of mind, he wouldn't show up, and if he did, he might clam up and not play ball. Ronnie had had a difficult upbringing, because his dad had been sent to prison for stabbing gangster Charlie Kray's driver in a night-club brawl while Ronnie was still a young lad. I had a quick lunch break scheduled, and then he was my first portrait of the afternoon session. I drifted over to the press room to see a relative of mine, fellow Black Country lad, Phil Yates, who worked for Clive Everton's 'Snooker Scene' magazine in Halesowen, and was also a regular contributor to the televised competitions as a statistician. Phil was a really good player himself, and could have turned professional, but instead chose the journalistic route. He also worked on many televised golf tournaments. By sheer coincidence (there's that word again) we are related, though when people try to explain that Phil's granny's uncle's second-cousin was married to Edna's aunt Agatha who ran the pub in Old Hill, I glaze over. He's a lovely chap anyway, and I've known him for years. I once got drawn against him in the Old Hill 'On Cue' Snooker Club knock-out tournament. I broke off and he totally fluked a 136 total clearance. I never touched the cue ball again. Anyway, Phil and I were catching up over a cup of tea, and I happened to mention that I had to draw Ronnie after lunch, which prompted him to tell me a quite remarkable story about Ronnie which he hoped might be useful in the interview. I listened, mouth agape, thanked him profusely, and returned to my set, shell-shocked by what I'd just heard. Ten minutes later, Ronnie arrived with two heavies, like he needed bodyguards to sit for a cartoon. The camera began to roll, and I nervously thanked him for agreeing to sit for me. He grunted, 'S'alright mate.' Then I seem to remember saying to him, 'Do you know I once changed your nappy?' I caught the look on the producer's face out of the corner of my eye. He seemed to be shrivelling up like a piece of fruit in one of those speeded-up film sequences. I almost expected him to become infested with writhing maggots and disappear at any moment. Ronnie, meanwhile, just stared at me with that Pound-shop Al Pacino Italian Mafia look of his. I decided I had best explain myself before he tore off his lapel mic and flounced off with his two minders.

'Your mother, Maria Catalano...' I began. I saw the cameraman and the BBC producer simultaneously look heavenwards and begin praying. '...she was my wife's best friend right through infants, junior and senior schools, back in Netherton in the Black Country. They were inseparable; people thought they were a pair of Italian sisters. After school, when I had begun dating Susan, we'd go to JB's rock club together as a foursome with her old boyfriend. Then she left to work down south as a Redcoat, or a Bluecoat, for Butlin's or Pontin's or whoever, and she met your dad, got married, moved to London and had a baby. Her accent changed from broad Black Country to Cockney in under a fortnight. We were invited to come for a weekend and look at the new baby, and they booked the babysitter so we could go for dinner.'

Ronnie, meanwhile, was still eyeing me as a mongoose would eye a snake. The film crew were glancing nervously at each other.

'I knew how to change a nappy, being a modern man,' I continued. 'Maria was busy putting her mascara on, so I changed your nappy for her. Obviously, I didn't know you were Ronnie O'Sullivan then, or rather, I did, but I didn't know you were a snooker player, which you weren't then of course, but anyway, 37 years later, we meet for the second time!'

And as I ham-fistedly explained all this, I was busy drawing him too. Who says men can't multi-task? Ronnie smiled and seemed to relax a bit. This loony artist was okay after all. He was my mother's mate. All good! I changed the subject then, and asked him a few questions about his most distinctive features. He reckoned they were his bottom lip and his Italian eyebrows. Ronnie and I were chatting nicely. The producer mouthed the words, 'Thank you, Jesus!' We'd got a decent interview from the man they feared would not participate, all thanks to Phil, my 3rd cousin twice removed, in the press room. After the camera stopped rolling, Ronnie asked, 'So you really know my mother?' I nodded with a grin. 'Very well, yeah, only I didn't know she was your mother till 15 minutes ago!'

'Then Lord help you is all I can say,' laughed Ronnie. We shook hands and he left.

After that, all the interviews went well, and I think the BBC people were pleased. When I got home, there was a letter for me. I opened it, and it was, quite incredibly, from Stephen Fry. I stared at it disbelievingly for an hour. He said that he'd been watching the snooker, as he always did (strangely, he's a massive fan of the game) and he'd been enjoying my sequences each day. He said that he wanted to congratulate me on my drawings.

To cap a perfect fortnight, I had secretly painted a cartoon of presenter, Hazel Irvine, for the BBC, which John Parrott and Dennis Taylor presented to her live on-air, halfway through her broadcast. She blushed in a very appealing way and said, 'Thank you, thank you, Geoff Tristram, I love you!'

I was on Cloud 9 for days after that. Susan reckons she actually said, 'I love it!' but I think she is quietly jealous of Hazel and me.

Chapter 20

I was still busy writing my comedies, and in 2009 I had just finished and published 'David's Michelangelo', which was a sort-of 'Da Vinci Code' spoof set in those elegant twin towns, Stourbridge and Florence...oh, and partly in Rome as well. The basic idea was that David Day, my chief protagonist for eight novels, had been asked by his mate, Laz (based on Larry Homer of course), to paint copies of Leonardo da Vinci's work on the ceiling of his new Italian restaurant venture. Laz had acquired an old Italianate chapel in the grounds of a posh country estate and wanted to call it Leonardo's, at least until David gently explained that the Sistine Chapel ceiling, which Laz wanted copied, was in fact by Michelangelo. The restaurant's name was hastily changed to Michelangelo's, and David then came up with an ingenious plan to get his art students to create the scene as a giant paint-by-numbers, to save time. He argued that Michelangelo had spent four long years on his back, with paint dripping into his eyes, and there was very little fun to be had from that. He would pay his students 50 quid each, which was a fortune to a student, and they'd have it done in no time. Besides, the ceiling was so high up, no one would notice if they'd left a few numbers showing.

There's a lot more to the book than that of course, with David discovering secret codes hidden in the Sistine Chapel ceiling and so on, but if you want to know more my advice is to spend £8.99 and buy the book.

Anyway, one evening Susan and I popped to investigate a new Italian Restaurant by the name of Michelangelo's that we'd heard about, in the unlikely location of Brockmoor, near Brierley Hill, a place that isn't renowned for *haute cuisine*, or in fact, anything. Having written a book about a fictional new

261

restaurant called Michelangelo's I was naturally curious. We were greeted by an old friend of ours, a waiter by the name of Giovanni, who used to work at Luciano's, Stourbridge.

'Just the man!' he exclaimed, giving me a big hug, as is customary with these Latin types. 'My boss wants someone good to paint Michelangelo murals on the walls, and I'd already told him about you.'

Giovanni called his boss over to see me. He was a smallish, animated livewire with a devilish twinkle in his eyes. He explained that he wanted an 'ignudo' (naked person picture, basically) from the Sistine chapel ceiling on one wall, some fluted Roman columns, and a giant blow-up of the famous two hands image that is in fact a small detail from a much larger piece featuring God and Adam, on another wall. I'd never painted a mural before, and in normal circumstances, I might have said 'thanks but no thanks', but these were incredible, extraordinary circumstances, in that life was imitating art. The only difference was, I intended to paint these pictures myself, not con a bunch of art students to do it as a paint-by-numbers project. I remembered that I had not yet been given the boss's name, so I asked what it was.

'My name is Leonardo,' he said. I gawped at him. The coincidences kept coming. 'But why on earth didn't you call your restaurant Leonardo's?' I asked. I was getting a bit giddy now.

'Because I prefer Michelangelo's work,' said Leonardo, smiling. I couldn't argue with that. I began work on the restaurant right away. The ignudo took over three weeks to complete. It looked great, I thought, but the man's willy (based on my own, some say) hangs right in the middle of where couples sit to eat, which is, well, slightly unsettling. I'm half-expecting people to start stroking it for luck, like that do with that bronze wild boar in the Florence market place. They've made its nose look shiny and golden now, with all that rubbing. I dread to think what will happen to 'The

Brockmoor Willy' if folks start rubbing that. It'll either go shiny or hard, I reckon.

The giant hands took just over a week and a half, which I reckon is going some, considering that they are 15 feet wide. I painted several other bits and pieces at Brockmoor, but all the time I was thinking, no restaurant can do well here; why did they choose this place? Leo proved me wrong. He is a shrewd restaurateur, I have to admit. The joint is heaving every single night; even Mondays. He then bought another place on the seafront in Weston-Super-Mare with his business partner, Danny, an Albanian lad that I love like a brother, but I wouldn't like to have a cage-fight with him. Weston, though undoubtedly prettier than Brockmoor, has a reputation for being a restaurant graveyard. Again, we questioned his judgment, and again, he proved us wrong. Now it is one of the very best venues in town, and just like its Black Country brother, it's packed most nights. I painted a huge, 20-plus feet long mural there, showing God reaching down to Adam – the famous scene from which the hands were taken. I even painted the cracks on the walls, just like the ones on the ageing plaster from the Sistine Chapel, to make it look even more authentic. One visitor wrote on Trip Advisor, 'Beautiful murals; they've obviously spent a lot of money on them, but it's a pity the plastering job is awful. There are already cracks appearing all over the walls, which is a real shame in a new restaurant'. I jokily replied on Trip Advisor that the author of that critique should think seriously about visiting Specsavers, but of course, I was flattered really, that my *Trompe l'Oeil* painting technique was so convincing. Visitors may also like to check out the Roman fluted columns closely. It's all an optical illusion. There are no flutes whatsoever, and the columns are completely flat and smooth, just as they are at Brockmoor.

Recently I completed work on the 3rd restaurant in their mini-chain, Mediterraneum, in Congresbury, not far from Weston. This time it's a 16-feet-long view of the Roman

Forum, circa 1750, with some 40 or so ruined temples, houses and so on, and a load of figures going about their business in the square. I don't exactly make life simple for myself, do I?

Painting the murals and writing David's Michelangelo also gave me a great idea for an invention of mine, 'The Giant Paint-by-Numbers Community Project'. I discovered that if I scanned one of my small paint by numbers conversions (the artwork that they use to print the canvas boards with, that show the segments and the numbers) and then put that into my laptop, I could project it onto a wall to any size I wanted. Then all I needed to do was to go over the projected lines and numbers with a blue fine-line felt-tipped pen, and I had a huge image that could be coloured in by a school, maybe, or a local community. All you needed was a group of volunteers who could paint neatly up to a line, and you'd end up with a very professional mural.

I was invited onto a Radio 4 arts programme in Salford to talk about the history of painting-by-numbers, which sounds extremely high-brow for a chap like me. The idea was to interview the man who actually invented it, way back in the 1950s. Max Klein, the owner of Palmer Paints, Michigan, and his artist, Dan Robbins, developed the idea and began selling the kits in 1951, and they sold like hot cakes, whatever they sell like. Klein had since died, but Mr Robbins was still with us, and lived quietly in a retirement home in the U.S.A., so he was very much the most important guest on the show. They also invited a snooty art critic, and a person who was still involved in designing the products, i.e. me. It was a real honour to speak to Mr Robbins, as I felt I was carrying the baton that he'd handed to me. I also thanked him for indirectly helping to pay my mortgage. Painting-by-numbers is, of course, awfully kitsch and chocolate boxy, but I think we all regard it with fondness, nevertheless. The presenter asked if I'd ever taken any liberties with it over the years, and I had to own up to my Last Supper/Mr Kipling Cherry Bakewell

264

incident, which had the studio guests laughing, I'm pleased to say.

Incredibly, the next day I had a phone call from the Chris Evans Breakfast Show. Apparently, Chris had heard our Radio 4 programme and told his researcher to get hold of me, as he liked the Last Supper story. Fame at last! I was told to sit by the phone from 7am onwards the following day, and they'd call me. This I did, for hours, until the programme ended. The researcher rang and apologized. Chris, he said, tended to do this. They'd run out of time, but could I do the same the next day and he'd make sure I was fitted in. I sat there for what seemed like an eternity, and for the second day running I was ignored. Once more the researcher rang apologetically. I told him that one day was no problem but two was taking the piss, and he never mentioned trying for the third time after that. I might send Chris this book to review, with a yellow post-it note attached to this page. You never know, it might be third time lucky.

It was not all bad news, however. A BBC reporter by the name of Jennie Dennett, from the Cumbria area, also heard the radio that day, and contacted me about doing a community PBN (for short) in Ulverston. She volunteered to trace off the image we'd chosen onto big sheets of primed MDF, and I, meanwhile, organised 20 numbered Tupperware tubs full of acrylic paint. We were based in the Town Hall and loads of shoppers popped in to help us complete the picture in two days. It was great fun, if a tad exhausting. Jennie organised two more such events in Sage, Gateshead, again, hugely enjoyable and successful, in spite of a mad Chinese woman who didn't quite grasp the BPN concept. She couldn't speak English, but gestured that she fancied having a paint, so one of our little team of helpers handed her a tub of paint and a brush, whereupon she attacked the boards like a deranged version of Yoko Ono (actually, come to think of it, Yoko Ono IS a deranged version of Yoko Ono), slashing paint hither and thither, as if trying to create a Poundland Jackson Pollock. The

265

security man was summoned and he had to drag her off, foaming at the mouth. Once our nerves had settled, Jen and I had to patch the picture up as best we could. It was maddening at the time, but I am quite philosophical about these things. I always say that an 'incident', whether it be life-changing, cringe-worthy, or just bizarre, serves two purposes. It is memorable when it happens, obviously, but it can also entertain us for many years afterwards, just as all these crazy reminiscences are hopefully doing now. These incidents truly earn their keep, filling the vacant holes in our lives with laughter, *ad infinitum*. I often wonder what percentage of our existence is used up by creating new experiences, and what percentage is dedicated to remembering old ones. I'm sure someone will work it out one day.

And here's a great example of that. I promised you two Jamie Tristram stories, and I must have retold these many times. He gets sick of being reminded of them, which is tough, because I don't.

Jamie had been catching the bus to and from Kinver throughout his school days, so he knew the bus route well. One day he was planning to visit his school and cricket mate, Ben Willis, and when he eventually returned home, he was moaning about the bus service. Apparently, he'd caught the same 228 bus he always caught, but this time it had gone all around the Wrekin to get to Kinver, which is normally only a ten-minute journey. That day it had detoured to Brierley Hill, Dudley, and Outer Mongolia, and he was not amused.

I was curious, so I probed deeper. 'Where did you catch this bus?' I asked. He explained that he usually waited for it outside the butcher's shop in Bridgnorth Road, but because it had started to rain, he crossed over the road and waited for it in the bus shelter instead.

I will leave you in peace for a few moments to work that one out.

Meanwhile, here's the other story. It is important to realise that Jamie is 6 feet 1 inch tall, with a big black hairy chest that makes Pierce Brosnan look like Shirley Temple. One evening, just as Susan and I had retired to bed, Jamie decided to take a late shower. We were in total darkness in our bedroom, dozing off.

'There's a dead fly in the bath,' he suddenly shouted from next door. There was a considerable pause, before I replied, 'Well, what do you want *us* to do about it?'

'How can I get rid of it?' he asked.

'Flush it down the bloody plughole, you cretin,' I shouted.

All was silent, as Susan and I lay motionless in the dark.

Fully five minutes had passed, when I heard a conspiratorial female voice in my right ear.

'He's hardly bloody Bear Grylls is he?'

Chapter 21

2014 was a big year for me, because Dudley Council invited me to stage my 40th Anniversary exhibition, '40 years Spent Watching Paint Dry', at Himley Hall, a stately home once owned by the Earl of Dudley. For those who like interesting facts, it was where Edward and Mrs Simpson used to fly to in his little bi-plane, so they could have lunch at the Himley House Hotel, and a bit of nookie afterwards at the hall.

I don't usually have exhibitions, but I thought that 40 years as a fairly successful professional artist warranted some form of commemoration, so I set about borrowing back loads of artwork from all over the country. I wanted the exhibition to be about all the aspects of my work, from serious portraiture, fine art, and commercial illustration, to cartoons, caricatures and comedy novels. I would like to take this opportunity to say a big thank you to all those who loaned me my work, especially as the exhibition was on for a massive 20 weeks, right through the summer, which of course meant that you had to live with those dirty marks on the wall where my pictures used to be. One man, who we will call 'The Shark', lent me two pictures, and then asked me to donate £100 to his favourite charity. He sent the pictures over first, and then hit me with that *fait accompli,* which I thought was a mean trick. I couldn't and wouldn't cough up £100, because money was quite tight at the time, so I sent the charity £25 with an explanatory note. If everyone who kindly lent me back my artwork had asked for money like him, it would have cost me around £2,000! I foolishly wrote in my letter to the charity that this man was a bit of a brash, forceful character, and he'd pressurised me into handing over more than I could afford, so I hoped my donation would suffice. It transpired that the lady at the charity was his daughter, and she told him what I'd said.

Let's just say that we didn't quite see eye to eye after that. There is a very interesting back-story to this which you may wish to read before you judge me to be mean. There was another reason that I was not keen to part with my cash.

This 'Shark' character had bought one oil painting from me, and he told me that a friend of his, who was not at all well off (unlike him) was crazy about Trivial Pursuit, and when he heard my Trivial Pursuit original artwork was for sale, he nearly wet himself. I wanted £1,000 for the artwork, but this was beyond his friend's means, I was told. Me being soft in the head, I let the not-so-well-off chap have it for £700 instead. Only there was no friend. 'The Shark' had invented him so that he could get the picture cheaper, even though he was a millionaire.

The heated exchanges caused by this charity donation threatened to sour the whole exhibition before it had even started, but we resolved the issue over the phone. He told me he would still lend me the pictures, but he never wanted to speak to me again. I can't tell you how happy both parts of his sentence had made me.

The exhibition was seen by 10,000 people, and was filmed by BBC's Midlands Today, with Satnam Rana. If you'd like to take a quick tour of the exhibition and see Satnam and me chatting as we walk around it, type in my name on YouTube, and it's usually the first item that comes up. So now I can advertise a 'free 40th anniversary exhibition video' with every book!

In the autumn of 2015 I had a phone call from Mike Flowers, a very old friend of mine who lived and worked in Stratford-upon-Avon. We'd been part-time lecturers together at Stourbridge Art College, but I hadn't seen him for ages. He got the all-our-yesterdays, art college nostalgia bit out of the way first and then told me that he might have a job for me. Stratford's councillors were planning an event to mark the 400th anniversary of the death of William Shakespeare on April 23rd, 2016. They celebrate The Bard's birthday each

269

year (it was also the day he died, which is a bit spooky) with processions in the town centre, but 2016 was going to be The Big One. People would be descending on the town from all over the world, and the councillors wanted to do it right. There would be the usual time-honoured rituals, of course, such as the annual replacement of the quill pen in the Shakespeare burial monument, and the strewing of Rosemary for remembrance, but this time they'd invited guests from many countries, including America, Australia and New Zealand. Flags of the nations would be unfurled in the main streets, a New Orleans' jazz band had been booked, film crews from 20 countries were descending on them, and a small sit-down dinner for around 1,000 folks was being staged in a marquee near Holy Trinity Church that was only slightly bigger than the Birmingham postal district. Oh yes, and they wanted to hand all the visitors a Shakespeare mask as they arrived, so that everyone in town on the day would look like the Bard. It was this mask artwork that Mike asked me to tender for. I must admit, I am not used to having to tender for jobs, but I knew that this was how councils operated. I attended a meeting, where I showed everyone my work, and I was thrilled to eventually be given the job, especially as I am a real Shakespeare fan. I duly painted the Bard's face from the necessary square-on viewpoint, which went down extremely well, and it was made into 10,000 masks, which the children from Shakespeare's old grammar school handed out to visitors. Seeing a whole town-full of people all looking like Shakespeare was one of the most surreal experiences of my life. It was not the day to be taking LSD - not that I tend to do that kind of thing, I hasten to add.

Before you ask, can I explain the problem we artists have with Shakespeare's features? The only picture of him that has actually been endorsed as a likeness is the rather crude etching that graces the cover of the First Folio, created by a young artist named Martin Droeshout. This was shown to Shakespeare's friend and fellow playwright, Ben Jonson, who said something along the lines of, 'Ar, that be the feller!' Everything else has no real provenance. It's not much of a thing, but it's all we have, so my brief from the council was to take Droeshout's etching and make it into a believable flesh and blood person, which is what I tried to do. To achieve this, I popped over the road to my neighbour, Ian, who has the same basic face type and no hair. Come to think of it, I would have fitted the bill too, but can you imagine the councillors' reaction if I'd been asked to paint Shakespeare and I'd just handed over a picture of me wearing a daft Max Wall wig and a ruff?

I traced out Droeshout's etching to life-size, and then transposed it from it from being slightly angled to the left to the square-on viewpoint that was required for a mask. Then I blew my photograph of Ian up to the exact size of my square-on Droeshout adaption - following this so far? – and painted the picture so that the shape and the details of the face - the likeness, in other words - was Droeshout's, but the flesh and blood, photographically-real part was Ian. Nowadays, most folks would do this on computer but I like the old ways best. The result, I have to say, was pretty bloody good.

When I delivered the artwork, I told the various councillors that, in my opinion, they had missed a trick. They really needed an official 400th anniversary portrait, by which I mean, the kind of thing you see in a stately home, preferably painted by Holbein. After several council meetings (these folks have meetings about meetings) they agreed, and told me to bloody hurry up and get on with it. The council didn't have a budget for such an expensive piece of artwork, but we agreed that I'd still own the original, and we'd share any proceeds from the sale of the limited-edition prints. I merely mention this in case any of you want one. If you do, ring me!

The first thing I needed to do was sketch out a rough scenario. I saw him in my mind's eye playing darts with a pint of Stella in his hand and nibbling a KVE pork scratching, but after more serious consideration I opted for picturing him at

271

his desk, writing 'Hamlet'. Original, I know. The Birthplace Trust in Henley Street offered to let us use the bedroom there as a backdrop, which was great, because he would almost certainly have been born in that very room. Next, I hired a costume that would have been worn by a person of his social class. I wanted an everyday outfit, not an ornate affair with a fancy ruff and sequins sewn all over it. That was far too grand, and more likely to be have been worn by someone like Sir Walter Raleigh. Once this was organised, and a date set for the reference photography, I asked my old mate Steve Jolliffe to take the pictures for me. Now all I needed to do was find a Shakespeare lookalike. I could, of course, have used Ian once more, but it meant him having a day off from the printing company he worked for, so instead, I asked my friend, Simon Millichip, who lives just around the corner from me. He has a job too, he owns a tool-hire company, but he'll do virtually anything for the promise of a cream tea afterwards. Incidentally, have you noticed that I am meticulous in my preparation and research, as long as it can be accessed by popping over the road to the house opposite mine or walking around the corner to Meriden Avenue? Anyway, Simon was thrilled senseless to be asked, and you know me, I aim to spread sweetness and light wherever I go. Hooked by the promise of a nice day out in Stratford, my trusty accomplices and I set off along the M40, only to run into an awful traffic jam. We arrived at the Birthplace late, and were rushed up to the bedroom after being warned that we only had around 20 minutes before the first tourists arrived on a coach. Simon struggled into his pantaloons and his baggy hessian shirt while Jolliffe ran around finding interesting corners and setting up lights. Meanwhile I paced up and down nervously and bit my fingernails down to the ankle. With ten minutes to go, Simon was plonked into an old oak chair, next to an ancient writing desk, both loaned by the house. He pretended to write on a parchment with a sawn-off quill pen, by candlelight, again, all loaned by the staff at the house, who couldn't have been more helpful. The sawn-off quill, by the way, was because most Tudors and Elizabethans did that to avoid getting the tip of the feather stuck up their nose. I was striving for historical accuracy, not some romanticized notion of what the era was like.

Steve, sweating profusely now, clicked away as Simon tried his best to look noble, which is difficult for him. We were forced to wrap up a few minutes later thanks to someone shouting, 'A coachload of Japanese folks has arrived and they're heading up the stairs.' They entered the bedroom just as Simon had removed his pantaloons, which I somehow knew would happen, it being us. It was as if Brian Rix was still with us.

Once Steve had printed off my reference photos, which were great, by the way, I set about the laborious task of composing the scene. It was a large picture, around four feet by two and a half feet, and loads of mini-tweaks had to be made to the photographic reference to make it work as a painting, which is usually the case. I won't bore you with all the technical stuff but it took several days before I produced the 'Master Tracing', as it's known. I ordered a posh canvas that wouldn't disintegrate after five years, from a company in Brum, and that alone set me back £120 – I was used to spending £30, max. I traced the line-work down onto the canvas and stared intensely at it for an hour, probably just like Edmund Hillary did with Everest before he took a deep breath and began to climb it. Then I took a deep breath of my own and started squirting out oil colours onto my old palette. I don't know if you are familiar with oil paints, but the first thing you do is to paint in a fairly quick undercoat layer, to get rid of the scary white canvas as soon as possible. For this you use something called Underpainting White to mix with the other colours, because it dries quickly. You also use turpentine rather than linseed oil for the same reason. Here's a fairly interesting fact for you (yes, I know - you'll be the judge of that). Oil paint takes at least 6 months to dry before you can properly varnish

273

a picture; a year is better, though you can apply a temporary 'retouching' varnish when it's touch dry. Once the quick-drying 1st layer is done, you end up with a very rough approximation of the finished thing, but it tends to look like your daughter's art homework. Then the real slog begins. I am not a quick, impressionist painter that can finish a picture in a day. I come from the Holbein school of portraiture, where you have to sweat real blood and risk serious eye damage to get the result you want. Add to that the fact that you are painting one of the most important figures to ever exist on this planet, which in turn means that the entire world will see, and bitchily criticize, your every brushstroke, and you have a recipe for nervous breakdown. I virtually locked myself in my studio. Susan slid pizzas under the door and didn't dare disturb me. She'd have varied the diet but the only thing that will slide under a door is a pizza, a biscuit or a flattened sandwich. I worked for 9, sometimes ten hours a day on that painting. I would retire, exhausted on a Monday night, happy with my progress, only to find that by Tuesday morning, the art fairies had visited it in the night and turned it into total shit. I would wipe the face (Shakespeare's, I mean, not mine) and begin again, and have several hissy fits. Then, bit by agonising bit, I progressed through the middle coats to the finishing coats, and talking about coats, why had I picked such an impossible to paint, ornate coat for him to wear? I was beginning to wish I'd hired a sack from the coal merchants instead. My advice, if you're ever considering painting a Tudor brocade coat, is don't. It will drive you to the point of insanity, and this was considered a plain one compared to those over-the-top Walter Raleigh outfits, remember. Then there was the parchment. I had to learn to write in an authentic Tudor-cum-Elizabethan hand so I could paint in the first soliloquy from Hamlet, in full: 'Oh that this too, too, sullied flesh would melt...' and mine nearly did, I can tell you.

I painted Shakespeare's actual gold signet ring on Simon's hand – the one that he lost at his daughter's wedding at Holy

Trinity Church, which was found a couple of hundred years later and returned to the Birthplace Trust. A walker found it in the dirt, and noticed the initials, 'WS'. A quick check of the parish records of that time revealed that the only person in Stratford with the initials 'WS', who could have afforded such a ring had to be the Bard himself, and this theory fitted exactly with the known facts. On his last will and testament, the bit at the bottom where he and the solicitor sign and seal the document, says, 'signet ring missing'. This, to me, is one of the most fascinating finds in history.

After nearly ten weeks, I finally finished it. I ordered a bespoke, Elizabethan-style frame from Frinton's Frames, of Frinton-on-Sea, and then inlaid a green leathercloth section that was inscribed with a quote from Cymbeline about mortality, 'Fear no more the heat of the sun…'

I don't wish to sound morbid, but I want that poem read at my funeral, if I'm ever unlucky enough to shuffle off this mortal coil. Can one of you remember I requested that, because Susan will forget.

I have to say, it all looked rather beautiful when it was assembled. I made a box to house it, and delivered it to the Town Hall, Stratford, and even that simple act was fraught with danger and tinged with farce, as befits anything that I touch. It was an incredibly heavy item, thanks to the huge frame, a solid hardwood canvas stretcher, and the protective case. It was also awkward because it was so big. I tried to carry it to the car but I was struggling and then I felt my back go, so I asked my next-door neighbour if he'd help me. Between us, we managed to place it in the car, once I'd folded the back seats down, but now my back was killing me. I rang my old mate, Mike, at his design studio in Stratford, and he arranged to meet me at the Town Hall so we could carry it inside. I arrived, parked up, and Mike insisted that he carry it in himself, as my back had got worse. Job done, we shook hands and then I drove home. The next day, my neighbour, who was now in agony, called me across the garden fence. His back had gone, and he'd fixed up an appointment with a chiropractor. I told him I was sorry, and added, 'if it's any consolation, and it won't be, I too have contacted the back specialist in Wollaston, after an awful night's sleep.'

I was just walking down the road to see this back-chap when my mobile rang. It was Mike Flowers, ringing from his osteopath's waiting area.

The lady mayor, the town clerk and all of the councillors loved it, I am pleased and mightily relieved to say, and it even made the national papers and the BBC, as well as the local Stratford papers. The picture was displayed at the council offices, and at various civic receptions. One notable event was the 'Stratfords of the World' afternoon tea at the Town Hall. Several commonwealth and ex-commonwealth countries have their very own Stratford, named after the original, and delegations from these places were spending a week's holiday in the town, some for the first time ever. I was invited to this event to tell people about the portrait. I mixed and mingled, but soon made a beeline for the New Zealanders, as Susan, Jamie and I had enjoyed a fantastic holiday there in 2007, that was the inspiration for one of my favourite self-penned books, 'Mr Maori Goes Home'. I sat and chatted to one lady who asked what I did when I wasn't painting the Bard. I told her that I was a cartoonist too, and wrote comedy novels, one of which was about their wonderful country. I then added that my brother was the senior comedy writer of the family, with 25 plays and 3 films under his belt, not to mention the accolade of being the '2015 Comedy Playwright of the Year'.

'What's his name?' asked the lady, and when I told her, she said, 'NO! You're kidding me! Not the man who wrote 'Last Tango in Little Grimley', 'The Opposite Sex', 'The Secret Lives of Henry and Alice'...'

My jaw dropped. 'Yes, him,' I said, 'but how on earth...'

'I'm in an amateur dramatics company in *our* Stratford, 'she smiled. 'We do a David Tristram play every year. He's our favourite comedy writer!'

To use an expression I don't much care for, I was completely gobsmacked.

'But enough about your kid brother,' she continued. 'You mentioned cartoons. What sort of cartoons?'

The first thing that came into my head was the Ravensburger jigsaws, so I told her about them.

'What, not Best of British, and What If?' Now it was her turn for the jaw to drop.

'Yes,' I gasped. 'But how on earth do you...'

'I'm a jigsaw fan,' she squealed. 'I've got *all* of yours!'

While we're on the subject, David, while I was lurching from one adventure to the next, had begun to make comedy films. His first two were based on his Inspector Drake theatre comedies, and his third was 'Doreen the Movie', with cameo roles by rock legend, Robert Plant, football legend, Steve Bull, and, erm, television legend, Nick Owen from the BBC. David had been filming a TV ad with a very talented local actress by the name of Gill Gordon, when he came up with a great idea. The pair of them filmed a mock documentary sequence featuring a benefits' scrounging ne'er-do-well called Doreen. The basic premise was that she'd seen the doctor, had some medical tests, and it was now confirmed. She was a Lazy Cow. She goes on to explain to us, with wringing hands and pathos-soaked close-ups, that she'll probably never work again, adding that her kids, Trojan, Tangerine and Taser have the same genetic condition, and they too will struggle to earn an honest living. David showcased his mini-masterpiece on YouTube, and it received something like 1,500,000 hits in a few months. Suddenly, he had a hit on his hands. Since then, he and Gill have staged one-woman Doreen shows all over the Midlands to rapturous reviews. She is now invited to open shops, star in professional pantomimes with well-known stars, and she has her own column in the Express & Star newspaper, albeit ghost-written by David. This, for both of them, was the perfect chance meeting. David is a genius (ok, I begrudgingly admit it) who writes every word, apart from the many ad-libs, that Gill utters. The entire Black Country seems to adore her, and, *ipso facto*, David's totally un-PC views, and she is a multi-talented actress who is not only a superb impressionist but a great singer.

If I may be permitted to return to Stratford Town Hall once more, Susan and I were also invited to another 400th anniversary event that was held there, this time full of civic dignitaries from all over the world. I was doing the rounds, showing people the portrait and so on, while Susan sat on her own up a corner, eating delicate ham sandwiches and sipping tea. When I returned, she had a daft grin on her face, so I asked what had happened. Apparently, a lady had approached her, and asked with hushed reverence, 'Excuse me, Madam, are you the French Ambassador?'
'No,' replied my wife with a Black Country accent and a face-full of sandwich. 'I'm from Netherton.'

I mentioned Robert Plant earlier, and here's a wonderful story about him. A businessman I know called Jim Cadman had an acoustic guitar signed by Robert, which he wanted to auction for one of Robert's charities. Jim asked if I knew anyone who might be interested in it, so I rang Luca Bonini in Italy. The Italians are mad about English rock bands and especially Led Zeppelin, and he offered Jim £1,000 for the guitar and the provenance photo of Robert signing it. Jim dropped the instrument round to my house, and I decided to whizz over it with the yellow duster and the Pledge before I sent it by courier to Lago Maggiore in Italy. Then I looked down at the Ibanez guitar and realised that I'd completely wiped the signature off, and all that remained of it was a black smear on my duster. I stared at that guitar, horrified, for something like half an hour. I may even have whimpered a little. I couldn't believe it. Robert had sprayed a lacquer on top of his signature to protect it, but tragically, it had the opposite effect. The ink had been sucked through the lacquer by osmosis (I think that's the correct term) and was now sitting on top of it, in dust form. I had just lost Jim £1,000 in one fell swoop. I hastily cancelled the courier and rang Luca to explain what had happened. In hindsight, I suppose it was marginally better than sending the guitar to Italy and getting an irate call from Luca to say *he'd* wiped it clean instead. At least Jim saw the funny side, once he'd sobbed brokenly for an hour or two.

They say that into each life a little rain must fall, which is a delicate way of saying that just when your life is going well, someone throws a bucket of shit at you. Susan had been diagnosed by our friend, Dr Firth, with an awful illness called Polymyalgia Rheumatica, which turns a fit, mountain-climbing woman into a struggling 95-year-old that can hardly get out of bed some mornings. The prognosis is odd. Apparently, this nasty ailment lasts between 6 months and 6 years, and then goes away. Interestingly, no one I knew had ever heard of it, and suddenly we became aware of three people who had it, including our neighbour, Anton, two doors away. Then, as it that wasn't enough, our benevolent God gave her breast cancer for her 61st birthday. The thought of losing my partner of 45 years was too much to bear, so I instructed her to see it off and tell it never to come back, or else. In true, stoic, Black Country Wench fashion, she just got on with it, even though she must have been in turmoil inside. She had to have a mastectomy, and I can't imagine how that makes a woman feel, but thankfully the disease was caught early, which is the real key to success with these things, and, well, so far, so good. I don't think it will come back. It wouldn't dare.

So where are we now?

Well, I'm still painting and writing every working day. I still create Ravensburger Jigsaws, the odd comedic auto-biography, various brands of greetings cards and anything else I'm asked to do, within reason - I draw the line at bondage and cross-dressing, though some people I know swear by it. Oh yes, and West End musicals, and I'd never, ever, get a tattoo. I hate them with a passion. Only graffiti is worse. I still give my illustrated talks (I did one only last night at Walsall Art Society as it happens). I still play the guitar, though only for my own amusement and certainly no one else's, and I get my beloved clarinet out once or twice a year (sadly, that's not the only thing I get out once a year nowadays). Larry Homer is still around, my oldest friend in more ways than one, and it seems a very long time ago that we met outside the cinema and talked about guitars. 48 years ago to be precise. Larry lives the good life now with his lovely wife, Anne, in a barn conversion in Kinver, where he spends hours in his home studio, recording music. My brother and his family are all fine, and we are still best mates that never have a cross word, even if I still haven't totally forgiven him for the pedal-car incident. Our beloved, wonderful, funny mother, Roob, is still going strong – well, maybe strong is the wrong word, but still going anyway, and she's as daft as ever. The other day David got her a Perspex bird-feeder that fixes to the window with rubber suckers. She asked him, 'Does it go on the inside or the outside?'

Susan is as lovely as ever (and that sentence stands or falls by how lovely she was deemed to be in the first place), but she could probably do with a new skeleton, as could I. We get on well and still make each other laugh, but recently she accused me of drinking too much and beating her. Thankfully it was only tea and Scrabble.

Last year saw the launch of the '100 Black Country Masters', which you may have seen advertised in the local papers. The public were asked to nominate people that had made their mark in some way, be it through the arts, or the NHS, sport or even cactus-growing, and I was thrilled that both David and I had been recognised; me for my art and David for his plays and films. I'd have been a bit miffed if he'd got in and I hadn't, I can tell you.

Peter Trafford, my old art teacher at Tipton, is also still very much with us, in spite of a prostate cancer scare. We've known each other now for an incredible 53 years, and I think he's as proud of me as I am of him. Sue's mom, Nancy, is still with us too, and she and Roob laugh like a pair of teenagers when they get together. Nancy has the hots for Aidan Turner, the Poldark actor, so there's life in the old dog yet, in spite of her wonky legs. I never realised she was the passionate type.

Ronnie O'Sullivan's mother, Maria, spent a day trying to find out where Susan lived, but couldn't, so she returned to London and they spoke on the phone instead. She invited us to watch Ronnie play in the world finals and then, most unusually, he got knocked out in the early stages, so they still haven't had a chance to meet up. Incidentally, Sue's dad, Derek, sadly no longer with us, was world champion boxer, Randolph Turpin's loyal best mate (as opposed to the rat-bag hangers on who helped ruin him), and we have a collection of letters from him that were sent to Derek, back in the 50s, that would make boxing fans drool. That's two famous world champions who are associated with Susan and her parents. Another weird coincidence.

Time marches on, and I was 64 in April this year, so I get a bit emotional whenever I hear a certain Beatles song, by which I mean that I repeatedly bash my head against my studio wall and scream 'NO, NO, NO, NO, this can't be happening to me!' every time it comes on the radio. Not that my age bothers me particularly. It doesn't concern me in the slightest, honestly! (cue sound effect of broken man, sobbing bitterly.) When I was around 40, I was actually quite a handsome chap, and I looked a bit like a young Phil Collins. Now, sadly, I just look like Phil Collins.

Anyway, here's a mind-numbing statistic for you. Having scanned my old invoice pads and done a few quick sums, it appears that I have created - and we're talking approximately here of course - some 10,000 paintings and 28,000 cartoons and caricatures since I became a professional artist, aged 22. That's 38,000 pieces of artwork in total, plus 15 books, a few of which are even well-written and half funny.

The Shakespeare portrait is now back at my house, under lock and key, so if you're well-off and you fancy something totally unique, let me know. It still owes me a fortune.

It's all been great fun, apart from the horrible bits, but I have a very strange feeling that it isn't over just yet. Another 100,000-word book like this one is stretching it, but I reckon there's at least a sizeable illustrated pamphlet left in me. I still live in Eggington Road, Wollaston, so if you're ever passing, well, as Oscar Wilde probably once said, keep on passing.

Finally, thank you for taking the time to read this. There's not much point in writing all this stuff down if people don't read it. Look after yourselves, laugh a lot with and at others and especially at yourself, and please don't waste your life. You only get one, no matter what some folks will tell you. Now, if you'll forgive me, I have some urgent colouring in to do.

THE END

I would like to say a big 'thank you' to Jonathan Pugh and Will Farmer for their kind words on the cover of this book.

*

Jonathan is a professional cartoonist who works for the Daily Mail. His style is completely different to mine. I am quite polished and craftsman-like in my approach, whereas Jonathan comes from the Bill Tidy, Larry, Quentin Blake, Loose Sketchers' School of Art, a style of drawing that I greatly admire. Maybe it's because he's my polar opposite that I love his work so much. It's one thing to draw and paint well and another to be hilarious, day after day after day in a national newspaper. I am a huge fan. Jonathan has kindly allowed me to include four of his cartoons on the next couple of pages, so that you can finally get a smile out of this book. *Pugh appears courtesy of the Daily Mail.*

*

Will Farmer is one of the directors of Fielding's Auctioneers of Stourbridge, and also a BBC Antiques Roadshow expert. I only met him two years ago, and after ten minutes I felt I'd known him all my life, for some reason. He's funny, easy-going and quite dapper. My only slight concern is that his reddish beard doesn't *quite* match his hair-colour. I have a theory about this. Will has friends in high places. Fiona Bruce is one of his best mates, for starters, and I daresay the Royal Family all watch the Antiques Roadshow, so I reckon that he did a secret deal with Prince Harry for one of his old ones.

283

*Tomorrow, men,
we will attack at dawn.
Unfortunately, I'll be
away on holiday.*

*I'd like to be in
the Rolling Stones
when I'm older.*

*It's too wide.
You'll have to drink it
in the kitchen.*

*Just be grateful you
haven't got your fathers ears.*

286

Books in the Adam Eve series:

THE CURIOUS TALE OF THE MISSING HOOF

Writer Adam Eve hires a pantomime horse costume, but forfeits his deposit when he loses one of the hooves. His obsessive efforts to locate it create mayhem!

MR MAORI GOES HOME

Adam Eve's hell-raising uncle has died and left him a substantial amount of money – on the condition that he returns a rare Maori carving to New Zealand.

LOSING THE PLOT

Adam writes a sure-fire best-selling novel, only to lose his only copy of it. Can he find his stolen laptop and bring the thief to justice?

A REMARKABLE CHAIN OF EVENTS

David Day and Adam Eve team up for the first time to make a life-changing discovery of global importance, thanks to the cryptic note found in Nosher's pocket.

Geoff has also written a stand-alone comedy entitled *The Last Cricket Tour*, as well as the splendid illustrated coffee table book, *JB's: The Story of Dudley's Legendary Live Music Venue*, which charts the rise and eventual sad demise of England's longest running rock club, a venue which played host to many of the biggest bands in the world before they became famous.

For more information, or to order a book by post, email gt@geofftristram.co.uk

Website: www.geofftristram.co.uk

287